Parenting by PERSONALITY

Printed in the United States of America
Second Edition

ISBN   978-0-9968318-0-2

This book is dedicated to the greatest family in the world... MINE!

To my sweetheart and husband, my rock, my Green-Orange, my cheerleader, my best friend, my absolute everything... words cannot express the depth of my gratitude and love... but you already know that! I love you.

To my amazing and talented son, thank you for your hours and hours of drawing, brainstorming, supporting, picking up the house, and especially for making me laugh when I felt like pulling out my hair and having a nuclear meltdown. You're the best, my Green-Orange, love you lots & lots!

To my beautiful, graceful daughter, thank you for hours and hours of organizing, for taking over my homemaker duties, for knowing my thoughts and feelings before I do, for being my intuitive assistant, for sharing every bag of chocolate that comes into the house, for all of the Jane Austin movie downtime, and for being my bestest girl friend. Most of all for being my Introverted Orange-Green shero! Love you with all my heart!

To my hard-working, lovable son-in-law, thank you for loving our daughter with all your heart, for believing in all this colors stuff, and for being a part of our family for eternity. That's brave!

To the rest of my family and my dear friends...
simply put... I couldn't have done any of this without every one of you!
I owe you an eternity of thank-yous and love. ;-)

Parenting
by PERSONALITY

The Everything Guide for PARENTING
YOUR CHILD or TEEN By THEIR
Personality Type or "Colors"

Introduction

Part One: Parent's COLORS

Discover Your Own COLORS as a Parent

Understand Your COLORS and Parenting Style

Part Two: Kid's COLORS

Discover Your Kid's COLORS

Parenting YOUR Child or Teen By Their COLORS

What's Left?

Parenting by PERSONALITY

Introduction Stuff...

Why Your Kids Do What They Do?

How To Read This Book

Are You Ever Puzzled?

Do you ever wonder why your child or teen do what they do?

Well, you won't be PUZZLED anymore!

The Simple Truth...

Why kids do what they do...

Your kids and teens do what they do quite SIMPLY because they think they are not getting their needs met. Now hear me out. I have no doubt that you are a great mom or dad, so don't throw this book across the room. This is not a "you've got to cater to your child's every whim" book... quite the opposite. So read on.

Back to needs... Now maybe they just *perceive* that they aren't getting their needs met or maybe they really aren't getting their needs met. Either way, they are acting out because they *think* that their needs are not being met. Here's where this book comes in... what they *think* is their need, and what they perceive about it being met or not has EVERYTHING to do with their particular personality type. At the same time, how much they are bugging YOU and what you need from them (and probably are not getting) has EVERYTHING to do with YOUR particular personality type. And guess what? Chances are your personality type is very different from your child's, maybe even the opposite. That can spell t-r-o-u-b-l-e. Or maybe you each have the same personality type and that spells f-i-g-h-t! Either way, you need more information, more insight, and more ways to neutralize that t-r-o-u-b-l-e and to stop the f-i-g-h-t.

Now all that sounds complicated, but it's not. I like simplicity, so I will keep it simple. To keep the personality type stuff simple we are going to use the language of colors. Yup, that's right, colors. It's all about "color." In **Parenting by PERSONALITY**, we use four colors to represent the four basic personality types to make it easier for you to understand and apply what you are about to learn about personality types and parenting. As you do just that, apply personality types, or colors, to parenting, a whole new way to build your family relationships, to discipline effectively, and to teach your kids to do what's right will unfold.

So let's get back to why kids do what they do. When kids (and adults) *think* that their needs are not being met they experience STRESS, whether or not those needs are *really* not being met or they just *perceive* that their needs are not being met. Experiencing stress leads kids to, consciously or unconsciously, choose actions that they *THINK* will *GET* their needs met. The actions kids choose come in two flavors: appropriate, good behaviors, and inappropriate, wrong, annoying misbehaviors. In other words, **kids and teens act-out in order to meet their real or perceived unmet needs**. Here's what's really cool, understanding your child's colors, or personality type, will help you figure out what's most likely going on with them and what need they *think* is not being met.

Still not sure you buy into this? I can understand that; it's a tough pill to swallow at first. Let's ponder for a moment. One of the basic aspects of being human is that we have needs, right? Right. Basic human needs include things like sleep, food, water, shelter, safety, love, belonging, and finding our niche. For more information ask Maslow in *Motivation and Personality* (1970). All this neediness starts when we are an infant. Think about it, a baby cries to

a) get your attention,

b) get a wet diaper changed,

c) get some food from you,

d) get to sleep or to stay awake,

e) get you to help them stop hurting,

f) get you to hold them,

g) or last but not least, because they can.

Whatever the need, that baby is crying because they either really need something, or they *perceive* that they need something. Either way, the baby is employing a real attention-getting action—crying—to get you to meet their need because they can't meet their own need. That baby is truly helpless and will die without you meeting all of it's needs!

Now, the older a child gets, the more creative they get about WHAT they DO to get their needs met. When kids, from toddlers to teens, are upset, stressed, and feeling needy the reasons often remain pretty much the same. They're hungry, wet, dry, cold, mad, happy, sad, or (as they get older) hurt, discouraged, overwhelmed, feeling ignored, frustrated, or boxed in. Then they DO what they DO to get something they think they need. End of story.

Here's a few examples...

1) Your 5-year-old cries in the store when you say "no" to buying him candy. Yup, he's VERY needy, from his point-of-view. He needed that candy and will probably die without it! At least, that's what he thinks. Now you and I are more likely to see the State of the Union as a life or death topic, but to your 5-year-old it's candy. Thank goodness that's all he has to worry about. He's got enough time to grow up and worry about the economy. So what's his action? Loud, obnoxious crying, a temper tantrum, throwing something, you name it. What's the (perceived) need? Candy.

2) Your 16-year-old is standing in front of you arguing (once again) about her curfew because you as the big meanie, freedom-snatcher mom or dad want her in by 11:30 when all her friends can stay out all night (with parents who are probably NOT reading a parenting book like you are). Furthermore, she is going to *die*—popularity wise—if you don't let her go out into the "safe and peace-

ful" night (yeah, right), alone (not on her life), without a curfew. The poor dear!! It's too bad that you love her enough to protect her from the not so safe, and not so peaceful, night so that she remains safe enough to argue with you yet another day. But back to WHY she is being argumentative and defensive: at that point in her young, and somewhat sheltered life, she thinks she *needs* that "no curfew" thing. So what's her action? Loud, obnoxious arguing and defensiveness, a teen-sized temper tantrum, maybe throwing a hissy fit, you name it. What's the (perceived) need? Freedom.

3) Your 10-year-old snaps at you when he gets home from school for no apparent reason. Then he ignores your call to come do homework. So what's his action? Snappiness and ignoring you. What's the (perceived) need? To not be bothered. But wait... here's the rest of the story: when you go check on him, probably a little ticked at him, he's on his bed, fast asleep, and guess what—burning up with a fever. Now here's a child with a REAL need. So, what's his action? Snappiness and ignoring you (same behavior). What's the REAL need? To get well, to sleep, maybe to get some medicine in him. He was snappy because he was not feeling well but probably didn't realize it enough to even tell you about it, and then ignored you because he'd fallen asleep. "Misbehavior" explained!

It's all about getting needs met whether they are real unmet needs or only perceived unmet needs. From toddlers to teens, kids do what they do to get their needs met. The older they get the more complicated and creative their behaviors get—and the more complicated it gets to figure out what they think or truly need. But never fear! You hold in your hand the key to understanding why YOUR child or teen is doing what they are doing AND how you are going to help them make better choices.

Now, speaking of choices... as kids turn into teens and even young adults their behavior choices can be more upsetting if they don't have the skills to get their own needs met in appropriate ways.

If, however, you teach your kids as they are growing up how to appropriately either get their needs met or learn that often restraint is the right thing then their behavior choices can be mature and healthy. Believe it or not, it's really that simple.

So how can YOU decipher what their needs are, when they are two, twelve, or twenty years old? That's simple too! Again, you are holding a sort of "instruction manual" in your hands right now.

As you learn about your child's colors you will learn three simple words for each color that will in a nanosecond remind you first, what YOUR child's most basic need is, second, what their greatest, hidden value is, and third, a single word, or phrase that summarizes the overarching discipline approach you must take with that child or teen, according to their personality type (or color) to be effective and successful. With those *"3 Words"* you will very quickly tune in to what's going on with your child and know in an instant how to work with them.

Here's the *really* comforting part, when kids, from toddlers to teens, do act out, they are not out to get you or make your life miserable. They are not plotting to take over the world (well, not yet anyway, at least not until they're teens ;-). The SIMPLE truth is that they ARE acting with their own self-preservation in mind. They ARE feeling stressed and needy about something. While they MIGHT BE imagining that they are in more peril than they really are, they ARE acting out according to a PATTERN: they are acting out using the stress behaviors of their personality type.

So what happens next?

We are going to **start** with personality types; yours and your child's. "Personality Types" have been studied by social scientists for hundreds of years (see the bibliography for more information and research). Today we use six different COLORS: BLUE, GREEN, GOLD, ORANGE, LIGHT PURPLE, and DARK PURPLE, to represent the four basic personality and two interaction styles of INTROVERT and EXTROVERT. Very quickly you will learn that those four personality types and two interaction styles mix and match to make up sixteen different combinations of colors.

All of us, parents, kids, and teens, came to Earth with a natural combination of one interaction style, Introvert or Extrovert, a dominant personality type, our first color, strongly influenced by a secondary type, or our second color. Each of the sixteen possible combinations have a unique blend of very different needs, values, communication styles, stressors, and motives for behavior. When you understand the combination of COLOR traits unique to you and to your child it changes everything in your family relationships. Your home becomes a happier place almost overnight because the people you live with make more sense and therefore you don't go quite as crazy as quickly as you did when they were just one big puzzle!

A final note: We use colors because they are easier to remember and a whole more fun to use at home with your kids, your friends, co-workers and extended family. Believe me, you are going love this stuff so much you will be talking "colors" to everyone in a matter of days!

What RESULTS can I expect from
Parenting by PERSONALITY?

This Parenting by PERSONALITY book will ...

- Change the way you "see" your child's, or teen's, actions, motives, choices, and attitudes virtually overnight;
- Help you understand why your kids or teens do what they do and why their seemingly wacko behavior bugs you so much;
- Help you be more patient with your child's inappropriate choices whether they are 2, 12, or 20;
- Teach you how to discipline your children and teens consistently and successfully with THEIR unique personality type in mind;
- Change the way you "see" yourself and improve your understanding of what frustrates you, what brings you joy, and everything in between;
- Provide a framework for teaching, guiding, disciplining, and growing the self-esteem of every member of your family including yourself without screaming, using "Command and Control" tactics, and without being their maid, servant, or constant rescuer;
- Give you the tools to communicate more effectively with everyone around you;
- Help you build trust in every relationship.

How to Read This Book

Reading Helps, Tips, & Explanations

I've tried to make this **Everything Guide** easy to read, fun to get through, unfussy to use, and exciting enough to act as a catalyst for real change in your life. I wanted to keep all the fluff out and make it down to earth for real people like you. Most of all I wanted this book to "feel" as if I was right there with you, every step of the way, to have as a friend. I've also tried to format the whole book with every "color" in mind; with logical information, action-oriented "to do's," sensitivity, and some structure. (The "structure" was the hardest part for me... I'm SO not Gold!)

Most of all, only read the parts that are meaningful to you. Don't think or feel that you must read the whole book. Once you determine your colors, and your children's colors, feel free to read only the chapters that pertain to the colors in your family.

Each ADULT COLOR CHAPTER has these sections:

The Quick [COLOR] Answer: Outlines **"3 Words"** that quickly describe the basic qualities of that color.

The Simple [COLOR] Truth: Provides a rich description of that color with all the fascinating facts and tidbits needed to understand adults of that color and how they relate to others' colors.

[COLOR] Parent Stressors: This section outlines all of that color's stressors through the parenting perspective.

Lower Your Stress as [COLOR] Parent: This section outlines several hints and tips for lessening your stress as a parent for that color.

(COLOR) Parenting Pitfalls :-(: This section outlines several of the liabilities that color needs to watch out for as a parent. In this section you will find dozens of ideas for negating these less-than-positive parenting stumbling blocks.

(COLOR) Parent Perks :-) : This section outlines many of the very cool qualities that a parent of that color brings to the table.

(COLOR) Parent Do's & Don'ts: This section outlines tons of Do's and Don'ts for that parenting style.

(COLOR) Parents: A Last Word or Two: This section is just a final word of encouragement from me to you... (I know... I'm SO Blue!)

Each KID COLOR CHAPTER has the following sections:

The Quick Answer To (COLOR) Kids: Outlines the **"3 Words"** that quickly describes the most basic and supreme need, the greatest value, and the "Parenting Strategy" for that color child or teen.

The Simple (COLOR) Kid Truth: Provides a rich description of that child's color with tons of details and specifics about how that child or teen sees the world. This is the section that really gives you a *Big Picture* explanation of how that color child and teen is wired, how they relate to the world, and what they basically need from the world. This section contains all the fascinating facts and tidbits needed to understand that child or teen.

A (COLOR)'s Greatest Need: This section outlines everything I could think of to share about that child's most basic and supreme need. This is an in-depth description of the first word of their **"3 Words"**. You will also learn from this section how to apply that understanding to your parenting efforts for that child.

A (COLOR)'s Strongest Value: This section outlines everything you need to know about that child's strongest value which is the second word of their **"3 Words"**. Use this section to under-stand how their strongest value influences their motives, their choices, and behavior.

The BIG Parenting Strategy for (COLOR)s: This section out-lines the overarching discipline approach for a child or teen of that color. If you will really study this section for your child and apply the information found there you will be well on your way to more effectively parenting a child or teen of that color.

Influence of A (COLOR)'s Second Color on Choices and Behavior: This section will be different for each color. It will cover rich descriptions of each of the four color combinations for that main color. As an example, for the Green child this section might contain information on the *Extrovert Green-Gold*, *Introvert Green-Gold*, *Extrovert Green-Orange*, and *Introvert Green-Orange*. You will learn more about the role of the second color on your child's choices and behaviors. This section may additionally include specific information on Introvert / Extrovert or gender differences for that color.

Understanding (COLOR) Stressors: This section outlines the main stressors for a child of that color including dozens of ideas for understanding why these things are stressors for that child.

Recognizing (COLOR) Stress Behaviors: This section outlines many of the frustrating misbehaviors that you will see in a child or teen of that color. This section can help you see that your child is not acting out in unique ways, but is acting out accord-ing to a pattern and that pattern is his or her personality type. This will help you understand that they are experiencing some form of stress related to who they really are. Understanding that misbehavior is a sign of stress can help you teach them more appropriate ways to act when they are experiencing stress. You can help them make more effective choices and isn't that what parenting is all about? This section is priceless!

Signs of Low Self-Esteem in (COLOR)s: This section outlines many of the red flags that can signal low self-esteem in a child or teen of that color. If you know what to look for, you can do things to build your child's self-esteem before it becomes too late.

Ways to Build Self-Esteem in (COLOR)s: This section outlines tons of ways that you can adapt your parenting style in order to build your child's self-esteem according to *their* color. This is SO important. Most parents make the naïve mistake to try to build their child's self-esteem according to what makes the parent feel more positive about themselves. This won't work and may even backfire. Study this section and apply its wisdom and you will be well on your way to growing mentally healthy children and teens. At the same time, don't forget, children and teens gain a lot of confidence from doing what's right. Also, don't forget to appropriately discipline bad behavior. Becoming inappropriately soft or permissive because you think your child or teen is too fragile to learn from their mistakes will do more harm than good. Follow the suggestions in this section and the other suggestions for you child's color and you will guide them to living a balanced, happy life.

Best To-Do's For Parents of (COLOR) Kids: This section is the end-all, be-all collection of hints, tips, ideas, and to-do's for parenting a child or teen of that color.

(COLOR) Kids: A Last Word or Two: This section is just a final word of encouragement from me to you about your child.

Now let's figure out your colors and then your kid's colors!

Parenting by PERSONALITY

Part One

Parent's COLORS

 This section will help you...

1. Discover you own Colors
2. Understand your Parenting Style based on understanding your colors
3. Learn how to maximize your gifts and minimize your stressors as a parent

Like using the best roadmap in the world, discovering and understanding YOUR COLORS and your parenting style is the fastest route to reaching your destination: a more joyful home.

What's Your Interaction Style?

Are you... an INTROVERT or an EXTROVERT?

The Quick Answer...

To be honest, there is not a "Quick Answer" for this chapter. If you want to find out what your colors are, and understand more about your unique combination of interaction style and personality type, then you will have to take the time to read all the stuff in this chapter.

The next few pages are to be used by adults and teens. You will first determine whether you are more of an Introvert or Extrovert. Then you will discover your first and second colors of
Blue, Gold, Green, or Orange.

(Don't worry, in Part Two you will find your kid's COLORS. In fact, don't try to figure out your kids COLORS from the grown-up descriptions in the next few pages, it will just drive you crazy! ;-)

The Simple Truth...

In the next few pages you will find in-depth descriptions about INTROVERTS and EXTROVERTS, the **two *Interaction Styles,*** first. Below are the steps you need to follow to determine your ***Interaction Style***.

After you determine whether you are more of an INTROVERT or an EXTROVERT, you can then read much, much more about INTRO-VERTS and EXTROVERTS in the pages that come after the descriptions. Please, don't read ahead, then you won't be prejudiced to one ***Interaction Style*** or the other. Read the information pages AFTER you determine your ***Interaction Style***.

Here's how...

1. Put aside any ideas you have about personally being "shy" or "outgoing," I'll explain why in a few pages.

2. Read the descriptions and stressors for adult INTROVERTS on page 25, and then for EXTROVERTS on page 26. Decide which description and list of stressors seem most like you, most of the time. Don't think in terms of what you want to be, or what you feel you ought to be. This will make the outcome inaccurate. Instead, focus on which one describes you best. Be honest with yourself about who you really are.

3. If you get stuck, don't worry; think about what description and list of stressors, seemed most like you in ***high school***. Here's why: high schoolers are mature enough to have their own unique "personality" show through, but are immature in developing the balancing life skills adults should have. Those balancing life skills are what can make it difficult for adults to discern between being a true INTROVERT or a true EXTROVERT. So if

you are stuck in the middle, right between **INTROVERT** and **EXTROVERT**, think back to your habits, behaviors, and stressors in high school, that should "unstick" you.

4.   Most of all have fun! After you've looked at the next few pages, ask your spouse, friends, older children, and family what they think.

5.   Jump in! Let's find out if you are an **INTROVERT** or an **EXTROVERT**!

INTROVERT Adults & Teens

I like doing things by myself or with a few close friends or family members. I prefer time alone to think and chill out. I need peace and quiet. It's important to me that I have my own space and stuff. I enjoy a few close friends.

I often need to take time to think before I speak and I tend to keep my feelings and thoughts to myself. With most people I usually only share the bare minimum, except with my spouse or a trusted friend. Even then I rarely say everything I am thinking or feeling. I think before I act.

I can be outgoing and friendly but it tends to wear me out and I eventually need some down time.

As an INTROVERT I need some time to be alone, to process and to think. I prefer some down time at the end of a busy or "people focused" day. I need to have others respect my belongings and space.

INTROVERT STRESSORS:

People who tend to talk a lot but don't really say anything too important or repeat the same thing over and over.
Real "huggy" people; especially if
I don't know them very well.
People who stand real close to me. Having my stuff touched, taken or rearranged.
Lots of loud noise for extended
periods of time. A room full of people I don't know, where I am expected to mingle.
Being expected to give quick
answers OR having someone else say my answers are not long enough or specific enough.
Being asked often: "What are you thinking?,"
"What's the matter?," or "Are you okay?"

EXTROVERT Adults & Teens

I like doing things with other people. I enjoy hanging out with several friends and/or family a LOT? I prefer to be in the middle of the action, but I don't need to be the center of attention. I'm comfortable meeting new people.

I often say things out loud and say much of what I am thinking or feeling when I think it or feel it. I can accidentally say whatever comes to my mind. I often act before I think.

I can be reserved, silent and quiet but it wears me out and eventually I find that I'm talking even if it's a whispered comment to a stranger.

As an EXTROVERT I need some sort of interaction with others, especially at the end of an "alone day". I am usually comfortable with appropriate physical contact. I need to think out loud with someone I trust and I need to be listened to.

EXTROVERT STRESSORS:

When I am expected to give short answers without being allowed to share all the details that matter or that complete the story. When other people don't talk or when there are uncomfortable lulls in conversations. When I have to guess what someone is thinking all the time. People who don't share their stuff.
Being quiet and/or still for long periods of time.
People who are stand-offish or stiffen when I hug them.
When someone wants me to "think it through" on my own when I really need to "talk it out". When I have a problem to solve and there is no one to talk to about it.
Long periods of time alone.

Okay, so what's your interaction Style?
INTROVERT or EXTROVERT ?

You're more of an _____

Your Spouse/Partner is an _____

Interaction Style goes way beyond
SHY or OUTGOING!

For all of us, our *Interaction Style* describes our natural tendencies for how we process our perceptions of the world around us and how we recharge our "batteries" after we are drained or worn out. Each one of us, including children and teens, have a very specific way that we interact with other people, things, ideas and information, and how we restore our energy.

INTROVERTs focus their attention inwardly.
EXTROVERTs focus their attention outwardly.
INTROVERTs process information internally.
EXTROVERTs process information externally.
INTROVERTs recharge by finding time alone.
EXTROVERTs recharge by creating time with others.

INTROVERTS ... Are people who process information by "thinking it through." They tend to keep their concerns, thoughts and feelings to themselves unless asked. When they are worried or stressed about something they need to be left alone long enough to process their feelings through in their mind before they can talk about it. **Introverts** MUST be allowed this "processing time" before they have to communicate their ideas to others. This can, however, be stressful for any **Extrovert** in the **Introvert's** life. **Extroverts** will want an **Introvert** to talk before they are ready which is then stressful for the **Introvert**. **Introverts** also need alone time to replenish their energy stores. They may spend a lot of time in their rooms or taking naps if their lives are busy, hectic or full.

EXTROVERTS . . . Are people who process information out loud. They tend to talk easily with others. When they are concerned or stressed about something they need to "talk it out" with someone they trust. If they don't have anyone to talk to they will talk *at* a complete stranger in an effort to solve their problem. **Extroverts** MUST get their thoughts out of their heads before they can make any sense of it all . This can be stressful for the "stranger" or for any **Introvert** in the **Extrovert's** life. **Extroverts** also need interaction with others to replenish their energy stores. These are the people who get their "second wind" in the evening, especially at a social gathering. They seem to just keep going and going.

> **If you don't know what an INTROVERT is thinking, *you're not asking*.**
> **If you don't know what an EXTROVERT is thinking, *you're not listening*.**

INFORMATION & ENERGY:
The TWO sides of Interaction Style

First, how we process **INFORMATION**, and second, how we restore our **ENERGY** after a draining day is what makes up our <u>Interaction Style</u>. **Introverts** process **INFORMATION** internally, through personal concentration, and restore their **ENERGY** by being alone. **Extroverts** process **INFORMATION** outside themselves through communication and restore their **ENERGY** when they are with others.

PERSONAL SPACE:
The "REAL ESTATE" of Interaction Style

Who we let into our **PERSONAL SPACE** and how close we get to others depends on our __Interaction Style__. **Introverts** have a very large **PERSONAL SPACE**. They tend to stand farther away from people and are less 'huggy' than **Extroverts**. **Extroverts**, on the other hand, tend to use touch more often in their communication and are very comfortable standing and being close to others.

HIDDEN ASSETS:
One CAUTION about Interaction Style

One very important point to understand is that **Introverts** tend to "hide" their natural color and "show" their second color to the world. They're not being secretive, they are just cautious. Their first color motivations, thoughts, feelings, and perceptions are very private. These things are private and not easily shared because they are an **Introvert**. Therefore, it is best not to try to guess another person's color because the guess could be wrong. If they are an **Introvert** they may be "extroverting" behaviors that are actually coming from the motivations of their second color, not their true color. On the other hand, with **Extroverts** what you see is what you get.

CONFLICT & THE CHASE:
The Rub Between each Interaction Style

When it comes to your relationships with other people, the differences in our personality with respect to **Introvert** and **Extrovert** often causes any initial conflict two people may be experiencing. If you are an **Introvert**, have you ever been really bugged by someone who just could not seem to shut up? Or by someone who is just standing way too close? Guess what, they were probably just an **Extrovert** being an **Extrovert**!

On the other side of the coin, if you are an **Extrovert**, have you ever been bugged by someone who keeps you guessing about what they were thinking? Or by someone who keeps backing away when you are trying to have a conversation with them? Guess what, the person bugging you is probably just an **Introvert** being an **Introvert!** Hmmm, go figure!!

Remember, **Introverts** tend to keep their private thoughts private, **Extroverts** tend to spill the beans about almost anything and everything. And the standing too close, or backing up thing... remember **Introverts** have a larger personal space and need to be farther away, distance-wise, from the person they are talking to. **Extroverts** have a smaller personal space and can be very comfortable being close to others.

The difference between "The Chased" (a.k.a. the **Introvert**) and "The Chaser" (a.k.a. the **Extrovert**) can cause real frustration in tight, closed spaces, like subways, stuffy offices, cramped hallways, and crowded places.

One really interesting example of this kind of conflict is in elevators. The Chased enters an empty elevator and moves to the center. At the next floor, The Chaser enters the elevator, looks right at The Chased, and says, "Hello." The Chased quietly nods and moves to one corner of the elevator to create more space between himself and the newcomer, who stands practically in the middle of the small enclosed space. The Chased thinks, "How rude, does he think he owns the WHOLE elevator?!" and turns 30° toward the elevator wall to create a bit more space between himself and The

Chaser. The Chaser, being uncomfortable with the silence, tries to start a friendly conversation with the man in the corner and gets only curt, clipped, short replies. The Chaser thinks, "How rude! Does he think he can ignore me in this tiny elevator? How unfriendly!" The Chased thinks, "Ugh! Save me from people who always need to talk! Silence is Golden!" The elevator doors open on the floor where The Chased works. He quickly shoves past the man STILL in the middle of the elevator thinking, "Good riddance!"

The Chaser, left alone in the elevator says out loud to the empty space, "Good riddance! Man, was he a grump!" and then starts humming to himself. Are you chuckling yet? I am. ;-)

ON THE HOME FRONT:
Interaction Style Within Your Family

The differences between **Introverts** and **Extroverts** can be exhausting and can cause great conflict in all kinds of relationships. Think of how these differences can play out in your family. Statistically, many husbands and wives marry their opposite when it comes to interaction style. At first this can draw couples together, you have a "talker" and a "listener" and you think that you are made for each other. But in just a few months, or maybe just a few weeks, after the honeymoon is over the "talker" needs the "listener" to talk. Or maybe the "listener" needs some quiet time when the "talker" isn't talking. Oops! We have a conflict brewing!

Now think about **Introverts** and **Extroverts** in terms of parenting a teenager. Let's say you have an **Extrovert** mom and an **Introverted** 13-year-old son. Holy cow, can you have a worse recipe for upset feelings, a Mom lecturing, the son withdrawing, and mayhem ensuing! I only use that as an example, because, um, yeah, well, that was me and my son, Zach. Good thing that about that time I learned a whole bunch of stuff about **Introverts** and **Extroverts**; I KNOW it saved us from killing each other!

What about the opposite? My very cool and amazing sister-in-law is definitely an **Introverted** Mom (Green-Orange, just FYI) and her oldest daughter is just an absolute cutie and quite the girly-girl. And, yup, you guessed it... an **Extrovert** (Blue-Orange to be exact). There are times when the **Extrovert** girly-girl just talks and talks and talks and talks and, did I mention that she TALKS, almost non-stop to my **Introverted** sister-in-law. Day in, day out, in the a.m., in the p.m. ALL the time! For my sister-in-law, coming to an understanding of the differences between **Introvert** and **Extrovert** was huge for her. She found that when her daughter is particularly talkative she can be more patient. And when she needs some peace and quiet she is able to explain her own needs in a way that won't hurt her daughter. A little information goes a long way to create harmony at home. Understanding how conflict comes from the opposite perspectives of **Introverts** and **Extroverts** can minimize, or even eliminate, most of the problem, most of the time.

Now that we've talked a tad about **Introverts** and **Extroverts,** let's figure out what your colors are. Just so you know, there is a whole boat-load more information on **Introverts** and **Extroverts** but we don't have the time or room here to talk about it all. For more information check out the resources in the last chapter. For now, on to GOLD, ORANGE, GREEN, and BLUE.

What Are Your Colors?

Are you a... GOLD, ORANGE, GREEN, or BLUE?

The Simple COLORS Truth...

In the next few pages you will find in-depth descriptions about each color: GOLD, ORANGE, GREEN, and BLUE the *Four Personality Types*. Below are the steps you need to follow to determine your first and second color. After you discover your first two colors, I will tell you more about each one in the pages that come after the descriptions. Read the information pages AFTER you   determine your *Personality Type*. Don't read ahead; that way you won't be prejudiced to one color or another.

1. Put aside any ideas you have about being a certain type. This happens most often if you have been exposed to some of this information at work. Well, that was work, this is all about your home life. Most of those work tests, surveys, personality analysis stuff is geared toward "who" you are AT work. This book is about "who" you are for real, at home, all the rest of the time you are AWAY from work. So, in two words: change gears. Forget all you've been exposed to before this and start fresh. (This is more fun anyway!)

2. Read the descriptions of qualities and stressors for GOLD, ORANGE, GREEN, and BLUE on pages 36 to 39. Again, decide which description seems most like you most of the time, not what you want to be, or what you feel you ought to be—but which one describes you best.

3. If you get stuck, don't worry. Think about what descriptions seem most like you in high school like you did for INTROVERT and EXTROVERT!

4. You will mostly likely find that more than one color seems to fit. That's okay. In fact that's good! Most people struggle between two colors. When that happens study the list of <u>stressors</u> for those two colors. Whichever list of stressors seems to fit you the best is probably your first color.

5. To determine your second color I have to share something with you that might not like... Understand that there are certain combinations for your first and second color that according to some very sound research are not naturally possible (for an explanation of this see pages 168 to 176). Soooo, if you are a BLUE or GREEN first color, your second can only be Gold or Orange. If you are a GOLD or ORANGE first color, your second can only be Blue or Green. Trust me on this, or go read page 173.

6. What if you are torn between some combination of BLUE, GOLD, and GREEN? You are not going to believe this but you are probably an ORANGE! Do me a favor: keep an open mind and look really seriously at ORANGE. ORANGE Freedom Fighters are chameleons. They've had to be their whole life. I'll explain more later. If you are stuck between the other three colors, in my experience (and I've had lots!) you're probably a really balanced ORANGE. That's a COOL thing!

7. There are two ways to approach this. 1) "Go with your gut" as you read the color descriptions on the next few pages –or– 2) if you are the more analytical type, use the little boxes on each list to check off qualities that describe you best and create your

own kind of informal tally thingy. You can compare how many boxes of one color seem to be more like you than the number of boxes for another color. Or don't; you decide. I deliberately choose *not* to create a "tally up your score" kind of measure here because we're humans and discovering your personality type takes a little time and can be messy. You can't just find your score and fit into a box. I choose to honor the human spirit and our ability to grow and learn and develop beyond a score. Remember, according to decades of research you do have a first color and a second color that don't change over time, even if you learn to develop qualities of the other colors over time. You are born with a permanent first and second color. Embrace them!

8. Most of all, HAVE FUN! Then ask your spouse, friends, older children, and family what they think.

9. Turn the page, jump in and get started. Let's find out what your colors are!

GOLD Adults & Teens

- [ ] Golds need structure and order
- [ ] They have a strong internal sense of right and wrong
- [ ] They are very organized in one way or another
- [ ] They are reliable and service-oriented
- [ ] Golds are traditionalists who value family, preparedness, steadiness, loyalty and trustworthiness
- [ ] They are dependable caretakers
- [ ] Golds are trustworthy and follow through on assignments
- [ ] Golds value time, details, cooperation, and productivity
- [ ] They work to preserve values, history, and traditions
- [ ] They create order from chaos and value structure, appropriate control, and rules
- [ ] They are usually focused on the task at hand
- [ ] Golds work responsibly until they have completed the job and it's usually done well
- [ ] They value and uphold social norms/rules of society
- [ ] Their talk is full of "should" and what others need to do

GOLD Adult & Teen STRESSORS:

(this is the stuff that drives Golds crazy)

- [ ] Disorder and inconsistency
- [ ] Unclear rules, policies, or procedures
- [ ] Lack of structure, powerlessness, lack of control
- [ ] Broken commitments
- [ ] Non-conformity that destroys proven traditions
- [ ] Change for the sake of doing something different
- [ ] People who are habitually late
- [ ] Lack of respect for position, rules, and traditions
- [ ] Disloyalty
- [ ] People who break social norms
- [ ] Lack of appreciation for service and contributions
- [ ] Other people being rude - not because it's hurtful, but because it's just wrong
- [ ] Loss of control or cooperation
- [ ] Being overloaded with responsibility
- [ ] Being overlooked for advancement
- [ ] Not enough time to complete a task on their "To Do" list
- [ ] Apparent irresponsibility
- [ ] Ignored deadlines

ORANGE Adults & Teens

- [ ] Oranges need freedom to be themselves and to act
- [ ] Oranges value rewards and enjoy competition
- [ ] Oranges are true chameleons: they often show traits from Blue, Green, or Gold but their core need is always based on freedom, rewards, and action
- [ ] <u>Extroverted Oranges</u> seem to be on the move all the time but may have trouble staying focused
- [ ] <u>Introverted Oranges</u> conserve their energy and action until the last minute, then they move quickly, and efficiently
- [ ] They are continually negotiating for what they want
- [ ] They are decisive, realistic, practical, and resilient
- [ ] They often seem to be care-free and easy-going unless under great stress, then seems controlling and bossy
- [ ] Oranges are very flexible about what they want, but may be stubborn about what someone else wants
- [ ] They live in-the-moment and can be bold in their actions and language
- [ ] They work hard to get done so they can play hard
- [ ] Their talk is full of verbs and what they are going to do

ORANGE Adult & Teen STRESSORS:
(this is the stuff that drives Oranges crazy)

- [ ] Any lack of freedom
- [ ] Limits, restrictions, and too many rules
- [ ] Unnecessary routines, boring work
- [ ] Waiting or having nothing to do
- [ ] Rules that are overly restrictive and detailed
- [ ] Inflexibility of others, lack of options and/or a way out
- [ ] Structure for the sake of having structure
- [ ] Inability to negotiate
- [ ] Detailed instructions and strict "how to's"
- [ ] Doing things over and over; excessive paperwork
- [ ] Lack of immediate rewards or outcomes
- [ ] Feeling used/overworked with no rewards or freedom
- [ ] Too much talk; not enough action
- [ ] Lots of theory, philosophy, planning
- [ ] Bossy people and slow decision making
- [ ] Lack of fun

GREEN Adults & Teens

- ☐ Greens are logical thinkers and need information
- ☐ They often ask "why" questions
- ☐ Need time to ponder incoming data
- ☐ They are analytical, problem solvers
- ☐ They are calm, cool, and collected most of the time
- ☐ They are "big picture" focused and make big plans
- ☐ Greens are continually learning and do their "research"
- ☐ They always check for accuracy
- ☐ They are insightful, subject-matter experts, interested in many topics but may become bored with routine tasks
- ☐ Greens feel their emotions deeply but have a difficult time describing, or discussing, their feelings
- ☐ When talking they say "I think" a lot, even when describing feelings
- ☐ Green moms are often nurturing and caring, and tend to see many, but not all, "Blue" traits in themselves

GREEN Adults & Teen STRESSORS:

(this is the stuff that drives Greens crazy)

- ☐ The stupidity of others; incompetence in self or others
- ☐ Unclear expectations
- ☐ Lack of a "big picture" mission or goals
- ☐ Illogical rules, restrictions, or limitations
- ☐ No time to think, digest, or process new information
- ☐ Being forced into a quick decision
- ☐ Errors or mistakes made personally or by others
- ☐ No appreciation from others for their personal competency.
- ☐ Too much "touchy-feely" stuff
- ☐ Systems failures or routine work
- ☐ People conflicts or emotional outbursts
- ☐ Unsolvable problems
- ☐ Blaming others or no problem solving
- ☐ Unfairness due to a lack of logical thinking
- ☐ Lack of a realistic, workable strategy
- ☐ No time to gather information
- ☐ Inaccurate or missing information
- ☐ Ignored recommendations

BLUE Adults & Teens

- Blues are people-focused and need healthy relationships; they are kind and often nurturing
- Blues are intuitive, and "pick up" easily on the feelings and needs of others
- Blues are naturally communicative
- Blues appreciate nature and connect deeply with a higher purpose
- They value authenticity, harmony, peace, and prefer being calm, but can be emotional when stressed
- Blues seek for balance and build trusting relationships
- They are natural mediators and try to solve "people problems"
- Blues promote enthusiasm, optimism, and look for the best in others
- They work to repair conflicts and hold to high ideals
- Blues use the words "I feel" when they talk and even when they share their thoughts or opinions

BLUE Adult & Teen STRESSORS:
(this is the stuff that drives Blues crazy)

- Disharmony, conflict, fighting, and mean people
- Insincerity, back-stabbing, inauthentic people
- Repetitive work and intense competition
- Personal rejection and criticism of others or self
- Being ignored, overlooked, or turned away
- Lack of appreciation for individuality and kindness
- Other people's non-supportive ways
- Loud, negative remarks - yelling
- Forced isolation (even for introverts)
- People who lie or who are aggressive
- Rules or procedures that become more important than people's needs
- Having too many people to please
- Inability to meet other's needs
- Bossy, controlling people
- Feelings of confusion
- Being forced into a quick decision, or one that doesn't matter to them, like where "the group" should eat. They just want to be with the group, where doesn't matter

Okay, so what are your colors?
GOLD, ORANGE, GREEN, or BLUE ?

First, I'm a(n) _____

And my second color is _____

First, My Spouse/Partner is a(n) _____

And their second color is _____

So to put it all together, I'm an...

_____, _____, _____
(Introvert or Extrovert)   (First color)   (Second color)

And my Spouse/Partner is an...

_____, _____, _____
(Introvert or Extrovert)   (First color)   (Second color)

Parent's COLORS!
Some Basic Information...
about Adult Colors.

GO BEYOND: Personality Type is more than

WHAT MAKES YOU TICK or WHAT TICKS YOU OFF!

As I explained earlier, each color has a unique set of NEEDS, VALUES, MOTIVES, STRESSORS, and STRESS BEHAVIORS. When you combine one of two interaction styles, and two of four personality types, **there are 16 unique combinations of needs, values and stressors.** In other words, there are 16 personality types.

Since this is a book focused on parenting your children I will mention, but not detail, the sixteen types. In the chapter on Kid's Colors you can read a brief description of all sixteen combinations. In the next few chapters you will learn more about each of the four adult colors of GOLD, ORANGE, GREEN, and BLUE from a parenting perspective. The 16 combinations are listed below with their Myers-Briggs Type Indicator format.

The 16 types are:

Extrovert Gold-Blue (ESFJ)	Introvert Gold-Blue (ISFJ)
Extrovert Gold-Green (ESTJ)	Introvert Gold-Green (ISTJ)
Extrovert Orange-Blue (ESFP)	Introvert Orange-Blue (ISFP)
Extrovert Orange-Green (ESTP)	Introvert Orange-Green (ISTP)
Extrovert Green-Gold (ENTJ)	Introvert Green-Gold (INTJ)
Extrovert Green-Orange (ENTP)	Introvert Green-Orange (INTP)
Extrovert Blue-Gold (ENFJ)	Introvert Blue-Gold (INFJ)
Extrovert Blue-Orange (ENFP)	Introvert Blue-Orange (INFP)

TIME & EXPERIENCE: Doesn't Change Your Colors Only Your Ability to Handle Stress

According to several researchers, your first and second color preferences don't change. In other words, it's been suggested by several social scientists that our core set of needs, values, and motives for our behavior choices and our general stressors don't change over our lifetime (Jung, 1979; Keirsey,1998; Keirsey and Bates, 1978; Myers and Myers, 1980).

While our colors don't really change, we can **choose** to develop qualities of each color that balances us out. For example, if you are a GREEN, you are very logical, but find dealing with emotions difficult. Let's say you marry a BLUE, or have a BLUE child. The BLUES in your life need affection and emotional connection. As a GREEN, you choose to become more competent at identifying and understanding your own emotions. At the same time you work to become more effective at communicating your emotions, especially your positive feelings about, and to, your BLUE family members. You've chosen to develop some of the traits of your other colors in order to be more balanced, to meet the needs of your loved ones, and mostly, to be a competent spouse and parent.

When we choose to become more balanced, it's usually due to some sort of stress in our life. When we experience stress, upset, difficult times, or tough circumstances we often suffer more than we have to because we lack the appropriate balancing skills. This often serves as a catalyst for changing our character and improving our skills. We make behavior changes so that we don't have to suffer negative consequences to the same degree next time. Sometimes we choose to go backwards in our progression. For example, a person who is hurt by love decides never to love again and therefore pushes possible partners away. Other times we choose to develop positive qualities. For example, when we are late for an important appointment and suffered because of our lateness, we later decide to be more conscientious of being on time. Stress causes us to develop new attributes. Hopefully those efforts are always focused on moving forward and becoming more balanced. Understanding about colors can help with this process.

BLUE, GREEN *AND* GOLD = ORANGE: How Does that *Add Up?*

If you are one of those who think that you are a combination of BLUE, GREEN and GOLD, and just can't narrow it down, then you're probably an ORANGE. Here's why, Oranges have not often been supported in our society, in our school system, or in our corporations because of their overwhelming need for freedom. Schools, corporations, and society are set up and controlled by rules, laws, grading systems, policies, and procedures. These institutions have "freedom-stealing" and "fun-sucking" written all over them. Don't get me wrong—we need structure to survive; but to an ORANGE these things can be stressful. As a result, an ORANGE child growing up under these structure systems has only three choices: conform, rebel, or find a creative way to balance their own brand of *conformity* with a bit of safe *rebellion*. Thus, an ORANGE child learns quickly to "play the game" by taking on the qualities of GOLD, GREEN and BLUE. They do this in order to navigate through all that structure without losing their rewards (which they love) and by preserving most of their freedom (which they need!). Thus we see the ORANGE becomes very much a chameleon early on. They are not A.D.D. or crazy; they are just very ORANGE!

REMEMBER: Introverts Keep First Color Private

Don't forget that **Introverts** tend to keep their first color traits hidden and their first color motives private. With **Introverts**, often what you "see" are the qualities and motives of their second color. Also remember that many **Introverts** have become experts at appearing very **Extroverted**.

So here's the danger: let's say you have a casual friend, a new co-worker, or your mature teenage baby-sitter who acts very **Extroverted Gold-Blue**. Remember, what you see in their outward behavior is them at their polite best since you don't live with them. In reality, each one of these lesser known individuals could be a true **Introverted Blue-Gold** because who they truly could be is an **Introvert** who's good at playing an **Extrovert** and therefore showing their true second color of **Gold** and keeping their first, and motivating, color of **Blue** more hidden until they know you better. This is precisely why it's best not to "guess" another person's color. Have your friend or spouse read the color pages for themselves. Pay them big bucks if you must, but don't try to guess on your own, you could be wrong. Just keep this in mind.

STUCK in the MIDDLE: What If You Can't Decide Between Two Colors for Your First Color?

If you are feeling "stuck" between two colors let me help you (hopefully) get unstuck. Your biggest stressor is the best "tie breaker." First get out a pen, pencil, crayon, or lipstick—something to write with. Next, in the list below, find the combination of colors you are stuck between. Now, I'll ask you to QUICKLY (without thinking) decide which of the two comparisons under your "stuck" combo is the most stressful for you. Again, don't think too hard, go with your gut. Put a check mark next to the one that bugs you the most.

If you are stuck between **GREEN** and **BLUE**, which is more stressful?

____ Somebody acting STUPID, making no sense at all?

-or- ____ Someone being really MEAN and hurtful?

Stuck between **BLUE** and **GOLD**? Which is more stressful?

____ Somebody being really MEAN and hurtful?

-or- ____ Someone who's always LATE because it's just WRONG?

Stuck between **GOLD** and **ORANGE**? Which is more stressful?

____ Somebody who's always LATE because it's just WRONG?

-or- ____ Someone taking away your FREEDOM with stupid rules?

Stuck between **ORANGE** and **GREEN**? Which is more stressful?

____ Somebody taking away your FREEDOM and your fun?

-or- ____ Someone acting really STUPID, making no sense at all?

Stuck between **GREEN** and **GOLD**? Which is more stressful?

    ___ Someone acting STUPID and making no sense at all?

-or- ___ Someone who's always LATE because it's just WRONG?

Stuck between **BLUE** and **ORANGE**? Which is more stressful?

    ___ Somebody being really MEAN and hurtful?

-or- ___ Somebody taking away your FREEDOM and your fun?

If your answer was: You're a...

    ... someone acting STUPID   GREEN.*

    ... someone being really MEAN   BLUE.

    ... someone who's always LATE   GOLD.

    ... taking away your FREEDOM   ORANGE.

Hopefully you are "unstuck." If not, don't despair. Read on. Consider your motives and ask yourself, "Why am I REALLY doing this?," and over a week or so your true colors will reveal themselves.

* Please understand, when I say "stupid" I don't mean anything unkind about individuals with a disability or lowered mental capacity. I mean when Greens are irritated by people not using the smarts they have and those who have no common sense.

COLOR DE-CODED: Information and Insights

In the next few sections you will find short descriptions on each of the four adult colors. These descriptions will shed some light on your first and second colors. The description of your first color will be the most representative of you, your needs, your stressors and your stress behaviors (the things you do when you are really bugged, angry, frustrated, overworked or worried).

Remember, there's only a little information here because this book is more about your kids. Check out the reference list for titles with an * at the end of the reference. These books or articles are focused on personality types.

Note: In the following Parent's Color chapters each color has a set of three words in **underlined bold**. These words are important and will help you remember the basic need, the greatest value, and the overarching approach to that color. I will teach you more about these three words when we get to your kid's colors; I just wanted you to notice them now. Have fun, read on!

Parenting by PERSONALITY

Parent's
COLORS

Understand Your Colors and Parenting Style

This section contains each of the
four adult colors in detail
and how your color affects
your parenting style.

GOLD Parents

In 3 Words... Structure, Consistency, Expectations

The Quick GOLD Adult Answer...

Needs <u>STRUCTURE</u>
Structure, order, and plans that make sense. Dependability from others.

Values <u>CONSISTENCY</u>
Respects things that stay the same: rules, order, conformity, and tradition. Change is very stressful, needs time to adjust.

Trust Tactic <u>EXPECTATIONS</u>
Operates best by knowing what is expected from them before they make commitments. Also has specific expectations for others and situations.

The Simple GOLD Adult Truth...

GOLD parents are structured traditionalists who are very focused on the moment and who have an internal sense of right and wrong. They are very action–oriented because they have a plan and tend to follow it. They like to have things under control and orderly. Their biggest stressors come from people, things, and situations that seem chaotic and unstructured.

Gold adults need **STRUCTURE**, order, and plans that make sense to them. Clear expectations, written directions, and concrete examples are needed by Golds. Loyalty, dependability, and responsibility from others are very important to Gold adults.

Golds value **CONSISTENCY**, rules, and organization because these things provide structure, which, remember, is their overarching need. They also value and promote order, conformity, and traditions because, again, these things contribute to a structured life. Golds are consistently hardworking because they are very focused in-the-moment and they take that "moment" and fill it with worthwhile things to do. They give that moment great structure and great meaning. They judge their own hard work and actions as "right" or "righteous." They fit all that hard work into a consistent plan for some future organized outcome that can be of service to someone: their family, community, or themselves.

Golds are very committed to their family, job and their community because of a strong sense of duty, responsibility, and safety. All of these things tie into their need for structure and consistency. They prefer, and often work best by, completing one task at a time. They appreciate being rewarded for a job well done, for being responsible, dependable, and loyal. When Golds are rewarded for reasons that might appeal more to the other colors, they are often annoyed instead of flattered. Depending on their second color, they may downplay compliments about their "kind feelings" (blue) or "cleverness" (green) because these are not what they, as Golds, perceive to be of highest value and therefore are not their own perception of their greatest contributions, and what they "contribute" is of high importance to them.

Because Golds value consistency and need structure, they often form very clear and specific **EXPECTATIONS** of what they want, or need, to have happen in almost every forthcoming situation no matter how small or insignificant. They also form very specific expectations of how they want people (and kids) to behave. Golds form expectations without realizing it. These ideas of how things *should* be, and how people *should* act, are the basis of why Golds often communicate in terms of "shoulds" and why they may seem judgmental. When their unconscious expectations are violated, or unmet, whether those expectations are of another's behavior, or how things *should* go, Golds can become upset, frustrated, and ultimately controlling. When this happens, they very seldom understand exactly why they are so upset and rarely, if ever, connect their feelings to their unmet expectations.

Most Golds don't realize how full of expectations they are until they begin to examine their own thoughts and feelings about what they want from the people and the situations around them. If they learn to examine their thoughts for strict, specific, and possibly unrealistic expectations, they will be much happier and more flexible, especially as a parent. They can learn to let go of some of their more unrealistic expectations when it comes to understanding their children (and spouse, friends, even co-workers) whose colors are different from theirs. They can learn to hold on to their high ideals, without being unreasonable with others' abilities. They can learn to balance what they think *should* happen with what probably *will* happen. They will be much happier and more patient when things don't go strictly according to plan. They can learn to see the positive and to be grateful for what is happening right now.

More to the point, Gold adults who don't learn to be somewhat flexible will be very controlling and unhappy as parents. If Gold children are not taught and expected to be flexible, forgive, control their judgments, and to "let it go" when things are out of their control, they will grow into Gold adults who are overly controlling of people and things when things don't go according to their plans.

While Golds have high expectations for others, they also have very high expectations for themselves. This can positively contribute to their sense of duty and responsibility but be detrimental to their sense of worth and level of happiness. They have a strong internal sense of right and wrong. They often think in terms of "right" or "wrong" or that things are "black" or "white" — that there is no gray.

Due to this internal sense of "either/or", Gold parents often have a more difficult time embracing the idea that different personality types really do exist and that not everyone, including a Gold's child or teen, thinks or feels like they do, or that they even should. Most parenting books, in my opinion, are written by Golds and teach how to raise little, obedient, cookie-cutter Golds. That's all well and good until you have an Orange child who won't behave like a Gold thinks they should, then we label that orange child as having A.D.D. or A.D.H.D. (Just some food for thought.) As Gold parents come to accept that their children are, in fact, a different personality type and as they embrace the "structure" and "consistency" of their child's color, the Gold parent will find parenting a much more rewarding occupation, even with an Orange child or teen.

A final thought on Gold expectations. Golds feel more secure when they understand the *expectations* others have of them. They want the structure, safety, and security of being able to choose to consistently do what others need from them: it's part of their duty as a contributing member of the family, or of society at large. Golds *want* to be responsible, they *want* to be dependable and they *want* to be loyal. This builds their self-worth. They can do these things only when they understand what "responsible," "dependable," or "loyal" looks like to the ones they love, respect, or work for.

Last but not least, Gold characteristics are highly desirable in our families for several reasons. Golds bring needed structure to the family. They are pros at teaching responsibility and accountability to their children. They are very loyal to their family members. They are really great at creating routines, bed times, chore lists, schedules and homework times. Golds are very responsible parents and care deeply about the service they do at home, at work, and within their community. They teach their children the value of work and service. They are often involved in their child's education and promote a feeling of getting things done on time and in order.

Their three biggest liabilities are that as a parent Golds can become controlling when things don't go according to their expectations. They tend to withhold rewards for good behavior choices because they see rewards as unneeded fluff (since kids should just be obedient and do what's right) and they become overly concerned about other's expectations of their parenting skills; so they often take their children's misbehavior personally and then emotionally overact.

GOLD Parent Stressors

**For each stressor, look at how your
child's behavior violates one or more of your 3 Words:
STRUCTURE, CONSISTENCY, EXPECTATIONS**

- Chaos in the form of unclean rooms, messy desks, unorganized backpacks, etc.

- Confusion and disorganization in how children want to complete a task or project—either because these things are just "wrong" and violates your expectations of how a child's room should look, or how a project "should" be done, or because of the lack of structure, order, and consistency.

- Crazy, ever-changing schedules, actions, moods, and explanations for bad behavior will prove frustrating because of the lack of structure and order and because you need and expect things to move according to a plan.

- Inconsistency with choices, making excuses, and lying.

- Lack of structure in doing chores the "right way." This is stressful because you will most likely want your child or teen to complete the chore or assignment in your structured way, over and over again.

- Watching your child or teen feel powerless or out of control will be stressful, frustrating, difficult to sit back and watch, and may at times embarrass you. This happens because as an adult you can probably see a clear and structured path to solve their problem. You also will worry about what others are thinking of you as they witness your child's inappropriate behavior. You will feel that they are judging you as a parent who is not doing your job right.

- When your child or teen keeps changing their mind, or can't make up their mind. This is stressful to Gold parents because it seems inconsistent, it shows a lack of commitment on the child's part, and because too much change for you threatens your sense of structure and blows your expectations.

- Feeling "forced" into doing something different than expected. For example, you've been planning a family weekend getaway for weeks, but your teenager was late to school twice this past week, for a total of four times for the semester, and now must serve a detention on Saturday, thus ruining your plans for the family getaway. This violates your expectations for some much needed family time. Some Gold parents even go so far as to assume that their teenager did this on purpose just to ruin the family's fun. (Which may or may not be true, in either case there's much bigger problems in that relationship than just missing a weekend camping trip and you better email me right away!)

- Children or teens who are late, who appear lazy, or who don't get moving immediately; this communicates a lack of respect and irresponsibility to the Gold parent who is forced to wait. It's also extremely embarrassing to the Gold parent when they walk in late wherever they are going, when their child lets others down, or when they are slow thus inconveniencing not only the Gold parent but others, too.

- Kids and teens (and all other people) who don't do what's "right" are huge stressors to Gold parents. This is because the "wrong-doers" don't meet the expectations of the Gold parent and communicate a complete lack structure or discipline through their behavior.

- Lack of appreciation and gratitude from children and teens for being cared for, taken care of, and given food, shelter, money, and time. This is very upsetting to a Gold parent because they think it's only "right" to be shown gratitude by their child for the things they do for them. Gold parents often feel that gratitude is owed them although they seldom want to openly admit they feel that way. Gold parents are often put off by kids who think that they are entitled to food, shelter, clothing, and money. Yet this comes from the same Gold parent who often doesn't believe that children or teens should be rewarded for doing what's right. Children should just do what's right because it's the right thing to do. The truth is, feeling unappreciated is a stressor to every-one—Gold parents and kids alike.

- Too much responsibility, too many tasks, too many assign-ments and too many "slackers" can be frustrating to a Gold be-cause it's "not fair." Golds often have very specific expectations of what's fair, just, and what "responsible" looks like.

- Not enough time to finish a task. This is because Golds may feel powerless to do a good enough job according to their own high standards or high expectations.

- Children, teens and other adults who are disrespectful. This is very stressful to Gold parents whether the kids are your own or someone else's. You don't tolerate it. Actually that's good. The other colors tend to tolerate it too much.

- Broken promises. Bottom line: they blow expectations. Gold adults expect promises and commitments to be kept.

They, after all, keep their commitments. Everyone else *should* too!

Lower Your Stress as a GOLD Parent

Here are some excellent ideas for lowering your stress.
Build STRUCTURE, CONSISTENCY, and positive or reasonable
EXPECTATIONS into your routines while allowing for the
needs of the other colors in your home.

- First of all, get acquainted with your 3 Words: **STRUCTURE**, **CONSISTENCY**, and **EXPECTATIONS**. Use these 3 Words whenever you are feeling frustrated, negative, unappreciated or overworked to self-diagnose what's really bothering you. This will help you be in control of what you can control (which is really only you) and let go of what you cannot control (which is really everything and everyone else).

- Learn to evaluate your subconscious expectations for yourself, your children and teens, and future events. Ask yourself if your expectations are realistic, fair to others or yourself, and do-able. If not, change them, or let them go. You'll be happier and you won't be let down so much. You don't have to lower your standards—just learn to be patient with "the growing season" needed by every human being, including yourself.

- Listen to your "talk." Are you using lots of "shoulds" and commanding statements such as, "Go get that," "Do this," "Don't do that," "Stop it," "Cut that out." If so, stop! Instead, say, "I need this to be done. Will you do that for me?" 90% of the time you will get what you need. What if they say, "No"? First of all, you are probably worrying about something that won't happen if you really try to do what I'm asking, but if they do, then fine. Don't get upset. Just give them a consequence for refusing to help. One consequence that really works is to let them know the next time they need help you will refuse. Say, "Since you are choosing to tell me no, next time you ask for my help I won't be able to help you. In our family we help each other." Then follow through, once, and calmly refer back to their moment of refusing to help you. Don't be vindictive, don't lecture. Let your non-helping speak for itself. Next time they will be more likely to help you. Kids learn pretty quick that it is far better to be cooperative. Try it. You will be surprised.

GOLD Parent Pitfalls :-(

This is a quick list of things that are often liabilities for your color when it comes to parenting. Each one can be eliminated first by recognizing the pitfall, and then by using the positive qualities of your second color to work past it.

- Using "Command and Control" (see page 394) tactics too often when your kids do something wrong, when they don't do what you ask, and when you are upset.

- You may be more resistant to change and less flexible than you think.

- When your child changes plans on you, you may go into "interrogation" mode causing your child or teen to become flustered, upset, or defensive.

- When you are stressed you may become moody or pessimistic, act short tempered or abrupt—often demanding that family members do whatever you tell them to do, right now.

- You may try to control children's behaviors, choices, time, schoolwork, activities, friends, clothing choices, and grooming responsibilities. This may work for awhile but eventually it will backfire.

- You may also try to control things like money, supplies, food, etc., as a way to get your child's behavior to change. Depending on your child's color, there are more effective ways to motivate your kids. You will learn more as you learn about their colors in the second half of the book.

- You may think that the only way to change a child's behavior is to impose stricter and stricter control. Again, check out your child's color later in the book.

- You may refuse to provide rewards because you feel or think that rewards are ridiculous, coddling, and soft. If this is you, then you probably believe that children and teens should just do what's right because you, the Gold parent, says so. Good luck with that. Is it working so far? Not likely. If you've got an Orange, providing rewards will change your life!

- You may think, or at least act, like you think that you are always right and justified in whatever you do as a parent. If you are stubborn and unbending, your child will be, too.

- You may blame others but will boldly justify your own actions—oftentimes talking over, or louder, than others who don't agree or who are arguing with you. This may be hard to admit, but if you blame others for what goes wrong, so will your child.

- Under stress you may become critical of your spouse, your children, teens, or others including your children's teachers, church leaders, and friends. You may also adopt a very narrow focus on the negative. If so, your children will mimic your behavior and your outlook when they are upset.

- You may be overly concerned about ownership, sharing, fairness, what's right, what looks right, and just getting the job done without considering the cost.

- You may create rules for everyone else but create "exceptions" for yourself.

- May become highly controlling of things, schedules, details, and telling others what to do. May appear bossy, very opinionated and judgmental under stress.

- May think that if your child or teen is acting inappropriately that it is ALL your child's responsibility and that it is not your parenting beliefs or actions. You may at first believe yourself to be a responsible, hard-working, no-nonsense parent and work to justify your actions and get other parents to believe you. As the child's behavior worsens, you may seek guidance for your child, again assuming that there is something wrong with the child. Eventually, a wise Gold parent will look inwardly and choose to change their own parenting beliefs and behaviors. This is when things start to improve and your child will change their behavior as you embrace effective but non-controlling parenting methods.

GOLD Parent Perks :-)

These are just some of the EXCELLENT qualities you bring to your parent-child relationship. Each quality is based on your ability to build STRUCTURE, CONSISTENCY, and positive EXPECTATIONS into your parenting behaviors.
This list may seem short but each thing is HUGE!

- You bring structure to the family's flurry of activities, often sorting through the chaos of conflicting needs and priorities in order to plan and juggle everything.

- You can create a solid sense of family purpose, often creating some kind of family mission statement, value chart, or guiding principles to live by.

- You are excellent at setting up chore assignments and reward systems aimed at teaching children how to work, and to be responsible.

- You instill a sense of tradition into your family's life and often communicate family stories, genealogies, and values.

- You are outstanding at providing stability, safety, and consistency in an ever-changing world, often upholding traditional or religious values.

- You are excellent at supporting your children's school projects, assignments, activities, and sports teams, often volunteering to help whenever and wherever possible.

- You have a natural ability to teach your children and teens about social norms, what's right and what's wrong, about being responsible, and about being committed to good causes.

- You have high expectations for your children because you see their potential. You rarely "give up" on your child or teen.

- You will defend your child and protect them as long as possible.

- You tend to not accept disrespectful talk from your kids and teens. This is good. Other color parents need to learn to communicate a "You must be at least respectful in your talk and actions" policy.

GOLD Parent Do's & Don'ts

Here's a quick and simple guide on what to do and what not to do as a parent, based on your first color.

- DON'T use command and control tactics to control your child's or teen's bad behavior. DO teach and model the right behaviors, then... DO give kids choices to do what's right or not.

- DO give them time (anywhere from a few seconds, to a few minutes, to a few days) to do what's right... or to show you they are really going to disobey.

- DON'T create unclear or unreasonable expectations for your children and teens because you assume your kids already know what to do, or how to be.

- DO teach your kids what you want them to do BEFORE you expect them to do it.

- DON'T take disobedience personally.

- DO look at misbehavior as some kind of communication. They are communicating that they are upset, uncomfortable, bugged, put out, or a host of other things. Then, again, teach them what a better response is and ASK them to do it. Give them a big "Thank you" when they do it, and a big consequence when they don't, but DO stay calm and don't command in all things.

- DON'T get too invested in how your children's actions make you look to other adults. Try not to care what others think, which is tough for a Gold or Blue parent to do.

- DO remember that YOU are the best authority on YOUR kids.

- DON'T look at your children as possessions. They have as much free will as you and will eventually exercise it, whether you are ready or not.

- DO realize that your kids make choices just like you and that the umbilical cord was truly cut at birth. All you can do is lead, guide, direct, and give consequences to your kids. It's ALL based on THEIR choices, not YOUR ability to CONTROL.

- DON'T hold your kids up as an object of pride if they are good, or a point of disgrace if they are bad. They are just human beings with minds of their own. Your job is to teach, give choices, provide appropriate rewards when they do good, and hold them accountable when they do wrong. It's that simple.

- DON'T jump to conclusions or decide ahead of time that your child or teen will, or won't, act a certain way. You hate that when others do that to you; why do it to them?

- DO give your kids (and others) the benefit of the doubt. Be pleasantly surprised by them at least once a day. Look for the good—not for how they will screw up. That's how you would like others to look at your actions. Your children deserve the same treatment, no matter what color they are or how bad they've been all day.

- DO, DO, DO have fun and lighten up. Golds often forget to have fun. Let your kids teach you how to be jolly!

Gold Parents: A Last Word or Two

Just the Gospel according to Shannon ;-)

Gold parents are amazing! I taught a class of a group of several Gold parents in Omaha in 2010 who had "multiples." That means they each had at least one set of twins, triplets, or more. WOW! I admired them so!!!

They juggled and parented and worked and played and loved their children. They also laughed, cried, and pulled their hair out like the rest of us but they did it double and triple! These parents showed me the wonder of the Gold parent. Each one needed structure and yet adopted some sort of "consistent" *flexibility*. They desired some semblance of order and yet "structured" in time to *go with the flow.* They naturally tended toward "command and control" and yet embraced the ability to parent their little Blues with sensitive -ity, their Oranges with some "organized" freedoms, and their Greens with more information and clearer expectations. When they butted heads with their Gold kids they realized that they were just a "Mini Me" of themselves. This special group of Gold parents and other parents just like them (without the twins) are certainly on my "hero" and "shero" list. (Probably even more so because I have NO natural Gold in me at all!)

We need the great examples of Gold parents who do pretty good with bedtime routines, getting their kids to do homework, and teaching their children the value of work and service and responsibility. They love their children and teens and definitely are an active part of their lives. Go, Gold Parents! We love you all and wish we were more like you!

The Quick ORANGE Adult Answer...

Needs <u>FREEDOM</u>
Freedom to act, move, and to be themselves. Independent thinker or feeler. Moves on.

Values <u>REWARDS</u>
Prefers quick results and outcomes. Wants some fun. Unconditional acceptance of who they are and what they do is a reward.

Trust Tactic <u>BOUNDARIES</u>
Operates best exercising freedom within clear boundaries understood BEFORE they make a choice, if possible.

The Simple ORANGE Adult Truth...

ORANGE parents are freedom fighters who are very focused on the moment and who often approach that "moment" with flexibility. At the same time, they may only be "flexible" about what they want. They usually need, or personally adopt, an outside source of boundaries, principles, or values that help them stay focused, productive, active, and doing what's right. They are very action-oriented because they are highly efficient and seek rewards in-the-moment. They must have personal freedom. Their biggest stressors come from people, things, and situations that seem to take away their freedoms and provide little or no reward.

Orange adults need **FREEDOM** to be and act for themselves. Choices, the ability to move and act, and some fun and adventure are also needed by Oranges. Oranges need others to understand that they are freedom fighters at heart, if pushed too far to conform they will rebel. Adult Oranges, like Orange children and teens, often want what they want, when they want it, but a balanced adult Orange will understand that they can't, or that it's not always right, to have everything they want right now. A balanced Orange adult will have learned to see that great freedom comes from following wise laws, rules, religious principles, and social norms.

Balanced Orange adults know how to control their actions in order to support the ones they love, to gain greater freedoms, and to experience more intrinsic rewards. Orange children and teens who grow up with a stable principle-based, value-driven family group grow into amazing, clever, entrepreneurial, successful, and adventurous balanced Orange adults.

Oranges value **REWARDS**, positive outcomes, fun, adventure, compliments, and cleverness. These things provide freedom, exhibit freedom, and promote freedom for themselves and others. They are the ultimate negotiators because they don't like closed options. There's no freedom, no reward in having zero choices. Many Oranges enjoy competition, but introvert Oranges will most likely compete against themselves, where extrovert Oranges will most likely compete against others.

Oranges also value physical abilities. They are often good with their hands and with tools. They like to build and create stuff. They are all about the action. There no greater freedom than choosing your own actions whether it's running or sleeping, cleaning or vegging, building something or playing video games. For these reasons Orange adults are very efficient in their actions, meaning they can move quickly to get things done and often expect the same from their kids and teens. They will move quickly through their chores and work projects in an effort to be rewarded either by the fun of doing something else they really want to do, or by the freedom to move on to another activity or location. Due to this trait to move quickly and efficiently, kids and spouses who move slower or with more forethought may drive the adult Orange crazy!

When Oranges move without much planning ahead of time or because some of their actions include verbs like sitting, sleeping, watching TV, or playing video games, other adults and Gold kids especially, may label these Orange adult behaviors as irresponsible or lazy. While it may be a sign of some self-centeredness, it may also be a sign of stress in the form of no freedom or rewards. While too many restraints can be frustrating to an Orange, they are very clever and efficient and work great under pressure because they are very in-the-moment and flexible with that moment.

Balanced Oranges can be very responsible, very accomplished, and very committed to their family, their job, and their community. This is because a balanced Orange adult chooses to see their commitments and obligations in one of two very distinct "orange" ways. They will either choose to look for and find the rewards and freedoms that naturally come from these commitments, OR they will find ways to create fun or freedom in some responsible activity simply because that activity is the right thing to do.

For example, as an Orange parent, it may be a real bummer that your Green son chooses to act up on your way to a family movie that you've been dying to see and the only consequence that will be logical to his young Green mind is to turn around and not go to the movie. An unbalanced, secretly self-centered, Orange parent will justify a way to see the movie anyway, thus reinforcing the Green child's idea that he can get away with bad behavior. On the other hand, a balanced and mature Orange parent will stay calm and opt to skip the movie, for now, and teach the Green child that there are consequences for their inappropriate behavior. The balanced Orange parent does this for one reason: because it's the right thing to do. There is no immediate reward and instead a complete loss of freedom for the Orange parent in that moment. However, the balanced Orange parent can create a personal reward or freedom later by getting a babysitter and going to the movie without the Green child or by creating some other fun activity for the family while the Green child learns their lesson (because they haven't misbehaved—the Green child has). Balanced Orange adults are very responsible and committed; we just have to understand it from an Orange's point-of-view.

Orange adults function best if they can have the freedom to do things their way within accepted **BOUNDARIES**. Oranges are actually very simple people to understand. They need freedom, they value rewards and have an uncanny ability to perform successfully, often pulling things together at the last minute. They really are that easy to understand. There is one concern for adult Oranges and Orange children alike. They must have boundaries. Boundaries are "rules" you can see, often put in place and reinforced by an outside source: another person (e.g. their spouse), a value system (e.g. their accepted religion), their job, or the law.

Because Oranges, both child and adult, are very in-the-moment and flexible with that moment, if they are not grounded with a firm foundation in true principles and values, they will tend to lack a strong internal barometer of right and wrong. This may often unconsciously lead them to "negotiate" what's right or wrong in their mind with the voice of what they want speaking louder than the voice of what is right. As mentioned earlier, if an Orange doesn't grow up with a firm foundation of values, such as being committed to correct principles or religion, they may make choices that serve their wants in-the-moment. They may lose sight of what they really want *later*, for what they think they want *now*.

Boundaries, or rules they can see, and avid use of their second color, tells them when they are about to go too far. For example, unless an Orange child is rewarded for kind actions, and given boundaries with respect to unkind actions, an Orange child may grow up being rude, abrupt, and matter-of-fact in their communication with those they love and think it's okay. They will continue to act that way as an adult until they are given a "boundary" by someone who tells them they have been hurtful and that it's NOT okay—thus depriving the adult Orange of a "feel-good" reward. Here's another example that you may not like: if an Orange grows up without being held accountable for being disloyal to friends and family they may decide that faithfulness in a marriage relationship is conditional and negotiable—thus justifying extramarital affairs. Every color has a dark side. This is the Orange's, if they grow up without boundaries, they arrive at adulthood without respect for boundaries. It's that simple.

An interesting perspective about the Orange adult is that in the business world, if you've been exposed to all this personality type stuff, Oranges (also known as ESFP, ESTP, ISFP, or ISTP) were probably described to you as "flighty, irresponsible party animals." But that is just not true. Extroverted Orange-Blues tend to be fun and very social "party animals" if you will, but not so with all the Oranges. Introverted Orange-Greens are extremely serious and prefer small groups, solitary activities, and do "quiet" really well. Their "verbs" often include sleeping, lounging, procrastinating, sitting, vegging, watching and zoning. They often seem pretty Green at first glance until they do something that doesn't make any sense at all because they were impulsive in-the-moment. Then you know they are not first color Greens. Greens are never impulsive, but Oranges are.

A word or two about Orange Introverts and Orange Extroverts. Introverted Oranges seem more reserved and quiet. They can often be sneaky about what they want and may cover things up. Introverted Oranges conserve their energy and put off any action until the last minute but when they decide it's time to move, they usually move quickly and efficiently.

Extroverted Oranges are almost complete opposites except they are still focused on the moment and may not think things through to the consequences. Extroverted Oranges seem to be on the move all the time but are not always focused. Most extroverted Oranges enjoy competition—often challenging others. They are usually decisive (although not always wise), realistic, practical, and resilient. They often seem to be care-free and easy-going as they approach life with flexibility. Since they live in-the-moment and can be bold in their actions and language, they are really expert in an emergency.

Mature, balanced Orange adults usually work hard and efficiently to get all their work done quickly so they can get on to the fun. Their talk is full of verbs and what they are going to do.

ORANGE Parent Stressors

For each stressor, look at how your child's behavior violates one or more of your 3 Words: FREEDOM, REWARDS, and BOUNDARIES.

- A complete lack of freedom in any form but especially if your child's behavior is the cause of your freedom being threatened.

- When your child or teen won't move as quickly as you want them to move or get something done. This causes a lack of freedom for you to also get moving.

- When family life and responsibilities are unrewarding and when you feel, or think, that you have no free time to just do a few minutes of what you want to do.

- When you work really hard and there's no money left over at the end of the bills to do anything fun with or to buy a reward for yourself or your family.

- Being told by your spouse that you can't afford something when you feel, or think, that you've worked really hard, either at home as a "stay-at-home" parent or working in your job for someone else.

- When the things that you want to do in your free time are not supported by your spouse. This feels like a lack of freedom.

- No time alone, or with just your spouse doing some fun or rewarding activity.

- When too many people all want something from you right now and there seems to be no solution or escape.

- When you keep losing things because you are distracted.

- When others give you strict "to do" lists, detailed instructions, or don't like how you helped or completed something around the house.

- When your kids or spouse demand something from you. Your impulse is to say "No!" just because you are feeling backed into a corner even though you would have said "Sure" if you had been asked.

- When your environment is restrictive and unrewarding. Oranges can do chaos unless it's taking away from their freedom. Most Orange parents are very good at keeping their home and office picked up with some sort of organization because it allows for movement, freedom, and rewards.

- Not having any boundaries. Too much freedom is also stressful even though this may be hard for you as an Orange to admit. When an Orange adult has too much freedom they tend to live large and take it all up only to suffer severe consequences sooner or later. Most balanced and mature Oranges would rather keep their freedoms within certain accepted boundaries and be able to consistently have those freedoms.

- Too much emotion and long, emotional "talks" or intense conflicts. Oranges tend to "check out" and seem to not care to those who are emotional.

- Unnecessary routines, over-scheduling, too many nit-picky family rules, zero flexibility, strict procedures for everything from the laundry to the dishes to getting the oil changed creates a lack of freedom with very little rewards or sense-making.

- Bossy children or spouse.

- When others, including children and teens, are slow to make up their mind or to comply with requests. Orange parents tend to use command and control tactics but it's about efficiency and a need to get moving, not about control and power like it might be for a Gold parent.

Lower Your Stress as a ORANGE Parent

Here are some excellent ideas for lowering your stress.
Build **FREEDOM, REWARDS,** *and reasonable* **BOUNDARIES**
into your routines while allowing for the needs
of the other colors in your home.

- First of all, get acquainted with your 3 Words: **FREEDOM, REWARDS,** and **BOUNDARIES**. Use these 3 Words whenever you are feeling frustrated, negative, trapped, criticized, or over loaded to self-diagnose what's really bothering you. This will help you be in control of what you can control (which is really only you), and to let go of what you cannot control (which is really everything, and everyone else).

- Learn to evaluate your freedom needs. Ask yourself if you are truly trapped and without options or rewards. Often, Orange adults just need to "reframe" their situation and realize that they have other, more important, freedoms and while their rewards are not immediate, they are on their way, or greater rewards are coming in the future. Use your natural ability to see the positive and move on quickly. You can choose to be happy and that in itself is a reward and brings more freedom. Listen to the wisdom of your spouse and loved ones when you want to do something right now. They will help you use your "freedom" in better ways.

- Even though you are an Orange and not a Gold, you need to examine your expectations, too. Your expectation of how fast your kids can move, how fast they can clean something, find their shoes and get in the van may be unrealistic. Whatever color your child is, there will be a reason why they are not going to move as fast as you expect them to. If they're Orange, YOU are now THEIR freedom sucker. If they are Blue, your harsh words confuse them and they will stand still and melt down because they don't know how to please you (because you sound so mad about shoes). If they are Green, you've not given them enough information and they secretly assume you are an idiot. ("If I didn't move when you just yelled, why do you think I will move faster just because you are yelling louder?") If they are Gold you've probably just given them what feels like ten things to do at once and it's not possible for them to get any sense of structure from your shouts and so to them you've, once again, proven that you shouldn't be a parent.

- Listen to your "talk." Are you using lots of "hurry-ups" and commanding statements? If you are saying, "Go get that," "Do this," "Don't do that," "Stop it," "Hurry up, we've got go," "Cut that out," then you need to change your tactics or your stress level will eventually lead to a heart attack. Instead, say something like, "I need this to be done. Will you do that for me?" 90% of the time you will get what you need. If they say, "No," fine. Don't get upset. Just give them a consequence for refusing that will help them see it is far better to be cooperative. Just try it. You will be surprised. If not, email me, or one of my coaches, and we'll figure it out together.

ORANGE Parent Pitfalls :-(

This is a quick list of things that are often liabilities for your color when it comes to parenting. Each one can be eliminated first by recognizing the pitfall, and then by using the positive qualities of your second color to work past it.

- Using "Command and Control" (see page 394) tactics too often when you need your kids to do something or when they don't do what you ask fast enough and when you are upset. Depending on your child's color, you will get various negative reactions but they won't move like you want them to.

- You may be very good at allowing your child the freedom you think they need but if they are not an Orange this will seem like you are too flexible making you their biggest stressor.

- When your child needs you to set solid boundaries, create a schedule, stick to your commitments or be dependable, you may appear to let them down.

- When your freedom needs are threatened you will become quickly frustrated and often go into "command and control" mode. Your child may see you as Dr. Jekyll and Mr. Hyde, going from fun one minute to bossy and short-tempered the next.

- You may not follow through on consequences and hold your child accountable for his/her actions. This often happens with Orange parents because they've become distracted and moved on. Being a parent, you've probably seen the movie, "UP!" Remember the dog with the voice-enhancement collar who, in the middle of a thought, will get distracted by something and jerk his head to the side quickly exclaiming, "Squirrel!" and then come right back to complete his sentence? Well, Orange's "Squirrel!" just like that!

- You may have a difficult time slowing down long enough to really listen to your kids when they are upset. You may instead minimize their concerns, hurts, and problems. This will only drive your children away and they will find someone else to listen. That's probably not what you want.

- Orange parents often have a tough time providing enough information to their children, especially their Greens, because it takes too long. Slow down and provide that information to your kids.

- You may ignore the need for rewards when your children do what's right, not because you feel or think that rewards are ridiculous, coddling, and soft, but because you've moved on. You've "Squirreled." Slow down and give the rewards and compliments that you value yourself and say, "Thank you."

- You are a lean, mean, move-and-get-it-done machine. You may think, or at least act, like you think that you know the best and fastest way to do something. Patience may not be your virtue but it needs to be. If you are stubborn, commanding, and always in a hurry your child either will be too, or they will be your exact opposite and made of molasses.

- You may get easily frustrated with your kids and others and prefer to either do it yourself or you may just check out and leave or give up. Fixing a problem, especially a people-problem, may seem to be more stress than it's worth. Be careful not to "write off" or emotionally abandon your kids because they seem to be a lot of work and no fun. Go ahead and get your freedom needs met in appropriate ways, but not at the expense of your children.

- Under stress you may become critical of your spouse, your children, teens, or others including your children's teachers, church leaders, and friends when you see them as restricting your freedom. You may also adopt a very narrow focus on the negative because you are so in-the-moment you may have a hard time seeing that things can work out in the future.

- You may be overly concerned with your child's freedom (even when they are not) and manipulate situations to get your child or teen out of restrictive situations or commitments.

- You may find ways to get around the rules for yourself and your children and teens. Without realizing it you may be teaching your kids to fudge rules and commitments.

- You may have little patience for emotional upsets, depression, wallowing, and the inability to get something done now.

- May easily make excuses for your child's or teen's inappropriate actions without holding them accountable because you may see a teacher's or principle's nature as too controlling and may undermine their discipline.

ORANGE Parent Perks :-)

These are just some of the EXCELLENT qualities you bring to your parent-child relationship. Each quality is based on your ability to provide FREEDOM, REWARDS, and specific BOUNDARIES for your child through your parenting behaviors. This list may seem short but each thing is HUGE!

- You respect and admire your child's unique personality and you naturally provide them with room to grow and develop.

- You generally like to DO things with your kids. You'll be the Mom or Dad that's out playing catch with your kids, building tree houses, baking cookies, and wrestling. I know of one Orange mom who, in the dead of winter, cleared room in her $500,000+ home for her kids to ride their bicycles on the tile floor from the kitchen through the dining room to the family room and back. I thought, "How COOL! Floors can be cleaned but bored kids can kill you!"

- Orange parents are generally "movers and shakers" so you

probably are pretty good at getting your kids to get stuff done as long as you don't use too many "command and control" tactics.

- You are usually pretty good at finding ways to have fun or to "reward" your children, unless you've been taught by your parents that rewards are to be used sparingly. I have worked with dozens of Orange parents who grew up with Gold parents who seem more Gold in their parenting behaviors. Once these parents embrace who they really are as Oranges, they become more rewarding to others and themselves.

- You probably don't lecture much. You most likely use short, specific and to-the-point words and phrases in your communication efforts. This is great for your Orange kids, but not for the other three colors. Greens need more information, Golds need specific instructions or expectations, Blues need to hear caring and consideration in your words.

- You don't dwell on your kid's mistakes.

- You are good at teaching your kids to move on pretty quickly with minimum drama.

- You are more likely to be open to negotiation as long as it doesn't infringe on your own freedom.

- You are very realistic and practical and teach your children to be the same.

- Orange parents are generally very skilled at all kinds of physical tasks and you will probably be more likely to let your kids try new actions, sports, and challenges. You may even be a little pushy about getting them involved.

- You are not likely to coddle or smother your children. You're more likely to be the parent who says to a toddler who just stumbled over his own feet, "Hop up, you're okay."

- You have a knack for being resilient with few real worries and you can teach your kids to be the same.

- You can be very bold in your actions and communication and this can help your kids in that you are more likely to tell them what they need to hear without worrying that you will upset them like many Blue parents might.

- You are good at getting many things done at once. This can be helpful in teaching your kids to multitask but be patient if this is not one of your kids' skills. Remember to teach them the skill rather than demand they be like you from the get-go.

- You are pretty flexible and this can be a good thing as a parent. You have a knack for "going with the flow" when you are juggling many kids, lot's of activities and multiple needs. Just be careful to have a little free time to yourself. Without a little freedom you will feel stressed and irritable. Watch out for that.

- You are highly efficient. I've admired Orange moms for how much they seem to get done in a day, even though they don't usually think they get enough done.

- As an Orange parent you usually have a pretty good sense of humor. Use this to have fun with your kids and help them see the sunny side of life—but don't be sarcastic or too lighthearted when your kids are upset. Listen first. Then when they are calmer, point out the humor of the situation.

- You are good in a crisis and get right down to the nitty-gritty of solving the problem. This is a good skill to teach your children. Your Orange kids will also have this characteristic, but your Blues will tend to be emotional and anxious, your Gold will get stressed, anxious, flee or shut down, and your Green will tend to panic or shut down. Teach them to focus, think only of their next action, and then DO IT. That's what you do even though you may not have thought of it that way before.

ORANGE Parent Do's & Don'ts

Here's a quick and simple guide on what to do and what not to do as a parent, based on your first color.

- DON'T be impatient, short-tempered, or commanding with your kids just because YOUR freedom is being sucked away in-the-moment.

- DO take a deep breath and speak gently.

- DO ask for your child's cooperation instead of demanding it.

- DON'T say, "Stop that!," or "Get the toys picked up, NOW!" Instead use "I Need / Will You" messages.

- DO say, "I need you to stop whining about not being able to go to the park and help me get the toys picked up so we can go. Will you help me now?" Trust me it works. If they don't help? Simple. The toys disappear and no park. Period. End of story. No lecture, just action. As an Orange you'll like that.

- DO get to the point when you talk.

- DON'T lecture. They heard you—they just may not like what you said.

- DON'T expect your kids to get to the point any time soon. All kids want to be heard and some can go on and on. If you need them to give you the short version, again use an "I Need / Will You" message. ("I need you to give me the short version, honey, will you do that for me?")

- DO understand that rules, or a lack of freedom in any form, is stressful to you. This will come up almost every day of your parenting career. You'll think babies shouldn't be equipped to cry so much as you get zero sleep. Then, you'll feel that the preschool is being stingy with their art supplies and too free with their 'time outs'. Next, you'll think your 3rd grader has too much homework. After that, you'll think the coach in middle school is having practice start way too early and it's cutting into your August vacation. Then, you'll think that the high school guidance counselor is requiring your teenager to pick a career before he even knows how to shave. Rules and policies in any form are going to bug you the whole time your kids are growing up.

- DON'T let all that get to you.

- DO use your Orange gifts to laugh at the silliness of it all and let it go.

- DO keep things fun for you and for your kids.

- DON'T be too tough on your kids, but don't be too easy either.

- DO be patient while your children, especially your non-Orange ones, learn new skills. They may never be as fast as you.

- DO give your kids choices, but also give them what THEIR color needs, not only what YOUR color can give. You want them to move fast? Then work WITH their color, not AGAINST it. It will be loads faster and more efficient. I dare you to try it.

- DO remember that you are all about the action.

- DON'T forget that your kids, especially if they are Green or Blue, are not. They will need you to slow down and do some listening and some explaining. This is good for both of you.

ORANGE Parents: A Last Word or Two
Just the Gospel according to Shannon ;-)

I love Orange parents! Most often in the classes I teach it's the Orange parents who are transformed once they learn that they are Oranges and they learn how to understand their kids who are not. Several have become very emotional when they realize that they are okay being an Orange and that it's okay to experience a little bit of freedom-loss as a parent; especially when your child or teen is your opposite color.

At the time of writing this first book, I've worked with more extraordinary Orange parents than I can count who have embraced the parenting principles and insights found here. They are still very action-oriented but they know how to "work it" so that even they get their needs met. In the process, they get more freedom as parents and their kids are more balanced, more fun, and parenting itself becomes more rewarding.

Orange parents often find this information extremely helpful in understanding their own parents, spouse, co-workers, and children's teachers, coaches, and friends.

Balanced Orange parents are very efficient at everything they do and get so much more done in a day than I personally could ever dream of doing. I have several Orange friends who have helped me refine the **Parenting** by **COLORS** information found in this book and the "Ask, Be, Do" Parenting Process shared in the next book; and for that I am extremely grateful. They've helped me shorten the "Ask, Be, Do" process. They've challenged me to shorten my classes. They've needed me to make my handouts more to-the-point. And last but not least, and my husband thanks them, too; they've helped me be a better homemaker. ;-)

The Quick GREEN Adult Answer...

Needs <u>INFORMATION</u>
Data, facts, details and to understand why things are the way they are.

Values <u>LOGIC</u>
Appreciates information and people that make sense. Desires to be calm, cool, and collected—even processing emotions logically. Values competency, problem solving, and logical communication.

Trust Tactic <u>EXPERIENCE</u>
Relates best to independence and autonomy. Operates best by gathering their own information through personal experience. They research, then act. Respects "big picture" expectations. Prefers results-oriented communication and creating their own "how to's."

The Simple GREEN Adult Truth...

GREEN parents are logical thinkers who are most often focused on future possibilities. They approach things in terms of the big picture and problem solving. At the same time, they are very logical in the present and don't appreciate things, situations, people, and emotions that don't make sense to them, (or "stupid"). They are very intuitive about whether or not things are logical or illogical, and about whether things make sense or don't make sense. This means they can see right through a teenager's bologna in seconds.

Greens are continually learning, and checking for accuracy in everything. I think that's why others think that Greens are being critical. They are being "critical" as in critical thinkers—looking for what makes sense and doesn't make sense. A balanced Green is not likely being as judgmental of the people in his/her life as others think he/she is being. Then again, if the Green is not very balanced, they might be critical as in judgmental. My suggestion... ask your Green, calmly, as if you were seeking information. In my experience, they don't *want* to be judgmental of the ones they love and if you calmly ask them to *think* about whether or not they are being judgmental, the process of thinking about how to answer your question often helps them to stop being judgmental and instead be more helpful.

A word of warning, if they do change their perspective, drop it. Don't become illogical and push, push, push for an apology or for them to tell you you're right. If you do, you will push them into a corner and you're just being selfish. Really, just drop it. You already got them to change their mind set. If they are being cooperative and more supportive, why ruin it by pushing another human being to their limit? Just drop it. If you give them a break, they will give you a break—and you will need it someday, too.

Greens are continually solving problems. Everything that comes at them they see in terms of a problem to solve, and most of the time they come up with some pretty great solutions. The problem is that most of the time we don't want to hear them and that's a shame, because I've found that my Greens really do have the best solutions 80% to 90% of the time. They are just really good at problem solving.

The down side to that is when a Green is married to, or parenting, a first or second color Blue there can be huge misunderstanding about talking and problem solving. Blues, first or second color Blues, build relationships through communication. When you have a Blue (first or second color) who is trying to be close to a Green, and that Green is naturally quiet, the Blue will tend to chat at the Green. The Green doesn't usually mind. If they do mind or get bored they tune out but may still look like they are listening.

Back to our chatty Blue. When the Blue chats, they often share their concerns, stressors, stories, and problems at the Green. Now, here's the interesting part, the Blue is chatting to build a relationship and the Green hears "problem to solve". So the Blue all of a sudden has an attentive Green interrupting him/her with fact-finding questions or "loving" solutions. The Blue doesn't interpret the interrogation or the abrupt, pointed and sometimes tactless solutions as loving at all. Instead they see the questions and solutions as impatient judgments and commands for actions that are offered without solicitation and without all the ins and outs of the story. The Blue is hurt, feels stupid, judged, and misunderstood and lashes out or withdraws. The Green gets defensive and wonders what the heck just happened, decides that this is stupid (the process not the person— another mistake the Blue makes) and decides to stop offering solutions for the meantime.

There you have it folks… conflict, hurt, misunderstanding, and miscommunication in the making. Is there a way out? Yes. It's simple and it works. The Blue must provide the information to the Green through communication up front that they are just wanting to chat, not to have their problem solved. The Green must choose to take the chatting at face value and relax, listen, bond, enjoy, focus on the one they love, and don't problem solve. If the Green does have a solution that is just bursting to get out, then ASK if you can share a solution. You'll get a Blue who is more likely to hear the Green out.

They are insightful subject-matter experts. They tend to become an expert in many areas because they love to learn and they are constantly seeking out new information. This is why Greens are often correct in their assessments, which can be infuriating to the other colors. It's because they have thought things through and done their research to a degree that the other colors just don't do. This why in my classes I always say, "Don't argue with a Green if you're not a Green because you will never win. So don't try!"

At the same time, it would be wise and competent of Green adults to seriously consider the thoughts, insights and ideas of others as having value and don't dismiss other's perspective so quickly. It just makes the Green man or woman look like an insensitive jerk and that's no way to be a competent parent, spouse, co-worker, manager, or friend. Greens who do act in this unbalanced way are not happy. Balanced, competent Greens realize that being, and acting, like they are an island unto themselves causes more problems to solve and in the end makes no sense if they value having functioning, productive, fulfilling relationships. I've watched many adults Greens come to this realization and change their behaviors. I've watched them smile more, draw their spouses, children and friends into their confidences, and communicate and demonstrate love more often. These Greens get happy and experience joy. It's a wonderful transformation to witness. They don't lose any of their wonderful, logical or thought-filled gifts, and they become a positive force for building relationships at home.

Another few, seemingly random, traits that all Greens seem to share is their drive to test the limits of their own understanding in ways that leave others scratching their heads. They use the words "I think" a lot, even when describing their feelings. They tend to have a dry witty, sometimes sarcastic, sense of humor, and they tend to secretly think they are the superior color.

Green adults can often seem slow to action and in-the-moment, because they need to think things through first. They must process everything in detail before they would presume to think they are competent enough on the topic to act, even about small things. Here's the interesting part: this "need" to think things out, is so internal, so ingrained, so sub-conscious, that most adult Greens have a difficult time admitting that this is true… until they have T - I - M - E to really think about it. Then they will see that it's true. They will tell the rest of us that it only makes sense to be that way and that, of course, it's the only smart way to be! (I live with three Greens, I've totally got your number.)

The rest of us, especially the ones who need to be constantly moving, need to realize that when Greens take the time to think first, act later, it's not a bad thing; it's just a Green thing. Be patient with your Greens when they need to process. If you need something done right away, provide that information and then give them three to five minutes of lead time. Your life will be less stressful, believe me.

Here's an example, when I'm doing the dishes really quickly and need the trash to be instantly whisked away, I kindly say to my Green husband of almost thirty years, "Hey, will you take out the trash (question, not a demand) in the next three or four minutes (a deadline in the form of information) so that I can get the kitchen cleaned up to make dinner (the "WHY" in the form of yet more information)?" Then in five minutes when he's still not done it, I don't get mad, I just say, "Hey, sweetie (my pet name that he doesn't mind), I'm not trying to nag (more info) but the trash (as a gentle reminder)… Are going to come take it out?" That's when he usually hops right up and does it.

Now some of you might think that's a lot of work. I don't think so. A) It gets the job done. B) It's respectful. C) It takes into account that I'm not perfect either and oftentimes get distracted and don't hop right to what he wants. I can't expect something I don't do. And D) it doesn't end up in conflict. So, how can that ever be a bad thing? Bottom line, just understand that you have a choice: you can understand and work around the fact that Greens take their time to process, or you can fight it. Either way, they don't care, AND they will still take the time to process. Period.

Now, to be clear, what are they processing? They are processing **INFORMATION**. Two of their biggest stressors are a lack of information and the lack of time to process it. Again, Greens are the logical thinkers and to be a "thinker" you have to have something to think about. You have to have information in the way that all the other colors can't even begin to comprehend. Information is like air to the Greens. Take away their information, and you suffocate them.

Greens need data, facts, figures, proof, evidence, research, the "big picture," desired results, and credible sources. They ask tons of "why" questions, especially about their spouse's and children's actions, motives, thought processes, requests, needs and wants. Greens ask "why" to get, pull, extract, and illicit more information out of whomever they are asking "why" of. Here's the funny part, if a Green is asking another human being "why", (or some form thereof) it's really a Green's way of saying "I love you." Yeah, I got your attention on that one, huh?

Here's how it works, Greens don't often really care what other random people think or how they feel. It's not insensitive on their part, it's just not logical to process information about what other people feel or what they want when they are not really connected to the Green personally. So, when a Green asks their spouse or child, "Why did you do that?," or "What were you thinking?," they are in essence saying, "I love you, or at least respect you enough to care what you were thinking that made you do that because right now what you did didn't make sense to me and I need more information to process your perspective." Believe me, "why," is a lot shorter than saying all of that. That's why they ask "why." Interesting, huh? Share this perspective with a Green and see what they think. When a Green's spouse or child doesn't make sense to them and the

Green sounds like they are being critical and judgmental, they don't mean to be. They are just frustrated and trying to make sense of what doesn't make sense.

Remember that Greens not only need information, they also need time to process it. Greens need others to give them at least a few minutes to think things through. Blues, especially take a Green's moment of thinking as if they've already said "no" and it feels like a rejection to a Blue. It's not. Give them a minute, be quiet, and let them think. Oranges will do the same thing if the Green isn't as fast as the Orange thinks they should be and will walk away or tune out and not wait for the answer. The Orange spouse, child, or teen will assume they've been told no and start hatching a plan to do, or get, what they want anyway. If someone makes a request of a Green, it would be a good thing for the Green to say, "Hmmm, let me think about that for just a _____ (second, minute, day, or week - the Green fills in the blank)." Just saying this is a competent way for a Green to communicate to the ones he or she loves that they need a little "think" time and that they are not immediately saying no.

The next idea to understand about Greens is that they value **LOGIC**. They are very analytical and try to be calm, cool, and collected. They are logical about everything, including their emotions. Remember, they are logical thinkers, so they even think logically about their emotions. This is why Greens do not share their feelings very easily or often. But don't misunderstand, while Greens have a calm, cool, and sometimes aloof demeanor, they experience very deep, strong emotions. In fact, when Greens experience strong emotions that hit very quickly without the necessary time to process them, they may do what I've come to call a "Wookiee rage."

These normally rare but sudden bursts of negative emotions for a Green can come on so quickly with no time to process, that the Green, momentarily looses control. Now when I say rare, I mean RARE, like once a year in a balanced, calm Green. But even balanced and mature Greens may, at these times, say cruel things to the ones they love. They will sound very illogical using absolutes that don't make sense to the rest of us such as "always" and "never." They can become physical, even violent, most often toward objects, shocking everyone around them. I've heard of wonderful, competent, balanced Greens slamming doors so hard the door jams come out of the wall or punching one isolated hole through a sheet of drywall.

Wookiee rages happen in our normally calm, cool, and collected Greens when a whoosh of strong emotions overwhelm their ability to logically process those emotions. For example, my very dear, logical, calm Green husband who's never shown a minute of anger towards me for at least three decades was hanging drywall in our basement. Over the course of the afternoon his drywall nailing gun repeatedly jammed. Finally, as he was struggling with nailing an awkward piece of drywall to the ceiling, the gun jammed again! Then it happened—the Wookiee Rage! Within the space of three seconds he angrily shot seventeen nails in the space of one square inch, then bare handedly ripped the piece of drywall off the ceiling except for the jagged corner where the seventeen nails securely held it in place.

As fast as the rage appeared it was gone, like nothing happened. He turned to his wide-eyed, stunned wife and 20-something son and with a frustrated edge to his voice, impatiently exclaimed, "WHAT?" Wife and son backed away. A few hours later we all had a goodhearted laugh about the whole thing, especially my husband.

It sounds like a really scary event but the Wookiee rage is actually very understandable. Most Green men, especially those who really love their families, who work hard and try to be logical, calm and collected 24/7, hate their Wookiee rages more than the rest of us. They don't understand why they just couldn't keep it together for just five more seconds because, truth be told, these good

Green men are really big gooey teddy bears on the inside.

Now what does a Green woman Wookiee rage look like? It's usually more of an emotional meltdown or more depressed-looking. Occasionally it may be a little more physical: a thrown pot or pan at the wall or slammed door. The most common action is that the Green mom or wife wants everyone to immediately clear out and give her some room or time alone. She may raise her voice and be suddenly commanding, saying, "Everyone OUT! Now!" That way she has the time and space to think things through. Don't bug her. Let her have her time to work it through.

Now the Green woman Wookiee rage may be the *result* of something her child or spouse did or said, but it's rarely if ever directed *at* her child or spouse. When a Green woman Wookiee rage happens they can be very hard on themselves and may even dive into the pit of despair for a time. They may feel guilty soon afterward and this will affect their self-esteem for a while until they can reason through it. They usually want to fix the situation or solve the problem right away where Green men tend to pretend it didn't happen. Again, a Green woman Wookiee rage is rare—maybe once a year—and it doesn't last too long. If a Green woman is going into Wookiee rage more frequently then her stress level is pretty high and I suggest that she gets help.

If a Green man or woman is losing control physically or emotionally more often than the rare occurrence I've described here and/or it is not as short lived as I've explained then it's not a Wookiee rage. It's serious and I would suggest they, or you, seek counseling. I've only seen my husband experience a Wookiee rage maybe three times in our whole twenty-eight years of marriage. I've seen my 26-year-old green son have a Wookiee rage since he was ten only four times. It is really rare once a Green grows up. I've also heard of dozens of other examples of the Wookiee rages that I'm describing with the same details in adults: rare and short-lived. Green children are different, they can Wookiee rage everyday, several times a day if they don't have parents who understand Green kids. For more information turn to the Green Kid's chapter page 293.

Once a Wookiee rage hits, my suggestion is to leave them alone to process it. Don't try to fix it, don't show an overabundance of compassion right then. Give them some space to process. Based on my personal experience living with two first color Greens and an Orange-Green and hearing dozens of other Wookiee rage stories, Greens are usually feeling frustrated with the situation and embarrassed that they lost control. Many times Greens can turn to other inappropriate behaviors such as blaming and rationalization after a Wookiee rage if they are pressed to talk, process, explain, or say "I'm sorry" before they have time to make some sense out of the situation.

Bottom line, Wookiee rages are typical but happen only occasionally in balanced Green adults. They are usually short-lived. They cause immediate embarrassment, maybe even denial, and are just the result of a momentary emotional overload for a logical thinker who needs time to think through their emotions. Period. If a Green adult is physically or emotionally out of control more than just one or twice a year seek other professional advice.

Now, believe it or not, the Wookiee rage brings us to a Green's need to have **LEARNING EXPERIENCES**. Greens really can only experience a Wookiee rage once a year, or even less. "How can that be?" you might ask when the rest of us can experience several emotional outbursts in a day on a really stressful day. It's because balanced Green adults learn by experience. As a child, a teenager and as a young adult, Greens experienced these times when Wookiee rages occurred and they didn't like the feeling of being out of control, illogical and emotional. These are things that they think are stupid in others, and really, REALLY stupid when they do it themselves. So they learned. They learned to shutdown, to act aloof, or to process emotional information faster. But as they grew and matured, they learned by experience to handle their emotions differently over time, thus the fewer and fewer Wookiee rages as they got older.

Greens learn everything by their own experience. When they have a problem to solve they often do some sort of research often even experiencing "analysis paralysis" when they need to stop researching and make a decision. Greens usually need to do their own research and are not likely to take the word of someone else easily. It's not that they don't trust others, it's just that doing the research themselves is all about gathering their own INFORMATION, in a LOGICAL way, so they can EXPERIENCE the LEARNING during the process. Are you seeing a pattern here? I hope so. For a Green, everything is about **INFORMATION**, **LOGIC**, and **LEARNING EXPERIENCES**. Period.

Learning for a Green is sort of a two-edged sword. Even a balanced Green adult will sometimes be like a Green child in that they, too, will bravely do things that others think they can't or shouldn't. Yet, at the same time they will shy away from opportunities and be reluctant to try for fear of looking stupid. A young and successful Green college student will courageously jump into going to law school but hesitates to start a workout program until he plans it out for weeks. Law school for this Green young man seems doable since he already knows that he is a highly skilled student, writer and researcher but he puts off starting a new workout program using the unfamiliar new law school workout facilities because he's never seen himself as athletic and he really doesn't want to workout alone or look stupid.

Very competent Greens can often be very successful in their work but may withdraw from family relationships or parenting. While they feel skilled in their work, they may feel incompetent when it comes to communication and people skills. This is often why Greens may seem preoccupied, deep in thought, or aloof at home with their spouses or with their children and teens. Greens struggle with showing their emotions and have little patience with the emotional responses of others, especially their family members whom they love but see their emotions as a problem to be solved or fixed. When it comes to emotions, don't be fooled into thinking Greens are cold and unfeeling. The truth is quite the opposite. Greens feel their emotions deeply and acutely, they just don't know how to communicate them or process them as easily as others.

It seems that I've shared more about the Green adult than any other color. That's just because typically Green adults can be difficult to understand if you are not one. They really are not that much of a mystery. Just remember their 3 Words: **INFORMATION**, **LOGIC**, and **LEARNING EXPERIENCES**. With the help of these 3 Words you can understand almost everything about the Green personality. Every lock has a key or a combination. The key to the Green is to focus on their 3 Words when you need to understand their behavior, perspective, or stressors. I wanted to give you as much information about either being a Green or about living with a Green. I hope this helps!

GREEN Parent Stressors

**For each stressor, look at how your
child's behavior violates one or more of your 3 Words:
INFORMATION, LOGIC, and LEARNING EXPERIENCES**

- When your child or teen does something that seems illogical and stupid because they didn't think, especially after you've already warned them about it or tried to teach them differently, like spilling milk after you warned them to be careful, or putting the car in the ditch after you specifically instructed them to slow down around that specific curve near your home.

- When you ask your child why they did something and they respond with, "I don't know." This is stressful because as a Green you cannot fathom that someone doesn't know why they did something; you ALWAYS know why you did something.

- Confusion and disorganization in how children want to complete a task or project because they (obviously) have not thought the assignment or project through.

- Having your child put off what seems to you to be a very logical assignment like taking out the trash or cleaning their room or picking up the toys before bed. You think, "What's the problem? This is an easy thing."

- Having your kid look incompetent (because you think it makes you look incompetent).

- Kids fighting, it's just stupid.

- Blue daughters who are very emotional. You don't see any logical reason for all the upset.

- Emotional sons, you don't even know where to start. They just need to suck it up, but mom wants to have them get in touch with their feelings.

- Dramatic Orange kids: you can see right through but your spouse wants to coddle them.

- When your spouse asks for help with a parenting issue and you have some answers but he/she decides that your solution is too harsh or abrupt and don't apply your idea. You think, "Then why did you ask me?" and refuse to help in the future.

- Lack of preparation when your older child or teen has an assignment, a project, or an after school or weekend event to get ready for.

- When your child is forgetful time after time.

- Lack of information about homework or other assignments they ask you to help with. You want to help but if you don't know what is expected or how can you help your child succeed.

- Having your child deal with stupid teachers, school counselors, or when they have to complete assignments that seem stupid to you, too.

- When the noise gets too high, especially when you have something to do, think through, or find.
- When you are blindsided or pushed to make a quick decision by an impatient child.
- When your toddler has a tantrum in public: this is just stupid and makes you look stupid.
- When your toddler won't stop crying and get themselves under control.
- When any age child won't take "no" for an answer.
- Parenting classes. Parenting experts. New parenting ideas that your spouse comes home with from some fly-by-night source.
- When you need some chill time and your kids are needy and can't give you two minutes to collect your thoughts.
- When you'd like some time alone with your spouse and your kids won't let you have five minutes to touch base without interrupting.
- When your teen acts immaturely.
- Your older child or teen won't try something new that you KNOW they will enjoy or be good at. You wonder why they won't trust your assessment when you have their best interest in mind.
- When any age child is not happy with what they have.
- Talking and jabbering that has no point.
- When your spouse says that you are not involved enough with the kids but then when you do try to do something your spouse is critical or wants you do it differently.
- When your spouse lets the kids wiggle out of their conse-

quences.

- When your son or daughter is standoffish and won't talk to you because you see yourself as very approachable and easy to talk to.

Lower Your Stress as a GREEN Parent

Here are some excellent ideas for lowering your stress. Give and ask for INFORMATION, be LOGICAL, but understand that others are not, and continue to have but also Provide LEARNING EXPERIENCES while allowing for the needs of the other colors in your home.

- First of all, get acquainted with your 3 Words: **INFORMATION, LOGIC**, and **LEARNING EXPERIENCES**. Use these 3 Words whenever you are frustrated, seeing only the negative, and when things seem stupid or illogical or both, to self-diagnose what's really bothering you. This will help you remain calm, cool, and collected when others around you are doing things that don't make sense to you. Understanding your 3 Words and working to process your emotions with less stress will help you be a competent spouse and parent.

- Learn to evaluate your unconscious expectations of competency for yourself, for your children, teens, and spouse. Ask yourself if your expectations of competency are possible given that not everyone around you is a Green. Is the level of competency you expect realistic, fair to others or to yourself, and do-able given the ages and learning opportunities that your family members have individually experienced? If not, be gentle—be a teacher. You'll be happier and you won't be frustrated with others as easily. You don't have to lower your standards— just learn to be patient with each person's "growing season," including yourself.

- Listen to your silence. Stress is greater where there is no exchange of information, no communication. Do you seem aloof and withdrawn from your kids and spouse? Are you spending a lot of alone time to de-stress? Are you engaged with your kid's activities? Do you ever smile at your family? Do you look grumpy even though you don't feel out of sorts? Choose to be happy and look that way. Smile, laugh, crack jokes, dance silly, snuggle. Don't be stingy with hugs; especially if you are the Dad and you have daughters of any color or Blue sons. Be engaged. As you engage with your kids, your stress will be lower because kids behave better when they are not trying to get your attention. Communicate your down time needs and take time to recharge/de-stress but set a time limit on your alone time.

- Are you silent when it comes to praise and telling your kids what they do right because you don't notice it? You will lower your stress level when you notice the good and praise your kids for what they do right, especially Oranges and Blues. They will want to repeat the good—that means less stress for you. You will lower stress at home if you point out the positive to each person in your family at least once a day.

- Listen to your "talk." Are you asking lots of questions? Do you sound like both halves of Good Cop/Bad Cop? If so, stop. You will experience more stress from their answers. Learn to ask better, color-related questions. Interrogations only serve to meet your needs. That is selfish. Instead, listen. Say, "I'm very upset and I don't understand why you did what you did. Will you help me understand *what led you to that choice*?" Then be quiet and listen. If the child is younger say, "Mommy doesn't understand why you're so mad. Please help Mommy understand." Again, listen. Put your questions on hold.

- Are you constantly telling your kids to settle down or be quiet? This will become more and more stressful as they ignore you. It's the perfect setup for a minor Wookiee rage. Instead say, "I need about twenty minutes of quiet time. Will you give that to me? If you do, when I'm done we will read one book together. If you don't, you will go to bed thirty minutes early." Given that kind of choice they will most likely comply. If not, gently but firmly follow through on the consequence and then YOU move to a more quiet place. Other consequences for their lack of consideration might be time in their rooms, no movie this weekend, no Wii time, etc. They'll be quiet the next time you ask. It's that simple.

- This is worth repeating. Most of your biggest parenting stressors can be alleviated as you participate in your child's life. Talk to them, listen to them, build a relationship of trust, communicate your love. These things don't often come naturally to a Green but just jump in and try; you will be better at it than you think. It's one of the best ways to lower your stress, especially when your stress comes from your kids not making sense to you. If you get to *know* them and learn to understand their colors, they'll make sense to you.

GREEN Parent Pitfalls :(

This is a quick list of things that are often liabilities for your color when it comes to parenting. Each one can be eliminated first by recognizing the pitfall, then by using the positive qualities of your second color to work past it.

- Being aloof, disengaged, or ignoring your child's bad behavior until it escalates to an absolutely unacceptable level.

- Becoming stubborn about what you want your child or teen to do and how you want them to do it because you don't want them to suffer the consequences you once had to suffer.

- Becoming embarrassed when your child or teen acts up, acts out, gives up, appears incompetent, or lazy.

- Agreeing with your child or teen that a school assignment is stupid.

- Thinking that your way is the only smart way to do something.

- Expecting your family to do things your way but rarely allowing them to do things their way.

- Trying to outsmart your teenager or spouse with intellectual debate. You may win the debate, but you've lost their trust and that's really stupid.

- When you get upset and you think that it's not your fault.

- Interrogating your family members when you don't understand what they are thinking or doing.

- Solving your spouse's or child's problem too quickly or without letting them give you more information.

- You need tons of information but you also have everyone else on a need-to-know basis with the idea that they generally don't need to know.

- Assuming you're smarter and that other people's information can't be trusted—so you have to go and recheck.

- Making others wait for an answer without communicating that you need a little processing time.

- Forgetting, or withholding, praise, expressions of love, acceptance, and hugs.

- Mostly for Green Dads: Not admitting your own mistakes. Assuming that your kids **aren't** intimidated or even a little afraid of you and your quietness.

GREEN Parent Perks :-)

*These are just some of the EXCELLENT qualities you bring to your parent-child relationship. Each quality is based on your ability to provide **INFORMATION**, **LOGIC**, and positive **LEARNING EXPERIENCES** into your parenting behaviors. This list may seem short but each thing is HUGE!*

- You bring great leadership strength to the family's flurry of activities, often sorting through the illogical tangle of conflicting needs and priorities in order to stay focused on what's really important. Don't hold back.

- You have a gift for seeing the Big Picture, for having a vision and for setting goals. You can create a sense of family purpose, often creating some kind of family mission statement, value chart, or guiding principles to live by.

- You can teach your kids how to dream and how to reach for the stars.

- You have a great sense of humor. You can teach your children and kids to see what's illogical and strange in the world without making fun of important things or people.

- You have a natural ability to learn from your mistakes and to logically process through personal motives, choices, and possible consequences. Teach this to your children in gentle, age-appropriate ways as your children are growing up.

- You have a knack for inventing logical consequences like no other color parent can. Use this ability to bless your children's lives with the characteristics of integrity and accountability. Be understanding and supportive of your spouse who may at first think that your consequences are too harsh. If your ideas for consequences are based on the love that you have for your child, chances are they are not too harsh unless the child is a Blue. If your child is a Blue, consider a consequence that is two or three "notches" gentler than you would originally issue. Note to the Green Parent's Spouse: If your child is a Green or Orange, and your Green spouse really loves that Green or Orange child, follow your Green spouse's idea for a consequence. Chances are you are being a softy. Sorry.

- You can help your kids learn to think and to ask good questions. Be patient while they are learning. We have these kids for eighteen years. There's a reason for that. For some of the colors, it takes that long to learn. Oranges and Blues will **learn** to be more logical but it may take all eighteen years. Use your time wisely.

- You can instill the value of education and lifelong learning into your family's activities. Engage in sharing your knowledge. Greens are subject matter experts and often know a lot about a lot of topics. Share it in fun, positive, self-esteem building ways.

- You are outstanding at providing wisdom and accurate information in an ever changing world. You can provide a safe place with a firm foundation where your children can "come in from the storm."

- You have a gift for seeing the possibilities in anything, especially your children. Communicate your vision of their possibilities and they will be your companions through anything.

- You have the ability to live what you preach. Be the hero or shero in their lives. Talk about your mistakes including what and how you learned from them. Uphold your family values; talk about the practical applications of those values.

- You are an excellent project manager. Teach these skills to your kids without making them the project. Work with your kids.

- You have high expectations for your children because you see their potential and you rarely give up on your child or teen.

- You have the rare gift to tune out the annoying, little things your kids may do. This is the bright side of being aloof. You can use it to your advantage to praise the good your kids do and to redirect negative behavior, especially when your spouse is "spent" for the day.

GREEN Parent Do's & Don'ts

Here's a quick and simple guide on what to do and what not to do as a parent, based on your first color.

- DON'T ask your child or teen (or spouse for that matter) "WHY?" or "What were you thinking?" when their behavior is mystifying to you. Ever. First of all, you're asking that for selfish reasons. YOU want information, and YOU want it NOW.

- DO train yourself to ask, "What would you do differently?" Another good way to ask for the information you seek could be "Help me to understand how you got to that choice. I want to understand but I don't." With both of these you'll get a better answer than the infuriating, "I don't know."

- DON'T forget to notice what your kids do right. It's easy for Green parents to be sort of aloof, so look for what they do that is right. Greens don't mean to be stingy with positive feedback, after all, it's good information, you just forget. Don't forget. Competent parents praise good choices. Period.

- DO be their Cheerleader when your kid's do something that's good or that's a right choice. Make an effort to not only notice but to overtly communicate your appreciation of their good choices. This is a very important element of parenting. You might be the only one who is their Cheerleader.

- DON'T always say NO first. Green parents tend to say no just to cover all their bases and perhaps sometimes to not have to deal with it, whatever "it" is.

- DO say YES as often as you can. When you hear yourself going for the "auto-NO" ask yourself, "Why would I automatically say no right now?" If your child or teen is pressing you for a quick answer say, "I need to think about that. If you don't want to give me a few minutes to consider it, then the answer IS no. What's your decision? Will you give me a minute or do you want the "auto-NO?" I bet they back off!

- DON'T go into Command and Control by telling your children what to do and how to do it. Most Greens are commanding not because of power but to save them from doing something dumb (something you've most likely done already and would rather not see them do the same dumb thing).

- DO teach them what's right and give choices. Then praise good choices or hold them accountable with consequences if they make the wrong choices. This process does take some focus but it's worth it. Say, "It's not okay to leave the toy room a mess. (this is the teaching part). You have a choice. You can either pick up your toys now, or I will pick them up and take them away in ten minutes. What's your decision?" (that's the choice part). See, no Command and Control, just smart parenting.

- DON'T be a "sideline" parent watching from the wings, aloof and disengaged.

- DO get involved. Dads: get off the couch at the end of a stressful day. Moms: get out of the kitchen or set aside the crazy mental list of to do's. Play ball, watch a movie, listen to your child chatter about nonsense, make up a game or story, wrestle, joke around, take a walk.

- DON'T be too serious.

- DO have fun, laugh, and smile a lot—especially at your kids and spouse.

- DON'T be so uncompromising and stubborn or need things a very specific, picky way.

- DO let you kid's be creative about the "how" of doing something—especially if you can see that it won't work. Let THEM learn that on their own; you had to. It's noble that you want to save them time, effort, money, consequences but…

- DON'T. Let them learn for themselves. Then, be there to support and not to say, "I told you so." You hate that; so will they!

- DO share your feelings. It's hard for a Green to do that. The other colors have an obligation to understand that and accept that Greens need time to process their very deep and real feelings. Work toward sharing your love, your good opinions of the people you live with, and your positive perspective of their cool traits.

- DON'T let Wookiee rage take over. If you start to experience that building sensation of frustrations take a walk and stop what you are doing. Say, "I need a minute," and glare if you need too. That's better than Wookiee rage. Take the time you need to process your feelings. It's the smart way to deal with a very normal and real sense of building emotions. It won't scare the kids. I know that you will be in control of even the Wookiee rage, but they don't.

- DO share your stories about anything. Work, your day, your ideas, your mistakes. They want to hear. You are most likely quiet and business like. Break out of that shell.

- DO tell your kids about how things were when you were growing up. Tell them about their grandparents. Keep it light. It's about storytelling, not about lecturing or even about having a point or lesson. Just be real and use that sense of humor to be funny. Get your kids laughing!

- DON'T try to get what you want or need through intellectual debate. To be honest, we all know that you're probably smarter, that you're way more logical, and that you're probably right, but that won't build family relationships. Using logical debate as a form of parenting is ineffective, creates barriers, and it's (to be honest) stupid. It makes other people feel stupid, and that's probably not your point. Your point is probably to spare your child or spouse the embarrassment of being wrong, but it doesn't come off that way. Try another tactic, like listening and problem solving—together.

- DO talk WITH your kids and spouse. Collaborate not compromise. Counsel together. Make plans and decisions together. You are a natural-born leader. Together with your spouse, lead your family to greatness.

- DON'T dismiss the feelings of your family members just because they are very uncomfortable to deal with. Take your time. Ask for time. Recognize that statistically speaking, you are more likely to have at least one Blue (the ones who do everything based on feelings) in your family than not.

- DO understand that first and second color Blues don't do "logic" like you do, they do "feelings" the way you do logic. They FEEL what's right or wrong the way you KNOW what's right or wrong. You would be incensed if someone questioned your logic. Blues are wounded when you question or dismiss their feelings to the same degree that you are frustrated by someone dismissing your logic.

- DON'T question a Blue's feelings. Gently ask them to explain their perspective. Listen for some logic to how their feelings are helping them "think" things through. Even respectfully and kindly ask them to calm down and talk. If it's not life threatening (whatever it is), just support them and back off. But don't dismiss the feelings of your kids or spouse just because they don't make sense to you. It will eventually destroy your relationship. Period.

- DO show love. And acceptance. And be fun. You will come to find that home is your favorite spot on earth.

GREEN Parents: A Last Word or Two

Just the Gospel according to Shannon ;-)

I'm so grateful for Green parents—especially because I live with one! I've learned over the years to value his wisdom, appreciate his calm nature, and depend on his quiet strength.

But this is not a book about my sweetheart. It is a chapter about Green parents. You, too, would be smart (if you have a Green in your life) to value their wisdom, appreciate their calm nature, and to depend on their quiet strength. Period.

BLUE Parents

In 3 Words... Relationships, Communication, Understanding

The Quick BLUE Adult Answer...

Needs <u>RELATIONSHIPS</u>
Positive relationships. Works for peace and calm at home. Very sensitive to feelings and needs of others. Unconditional acceptance.

Values <u>COMMUNICATION</u>
Prefers clear, calm, honest, open communication. Uses gentle words often. Give them benefit of the doubt. Let them vent, but not wallow.

Trust Tactic <u>UNDERSTANDING</u>
Relates to kind examples and calm requests.

Authentic, trusting, kind. Don't problem solve too quickly. Let them "fix it" or try again.

The Simple BLUE Adult Truth...

BLUE parents are intuitive feelers who are most often alert to the potential of the moment and care deeply about the potential of the people shaping that moment. They are people focused and driven to create harmonious relationships at home. They enjoy helping others feel comfortable and happy until they feel taken advantage of and then the situation will become stressful. Don't mistake a people-focused orientation for being weak or walked on. Blues are sensitive, yes, but balanced Blues are tough and stand for what's right according to their very strong set of core values. Blues are principled. They have an uncanny sense of empathic understanding. When it comes to intuitively understanding another's emotions, they are usually spot on. The down side is that without the right skills they may be misguided with what to do with that intuition. They may rescue when they shouldn't, make excuses, cover up, or downplay another's inappropriate actions. A balanced Blue adult will use that intuition to help others grow even if it means allowing them to suffer consequences. This is especially true with the Blue parent—most likely the Blue mom.

Blue adults have an undying need to build positive **RELATIONSHIPS**. They see the potential in people and have a natural faith in their ability to be good, do what's right, be kind, and understanding of others. This may sound somewhat of a "Pollyanna" attitude but it's really not. They are just born with an innate ability to believe in people. Now this ability can become jaded over time. If that individual Blue adult has been repeatedly hurt or neglected, then they will become very leery of people becoming guarded and protective. They may also be co-dependant and needy—looking for acceptance from unhealthy sources.

When it comes to building healthy relationships, Blue adults are the champs, hands down. Mature, balanced Blues are very adept at meeting the needs of others in a way that seems like they are mind readers. Balanced Blues can be so positive and supportive, often to the point of seeming self-serving or unbelievable to the other colors. I often hear of people who, upon meeting a balanced, happy and healthy Blue adult, think that the Blue is too good to be true. Too kind, too nice, too authentic. But, nope, that's just a balanced Blue. They really are that genuine and kind. They really do have a knack for being supportive and friendly. They really will give you the shirt off their back. They really are nurturing. They tend to forgive easily and be painstakingly polite. They focus on the person they are talking to and are encouraging whenever possible. They befriend the friendless, fight for the underdog, and will help others to the point of personal exhaustion.

The down side to all of that natural goodness is that Blues can say yes to too many things overwhelming and immobilizing them. They are prone to being down or "bluesy" and when pushed too far they will choose flight over fight, but can fight nasty if they have no way out. Then your normally balanced Blue not only looks like a loon, but, believe me, they feel like one, too. This is especially up-setting for everyone because a Blue parent (usually the Mom) seems for all the world that they've got it under control until all of a sudden they just lose it. Well, they didn't just lose it, it's been build-ing for hours or even days or weeks. The usually balanced Blue doesn't want to bother anyone, so they hold it together, trying to not let anyone down, day after day, until the stress level overwhelms them and they have a meltdown or explode.

One of my parents with a Blue child came up with a Blue anal-ogy and it's perfect! Think of a sponge. A sponge that is set in the middle of a puddle of water on the kitchen counter soaks up all the water. Then what do we normally do with that sponge? We wring it out. Now there is still some residual water left in it but it can go back to work and soak up more spills. If we let it sit for a time to "recharge" it will dry completely and then it is doubly efficient the next time it's needed. The dark side of sponges are that if they are not wrung out they eventually become saturated and can't soak up any more and instead make a mess. Or, left to dry completely out in the dark without proper care, it gets musty and sours.

Blues can be like sponges. First of all, they soak up all the emotions, concerns, worries, and stress around them. They keep on soaking up these emotions until, like a sponge, they either get "wrung out" or become so saturated that they can't hold any more.

Then they leak (cry or get snippy), burst (have a melt-down or lash out), or stop working all together (become immobilized or depressed).

What comes next is even worse: guilt, negative thoughts about themselves and their worth, and all out self-loathing. It's not a pretty battle and every Blue mom fights this battle. (And lots of Gold-Blue moms and Orange-Blue moms do, too!). Three things to note at this point: 1) I haven't heard of this happening to Blue dads very much; 2) every first color Blue mom I've ever taught, met, chatted briefly with, or coached has had this happen to them, and, 3) they don't realize that every other Blue mom does the same thing. They think they are the ONLY 'crazy' in the world. Well, not so! Blue moms unite! You are all experiencing the same cycle, and you are not crazy! Let me say that again: YOU ARE NOT CRAZY! You're Blue—and you are as normal as they come. You're just Blue. Feel better? I hope so! ;-)

Here's the cool news, if the Blue develops the skills to "wring" themselves out through communication with a trusted spouse or friend, manufacture some reasonable down time, or learn to control the emotional input (by saying no, by delegating assignments, by letting go) they stay balanced and have more to give the next day, keeping emotional meltdowns or freak-outs to a minimum. If a Blue can learn to communicate stress and ask for what they need in appropriate ways BEFORE they become saturated, they will rarely get to that horrible, fall-apart place. Without those skills, or if they put off the "wring out" that's needed, they will eventually became saturated, overloaded, and will act badly.

DISCLAIMER: I'm about to be blunt and be a bit abrupt, but I know you Blues can handle it. Do yourself, and your family, a huge favor: ASK FOR WHAT YOU NEED BEFORE YOUR SPONGE IS SATURATED AND LEAKING. When you hold back your early frustrations and don't communicate your needs (appropriately) and give and give and give until you are spent, whose needs are you *really* meeting?

If you become the martyr you're really meeting YOUR OWN need to meet others needs. When you rescue and coddle and continually fix things for your kids, husband, or anyone else, you are most likely being selfish; it becomes more about you than them. Being selfish is NEVER what a Blue wants to be.

Blues, your family needs you to be a support, not the fixer. They need you to be dependable, not the wall that continually protects the fortress. They need you to listen, not rescue and make everything perfect. If you've done all that for a long time, you've trained them to expect it from you. Here's one more bit of tough love: if you've trained your family to expect all this perfection from you as part of your relationship with them, you can "un-train" them too. You can un-train them with loving communication, by backing off, and by letting go and learning to balance your needs with theirs. It may tip the scale for a few weeks, but if you do it the right way, you will gain their respect and help. The other colors really don't respect a doormat but they will use it if it's offered!

On to a happier note: **COMMUNICATION** is one of the Blues best qualities. They are great at communicating love, emotions, acceptance, and details. They are usually natural story tellers and pass on verbal histories of family events, yesterday's news, or an upsetting conversation between themselves and someone else.

Blues are usually very adept at identifying their own feelings and putting their emotions in words in an effort to authentically communicate what they are experiencing. They speak with great feeling in their voice—often putting their hand over their heart unconsciously when they are sharing something vitally important to them. They often use the words "I feel" to share not only emotions but also their thoughts, ideas, and values. There is a degree of absoluteness to their feelings and thoughts when they say "I feel..." that is equivalent to another person's (particularly a Green's) "I think."

Blues tend to avoid fighting with words in "real life" though many Blues will rehearse in their heads great and meaningful conversations with powerful and sometimes cutting words they will never utter out loud. They just can't bring themselves to be that mean. They know that IF they could say it out loud they would expect their words to change the life of the other person profoundly. (Yes, Blues are also a bit romantic with a flair for drama - but that's why a balanced Blue doesn't actually say it, they know it's a little dramatic. At the same time, an unbalanced Blue will opt for the drama.)

Blues usually have a soothing, mellow tone of voice. It's part of that whole nurturing thing. They also try to make their voice match the emotion that they are experiencing unless it will cause a conflict. That's when a Blue parent will say, with great resignation in their voice, things like, "Fine, do what you want. You will anyway." or "Go ahead. Go. That's fine." If a Blue mom says, "fine" in any form, it's probably not fine. They are just about to blow. They are trying to avoid a conflict (probably with a Green who is demanding logic) and all they have is a feeling that they should say, "No" but are feeling pressured to come up with a good logical reason but doesn't have one. They just have a nagging feeling. Greens are notorious for exploiting this "flaw" in a Blue. Oranges will negotiate and do the full-court press wearing down the Blue parent, and Gold kids will emanate their "you're not a very good parent" vibe which makes the Blue mom or dad give in because they question themselves as much as the Gold child. Green, Orange and Gold kids don't need a best friend—they need you to provide Learning Experiences (for the Green), Boundaries (for the Orange) and clear Expectations (for the Gold) of who the parent is and who the child (or teen) is. Don't buckle under pressure. You can do it gracefully and with a little tough love.

Blue parents are also really good at **UNDERSTANDING**. This is a cool thing. While I've only mentioned times when kids, teens, or other adults may run over a Blue when they want something, this is not one of those times. Blues are awesome at understanding when their child, teen, spouse, friend, or co-worker is genuinely upset. When another human is upset and needs understanding Blues are at the top of their game. This is when a Blue's intuitive ability to empathize is crucial. Blues have an uncanny ability to listen, describe feelings, siphon off the hurts and abuses of others, and help others heal. This is a great gift. For a parent, this ability is at times essential; yet this is not a natural talent for the other three colors. It's only natural for a Blue. From 2 to 18 to 98, all human beings have times when they need understanding and acceptance. Because Blues focus on the potential in people they have the unparalleled skill to have faith in people, which often translates into unconditional acceptance.

Balanced Blues are able to communicate love, hope, and faith to others. They can often be the unsung cheerleaders, usually in the background cheering others on to greatness. Blues tend to look for the reasons behind a child's or teen's inappropriate behaviors— sometimes to excuse or to rescue.

Blue adults also need extra doses of understanding themselves. When faced with criticism a Blue adult will often become even more self-deprecating and negative. They need support, a listening ear, and compassion when they fall apart. They are already being 150 times harder on themselves than someone else would be. Harsh criticism, judgments and accusations are not helpful.

Healthy, balanced Blues also find it difficult to handle someone who rushes their need to process a problem by instead solving the problem without hearing all the details. Balanced Blues often need to just talk things out. They are perfectly equipped to come up with a solution themselves or are able to "dump" the problem by talking it out (and don't need a solution). They only need a listening, understanding spouse or friend who won't rocket into problem solving mode.

Blues tend to be good listeners. They want to be involved with their children and spouses. They want to build relationships and to do that they use communication, togetherness, understanding, and service.

The dark side of the Blue is when they need too much in the way of affection, attention, communication, or togetherness. This may come out in the form of never-ending venting, seeing only the negative, stirring up drama to get attention, or by gossiping. A Blue who makes a show of being depressed is crying out for different needs than a Blue who is quietly trying to hide their real depression and low self-esteem. The first is usually lonely and seeking attention; the second may be truly depressed. Both may need professional assistance. A balanced Blue will have times of frustration, bluesy moments, and have a difficult time processing through very hurtful people issues, but generally they will find peace and balance given a few days and some extra doses of understanding and support from their children and spouse.

BLUE Parent Stressors

*For each stressor, look at how your
child's behavior violates one or more of your 3 Words:*
RELATIONSHIPS, COMMUNICATION, UNDERSTANDING

- When your child or teen does something that seems hurtful and unkind such as fighting among themselves or hurting other children or teens. This is also embarrassing because you feel that it's a reflection on you and your ability to be a good parent.

- When your children or teen lies to you. You don't really understand how people can be inauthentic; this is very stressful for you. Storytelling, if not for entertainment, is also worrisome to you. You may perceive that this is just another form of a lie. Lying assaults all three of your 3 Words.

- Homework time will be a complete stressor for Blue-Orange

parents because of the fights and the loss of freedom for you as a parent. It will be stressful for Blue-Gold parents because of the fights and the lack of structure and because you will feel like you are letting your child's teacher down.

- Some Blue parents have a hard time watching their children and teens in sports and other competitions. You feel deeply the win/lose scenario even when it's often irrelevant to your child or teen. Competition by it's very nature means that there is a winner and a loser. This is stressful for a Blue parent and you may find that you become emotional during the process. Don't embarrass your kid by being too involved. Take a cue from your child's response as to what yours should be.

- Watching your child or teen being rejected, slighted, misunderstood, judged, or criticized can be very stressful. Again, guard against taking it so personally, let it go and take a cue from your child. If your child is a Blue, help them cope by being understanding, then move quickly to problem solving, don't add to their wallowing. Show some toughness and expect them to grow theirs.

- One of the biggest stressors for a Blue parent, especially a Blue mom, is trying to do everything perfectly while trying to please too many people. "People" include your kids, your spouse, your parents and/or siblings, the neighbors, your boss, your friends, your church, and your own self-image of who you feel you should be but that you feel you are not. Whew! That's a lot! No wonder you are feeling stressed out, unloved, unlovable, overwhelmed, and immobilized. Stop. Just stop. Blowing your commitment for a dozen cupcakes for the second grade Spring Fling is better than being admitted to the loony bin. See the Do's and Don'ts for more suggestions.

- Bossy, controlling people, and other mothers who seem to be overachievers and perfect are huge stressors for Blue moms.

Embrace your own special gifts and realize that a perfectly clean house is virtually impossible for a Blue (and, might I add, overrated?). Stop trying. Don't settle for a home that would win a spot on Hoarders, but don't worry about being able to eat off of the floor. It just isn't going to happen, unless you are a first color Gold or Orange. Since you're not, be thankful for the great relationship you probably already have with your kids and that they come home to talk to you. Quit trying to be someone you are not.

- Another Blue parenting stressor is when your kids or teens ask to do something or go somewhere and you feel like you need to say "no" but there is no logical reason to say "no." For example, your daughter wants to go spend the night at a friend's house and you have a bad feeling about it. You have no logical reason for saying "no," you simply don't feel good about it. You don't know why you feel that way and she's pushing you to just say "yes." Boy, is that stress! Stand your ground. Let her be mad. You are right, for some reason, and you DON'T have to justify it or explain it, to your daughter, to the other mom, to anyone. Having your daughter safe but mad is better than happy and unsafe, or worse. Make excuses if you must but trust your gut. You will regret it later if you don't stay true to your feelings.

- Another stressor for a Blue mom is when you don't know how to get moving because you are overwhelmed and overcommitted. This is a real stressor. Don't dismiss it as just being a ditz or a bad mom. Use your second color to get moving with organization and to do lists. Pick one "next action" and focus on that. Then move on to the next "next action" and focus on that. This strategy works every time. Another strategy: ASK FOR HELP! Quit being the lone ranger. You are not an island.

- You will also feel great stress when you are faced with a parenting problem you don't know how to solve. You already have a great solution in your hands. My next book, "Parenting By Colors II: Ask, Be, Do, and 4 Colors True" will teach you what to do in any parenting situation. Also, tap into the power of your spouse's color. 80% of the time your parenting issue is probably because you are being too easy on your child or teen. A Green, Gold, or Orange spouse will tell you this. They may not say it gently but they are a good reality check. Listen, absorb, follow their counsel. (Now, don't get your panties in a twist. I didn't say "obey" like you're a child; you're not. But they are probably right if they are telling you that you are being too nice.) As a Blue it took me years to follow my Green husband's counsel when our kids were trying to pull one over on me. I thought his ideas were harsh. Not so. He was right. I was right when our kids were hurting, sad, or faced a problem, but he was right when they were disobeying, negotiating, being sneaky, rude, bossy, or ungrateful. When your spouse is a good mom or dad with your children's best interest in mind, take his/her counsel even if it seems harsh to you. If you have a Green, Gold or Orange child, your spouse is probably right to show a little tough love.

Lower Your Stress as a BLUE Parent

Here are some excellent ideas for lowering your stress. Understand that building RELATIONSHIP happens differently for each color. COMMUNICATION is essential but match your communication style to the color needs of the person you are communicating with for greater UNDERSTANDING.

- First of all, get acquainted with your 3 Words: **RELATION-SHIPS**, **COMMUNICATIONS**, and **UNDERSTANDING**. Use these 3 Words whenever you are overwhelmed, frustrated, feeling like you are not doing good enough, or when people (especially your spouse or kids) seem hurtful or demanding. Understanding YOUR 3 Words will help you "self-diagnose" which parts of your needs or values are feeling attacked. Understanding which one (or more) of your 3 Words are being assaulted or going unmet can help you be calm and handle things in a way that you can be pleased with later on. You can better determine if you need to ask for help, if you need to stand your ground, or just let the upset go because you are not being as threatened as it initially felt like you were.

- Understanding your 3 Words and working to process your emotions with less stress will help you be an understanding, supportive spouse and parent who helps to meet the needs of your family in a way that is really best for you and them. You want to be a giver but you can't give from an empty or upset bucket.

- Learn to evaluate your feelings of inadequacy. Chances are they are linked to unrealistic expectations, feeling overwhelmed, and unfair comparisons. Ask yourself if your expectations of competency for yourself, for your children, teens, and spouse are realistic. Determine who exactly you are comparing yourself to. Is that a fair comparison? As a much older Blue mom with grown kids, this was my single biggest parenting pitfall and stressor. I needed to lighten up on myself and just breathe. I give you, Blue Mom, permission to do the same. Lighten up! The dishes won't really be done till you die, if your toddler's clothes don't match the world will not end, and that "perfect" mom at church... well, she yells every once in a while, too. If not, she'll be in the loony bin before you!

- Have fun! Laugh! Be silly! Do your best and be content with your best being good enough. Believe me, Blues work so hard to do what's right for others that your best probably IS good enough. It is!! Don't miss the crossroads of your children's lives because you were too intense. Don't let yourself fall into depression. If you are down or truly depressed, quit being a hero and get help while you work to get healthy. You'll be happier and you won't be frustrated with others as easily. You don't have to lower your standards, just learn to be patient with each person's "growing season," including yourself.

- Learn to let go of what others think of you. Don't fill in "silence" with assuming the worst. What I mean is that Blues are notorious for interpreting silence, especially from a Green or Gold, as negative. Blues cause themselves tons of stress by assuming that someone else is assuming the worst of you. Stop that! It's not true. They are usually thinking of something completely different. If they are thinking bad of you, they're judging and that's their problem. You're trying to do the best you can, right? Okay, then. Don't waste your time on what other's think. Let your toddler have a fit in the grocery checkout line. Smile, be gracious and get out as soon as you can. Let your teen have green dyed hair as long as that's all they are doing. Either people want to help and they don't know how, OR someone is being a jerk and thinking, "Why can't that parent control their kid?" Can you really do anything about them being a jerk? No. So stop worrying and concentrate on the wonderful, upset child that God blessed you with or that free-spirit, green-haired teen who's not doing anything else wrong. That's what is really in your heart. I know. I'm a Blue. You are actually a great mom with an upset toddler and/or a green-haired teen, end of story. Don't complicate things.

- Listen to your self-talk. Chances are it's negative. Stop that, too. Negative self-talk is based on trying to do everything perfect and failing. It's not the failing that's the problem, it's the trying to do everything perfect. Again, do your best. It's better than most people's awesome. Blue's are so hard on themselves and you (we) need to be very careful about this. It's the best way to NOT be there for your family. If you let depression and negative feelings overwhelm you, then you're not there for your family, which is what you wanted to do perfectly in the first place.

- To lower stress, do your best and give yourself a break. Today, as I'm writing this book, today, I have dishes in the sink, there's a several wisps of dog hair under the table that need sweeping, I need to move on to the laundry, (where there are three loads, clean, in baskets, unfolded) and we've been fast-fooding it for a week. Welcome to my world! But here's what I did right: I'm insanely focused on working on this book to bring you hope.

- Now that I said all that, what if you are a Blue and you do have people who are being critical of you (including your spouse and/or child)? Stress is greater for a Blue where there is a strained relationship, no connection, negative communication, no under-standing, and criticism. This is a toughy. To lower your stress there are a few things to try. See the solutions below. Get help, talk to a friend, a counselor or therapist, or your religious leader.

- ***Stress Solution Number 1:*** When you are being criticized, are they somewhat right? Have you let things go because you are down or depressed? If so, seek professional help, now. Ask for help. Delegate. Tap into your second color to get moving. Blue-Golds—start with listing all your good traits. Read that list everyday. Do your real best, then let your best be good enough. List your To Do's, then prioritize them - do the first one, then the second one and so on. Break the rut by using the good traits from your list to overcome your less-than-wonderful habits. Blue-Oranges: don't make a To Do list. Instead think of "Next Actions." Ask, "What do I need to do next, right now?" That little voice in your head will tell you something like, "Get up" or "Put in a load of laundry" or "Apologize to Steve" or "Stop fretting." Then go do it, just that one thing. Don't think about the other 230 things that you should do. Just concentrate on one.

Then ask, "What do I do next?" Listen, then do it. It may say, "Take a shower" or "Fold the white clothes" or "Say three kind things to Steve today" or "Have faith, it will be okay." Sooner or later all those Blue-Orange Next Actions will get you out of your rut. Then for all Blues, Choose to be happy. Choose to exercise faith!

- **Stress Solution Number 2:** Are family members telling you that you are overly involved in their lives and activities? You won't be happy and supported yourself until you can learn to stop rescuing, stop lecturing, and stop being too nurturing. Let your family members grow their own wings. Over-nurturing by a Blue usually stems from fear. You're probably, deep down inside, afraid that something bad is going to happen because you didn't take care of it, because you didn't warn someone at the right time, or because you did the wrong thing. Here's where your thinking is faulty, you're assuming that you can control a lot more than is humanly possible all in the name of 'taking care" of your family. Blues are great communicators, they are naturally full of faith, and they see the positive potential in people and situations. Fear is the dark side of all of these positive Blue traits. The cure is to replace fear with faith. Choose to be happy. Communicate your love to, and faith in, those around you and understand that when they walk out the door they may come back, they may not. You cannot control that. However, you can control that they know that you love them and support them when they walked out the door.

- **Stress Solution Number 3:** For my sanity, and to control my fear, I've learned a lot that would be a book of it's own. Someday I'll write that one, but for now, here's my council.   **A**. Stay grounded in your faith. Believe that there's a God, a supreme being, Who really is in charge and trust Him.   **B**. Always leave things with your family members so that they know you love them. *C*. Quit being critical of others, even if it's just trying to help. It's not helping, they hear criticism. *D*. If you are down, get help, now. *E*. If you are truly being unappreciated, criticized or walked on (and you are not being oversensitive - read about the other colors first) then stand up for yourself, ask for what you need, stop thinking you are bothering others. If they love you, they will help. *F*. If you are being abused, talk to someone, be brave, and get help!

BLUE Parent Pitfalls :-(

This is a quick list of things that are often liabilities for your color when it comes to parenting. Each one can be eliminated first by recognizing the pitfall, then by using the positive qualities of your second color to work past it.

- The biggest parenting pitfall for a Blue is being too compliant and easygoing. Blues are completely stressed by conflict. Because of this, you may tend to let your kids and teens get away with too much. You might plead and beg your kids and teens to obey by asking them to do something over and over again within just five minutes' time, or over several weeks' time. Either way, it's the same outcome. They don't do it, you keep begging, and they learn that you are not really that serious until you yell. Even then they may still blow you off.

- Using "Command and Control" tactics when you've reached the end of your rope is another Blue parenting pitfall. You've reached the end of your rope because you are not asking for, or expecting, help. Blues tend to let frustrations build and build until you blow. When a Blue blows up it's not good—then you feel terribly guilty. It's best to diffuse your frustrations before you blow by asking for help, making assignments, then holding people accountable for doing what you've asked.

- You may have a tendency to overreact when your child is

upset. If another child or adult has somehow wronged your child you can become overly protective and emotional. You can turn into a Mama Bear, or Papa Bear, pretty darn quick. You will rush in and rescue. It's definitely a parenting liability to over-react. Instead, keep your cool, get both sides, and remember you have time to think, not feel, your way to an answer. Take that time and stay calm and neutral.

- You might find that you struggle with being firm with your kids and teens. This happens because Blues don't want to create a conflict which can carry over to not wanting to upset your kids. Most mature Blues, when faced with understanding that per-spective in the harsh light of day, realize that it's not wise or possible to be a good parent AND not upset your kids by being a parent. You need to learn not to worry about upsetting your kids by being firm, by saying no, and by holding them account-able for their choices by following through on consequences. Blue parents can end up with rotten kids that no one likes to be around, and it's not the kid's fault. It's the fault of Blue parents that are not firm. Don't be that kind of Blue mom or Blue dad. Actually, not being firm appeases YOUR emotions, and that's selfish. Being firm with your kids is selfless. Make a choice and don't back down.

- Blue parents can get sucked into justifying their parenting deci-sions to their kids, especially an older child, pre-teen, or teen-ager who says, "But WHY can't I... (go, stay, leave, skip my homework, you fill in the blank)?" Immediately, as a Blue mom or dad, you switch sides from parent to defensive back without even noticing and go into "I've got to win you over" mode. You start to explain, persuade, justify, argue, and re-word your per-spective. Stop that right now. We don't negotiate with terrorists and your teen is being a terrorist when they get you to switch sides like that. Pleasantly but firmly say, "Oh no you don't, I don't negotiate with terrorists. The answer is no, sweetie. YOU need to tell me why you think I should say yes. And just so you know, the answer will still probably be no but I'll hear you out if it will make you feel better." Nine times out of ten they are dumb-founded and give up. They don't have a good reason to go, or at least all they have is a lame one and they know it. Being lighthearted but firm goes a long way for a Blue parent who doesn't want to cause an uproar but who needs to say no.

- You are probably slow to make parenting decisions. At first you may not think so but watch yourself for a few days. You will see that this is true except when you are upset because your kids are upset—then will be too quick to jump the gun.

- Blue parents can be pretty weak at goal setting and undisciplined with time. If I had no answer for this one, I'd be writing a different book like one of those, "How to organize your life in under two days and on $100 bucks." Remember, I'm a Blue. This book's taken me four years to write! My best suggestions for this one are: 1) Realize that this is a liability and plan around that (yikes, did I say "plan" - yes I did). Don't make promises you can't keep. Say, "I'll be there about 2-ish," not "at 2:00 pm." If you think something will take you an hour, double that and you'll be closer to the truth. Understand that you were born to drive Golds (and some Oranges) crazy. Communication goes a long way to bridge those gaps. Understanding colors helps, too. 2) Find a Gold friend or spouse and tap into their natural ability to do what you can't. They will love to either organize you (Golds) or help you be more efficient (Oranges).

- As continuation of the last point, you may be disorganized to an extreme. Use your second color to build in some sense of order. If you are Blue-Gold set up a few systems to address your biggest disorganization stressors. Seriously, ask a Gold friend for help, but set up early expectations for your Gold friend that you ONLY want three ideas for two problems or your friend may want to do a complete overhaul. Blue-Oranges: you can build in some ordered flexibility by being creative. Snacks for my kids used to drive me crazy. I was inconsistent and all over the place when it came to meals, snacks and nutrition. So I got creative. Of course there were limits, boundaries, and consequences for being piggish without me having to be the snack drawer police. I never had a problem from day one. Our kids followed the rules of the snack drawer almost to an extreme. They were even self-regulating with their friends. They did not want to lose the privilege of such an amazing freedom and I got some peace out of what was once a daily disorganized fight.

- Blues tend to over-commit because you don't want to let anyone down. This can cause a lot of anxiety and stress. Check out the Do's and Don'ts section for some pointers on this.

- The last liability I'll mention for you Blue parents is something I've talked about several times already. It's that whole rescue thing. If your 7-year-old has a project due tomorrow you will want to stay up all night to "help" them finish. (It's a rescue.) If your teen has a friend that is in a tough situation you may let yourself be talked into having them move into your happier home. (You're still rescuing.) If your 3-year-old is crying because you took his toys away after he refused to pick-up, you'll give him one back so that he will know you still love him and because, now that you think about it, losing ALL his toys was probably too mean. (Big rescue!) Your 10-year-old son is being pushed around in soccer and you are ready to let him quit. (Dangerous rescue!) GROW A BACKBONE! Kindly, but lovingly, let your 7-year-old get an 'F' on the project. F's are not the end of the world. Let them fail. NO, you probably can't let another teen move into your happier home. How long will it stay happier. Help the friend, support the friend, be a safe haven for that friend after school for a few hours. But you must protect your own family, first. No one family can save the world, save your own family first. The 3-year-old does not need a toy back, and your 10-year-old is probably old enough to stick it out. Go to each practice but stay on the sidelines and help them to grow a backbone, too. Bottom line, if you rescue, all you are teaching is that you will always rescue and you will cripple them. That 7-year-old who got you to stay up to help will definitely turn into a 17-year-old that you are still staying up all night rescuing—and not always with a homework assignment. Honestly, the rescuer is as guilty as the rescued. Grow a backbone—you owe it to your kids.

BLUE Parent Perks :-)

These are just some of the EXCELLENT qualities you bring to your parent-child relationship. Each quality is based on your ability to provide positive RELATIONSHIPS, effective, clear COMMUNICATION, and UNDERSTANDING into your parenting behaviors. This list may seem short but each thing is HUGE!

- You bring great caring, nurturing and understanding to the family's flurry of emotions, conflicts, worries and concerns. You can often sort through the tangle of conflicting needs and priorities in order to stay focused on what's really important: each other. Don't hold back. Expect kindness, understanding, giving each other the benefit of the doubt, and managing conflict in a way that is uplifting at home no matter what the world tries to say is normal for everyone else.

- You can make your home a safe haven. Whether you are the mom or the dad, you can be the heart of the family.

- You have a gift for seeing the best in everyone as long as life has not jaded you. If you are a bit cynical, it's not who you really are. Work past those negative feelings and judgments and be the positive loving person you are wired to be.

- You are exceptional at seeing the potential in each member of the family too, even when they are not acting their best.

- You can communicate love and acceptance.

- You are a natural listener as long as you remember to put your story on hold first. Remember, that when others are upset, they need to be understood—not lectured or given advice. Is that what you need when you are upset? I didn't think so. Listen the way you would like to be listened to.

- You have a wonderful grasp on the family values that need to be incorporated into our families today. Things like virtue, faith, love, forgiveness, work ethic, gratitude, and an abundance mentality. Work to weed out an "entitlement" mentality in your children and teens by NOT rescuing them. Rescuing breeds an entitlement perspective.

- You have a natural ability for faith. Teach your children to have faith in the future, in other human beings and in God. Each color child will have a different way that they deal with faith. Look for more information on this in the Kid's Colors chapters.

- You have a natural ability to learn from your mistakes and to process through your own feelings, motives, choices, and possible consequences. Teach this to your children in gentle, age-appropriate ways as your children are growing up.

- You have a knack for empathic understanding like no other color parent can. Use this ability to bless your children's lives with the characteristics of charity and compassion. Be understanding and supportive of your spouse who may at first think that your understanding ways are too mushy. Again, don't rescue. Listen, be understanding, but don't cripple them.

- You can help your kids learn to be sensitive to the needs and feelings of others—a trait that is sadly lacking in the world today. If you have Gold-Greens, Green-Golds, Green-Oranges or Orange-Greens this is very important. Be patient while they are learning to understand feelings. It will be hard for them and may take almost all of the eighteen years God had given us to teach our kids what is right and good. Use your time wisely.

- You can instill a love of education and lifelong learning into your family's activities. Make learning fun and low stress and don't expect perfection tomorrow. Look at it as a process. Teach yourself about learning styles and help tune in to how your kids learn and nurture those abilities. For example, my Green-Orange son and Orange-Green daughter never (and I mean never!) could get that whole Gold "make an outline, then note cards, and finally a rough draft" way of writing a research paper, a speech, or other projects. So I taught them how to brainstorm using mind mapping to get started, then transfer their ideas to the "assigned" way of doing it. Neither one was very good at memorizing but they were good with visuals. So I taught them how to use colored pens and colored note cards to study with. When I saw them struggling, I researched better ways of learning or processing information. Greens are subject-matter experts and often know a lot about a lot of topics. Share it in fun, positive, self-esteem building ways. Think of creative ways to augment what and how your kids are learning in school but don't rescue or do the work for them. Help at home, support at home, but don't convince yourself that you should home school (see page 137). That's a two-edged sword for a Blue.

- You are outstanding at providing wisdom and instilling values in an ever-changing world. You can provide a safe place with a firm foundation where your children can "come in from the storm."

- You have a gift for seeing the possibilities in anything, especially your children. Communicate your vision of their possibilities and they will be your companions through anything.

- You have the ability to practice what you preach because you are authentic, honest, and genuine. Be the hero, or shero, in your child's life. As you share with your children and teens how you are able to overcome your weaknesses, they will learn to be humble and teachable too.

- You have the natural ability to build rapport and to be encouraging. You do this through communication and your ability to see the best in others. Kids and teens need this from you. This helps to make them feel safe and build their self-esteem.

- You are also a team player and a team builder. Think of your family as a team. You have the natural ability to rally the troops and to get everyone on the same page. You are inspirational. Go for it!

- Last but not least, a healthy, balanced Blue has the gift to stop and smell the flowers or to appreciate a starry sky. Share that with your kids. Be careful to nurture your sense of balance so that you can nurture balance for your whole family. You will be glad you did.

BLUE Parent Do's & Don'ts

Here's a quick and simple guide on what to do and what not to do as a parent, based on your first color.

- DO be intuitively aware of your child's and teen's needs, feelings, concerns, ideas, and stressors. You may be the only one who can read them like a book. That's a good thing and it builds your bond of trust with them. They will know where to go for understanding. Trust your intuition and your instinct even if you can't justify them logically. You are probably right.

- DON'T smother them, though. Too much nurturing can be detrimental to independence, self-esteem, and problem solving. It's a balance. Listen to that little voice in your head that says, "Back off, trust them." Listen to your spouse or best friend who is telling you that you are too invested. If others are noticing it, you are. Listen, and back off. If they are wrong you can always swoop back in, but I bet they are right. Your adult kids will be all the better for your support from a distance. Parenting is the art of letting go, someone wise once said. It's true. Embroider that on a pillow and live by it.

- DO recognize your faults, but...

- DON'T apologize too much. Constantly saying, "I'm sorry," is really annoying to the other colors. You probably didn't do anything wrong and you are probably worrying too much about what others are thinking of you. Communicate. Ask if you did/ said anything to offend. When they say, "no" (and they probably will) let it go.

- DO your best and remember that your best is probably good enough. Be the best parent you can be. Blues have a gift for being great parents. Every minute of the day and night, live for you kids. That's very cool. Be there at the crossroads of your child's life. Love them. Nurture them. At the same time...

- DON'T forget that you are human, that you are allowed to not be perfect. You have natural liabilities. You need to ask for help. Ask, don't give hints. Blues are the only ones who even come close to "getting" hints so of course Blues think that others will get hints, too. They don't. You deserve to expect help, and kind support from others, from your children and teens, and from your spouse.

- DON'T give in to that "you're a bad parent" vibe that can lead to real depression, self-loathing, and immobilization.

- DO fight it with your second color's common sense. Blue-Golds, list all the ways you are good and get moving on only

Today's To Do list. Write three things that are good about you on your mirror in shaving cream or red lipstick. Have some ice cream or chocolate at the end of the day to celebrate all the things you did. Blue-Oranges, take a break, run away with your family. Have some appropriate fun. Reward yourself in a small way for all that you're doing. Only think of one thing, that "Next Thing" that needs to be done. Then have one scoop of ice cream or piece of chocolate. Do the "Next Thing," have another scoop or one square of chocolate. Get the idea? Good. Now, both of you, go help another Blue mom or dad who's feeling the same way!

- DON'T fall prey to the "you've got to justify why you're telling me no" from any color teen. Remember, you don't negotiate with terrorists. You don't owe them an explanation. Period.

- DO be the parent, pull on your big-mom panties, or your big-dad shorts, and tell that teen that THEY need to tell YOU why they should do whatever it is they want to do so badly. Parenting is about being the Influencer, not the Influenced. Which may mean you might offend your child once in a while. Too bad, so sad. Keep them safe, don't play defense.

- DON'T wig out if your child lies or tells a whopper of a story the first time or for the first time in a long time. This is tough for a Blue parent because being authentic and truthful is very important to Blues.

- DO calm down first of all and see "lying", especially in small Oranges and any color teens, as an attempt to win back some freedom. As a Blue parent, are you smothering your child or teen with too much involvement and too little freedom for their color or their age? Give back some freedom or control with choices. Ignore the occasional lie as much as possible. Reward the very next "not lie." Lessen the consequence of a wrong choice IF they told the truth. Make telling the truth the best thing in the world. Start this pattern young. You'll end with teens who know they better tell the truth.

- DO address habitual liars with consequences that really hit home for their color. See the sections of each Kid's Colors for more information on consequences.

- DON'T give too many chances by begging your kids to do what you ask them.

- DO give toddlers to teens choices, but do it only once. If you restate the choices a second time because you are trying to get them to listen, obey, pick one, or you are cajoling them into do- ing what you need, you've gone too far and now you are just giving chances, not choices. Here's the rule, give kids all the choices you can live with, but they get one chance to obey. One. That's it. One. Then it's time for a consequence.

- DON'T feel pressured into making quick decisions.

- DO be firm about taking time to answer your kids and teens when you need it. When faced with a tough parenting decision or a child or teen who wants an immediate answer, wait. Don't negotiate with terrorists—and a pushy kid is a terrorist. Tell them, "If you push me for a quick answer, the answer is no. If you give me a minute to think this through, it may still be no, but your chances for a yes get better." Then take your minute. If pushed again, stick to your 'no' this time. They'll learn not to be a terrorist next time.

- DON'T jump into an overly emotional response when your chil- dren or teens are hurt, upset, treated unfairly, or come home with an emotional "they did it to me" story.

- DO get both sides of the story. When faced with an emotional situation, don't jump the gun. Take your time to decide on a course of action that considers all sides of the situation. Then you won't look like a Mama Bear AND a fool. Unless someone is bleeding or the place is on fire, you have all the time you need. That bully will still be there tomorrow. That grumpy teacher will still be there tomorrow. That nasty mean girl group will not only still be there tomorrow, they will be there until your daughter graduates high school—you have time to plot.

- DON'T be too intense, too serious, too hard on yourself, and don't allow yourself to get down or depressed. Stop second-guessing yourself. It's never too late to fix a problem.

- DO focus on your gifts, and ask for help when you need it. You are most likely a wonderful parent. Blue parents who are not great parents don't buy and read books like this. Celebrate your strengths. Manage your weaknesses with help from others.

One Final Do or Don't... You Decide.
Blue Mom Home Schooling

Over and over I see that at least once in the career of the Blue mom comes THE big stressor, "Should I, or should I not, home school?" My last bit of advise for Blue mom's... and you may hate me for this but here goes anyway... don't home school unless you can turn yourself into a Extrovert Gold-Green everyday during your school hours and then switch back into a True Blue during mom hours.

Okay, so take a deep breath and just hear me out, but be careful not to dismiss what I'm about to say as not pertaining to you. Read this with a trusted friend or your spouse and take their objective feedback as to whether or not this applies to you. It applied to me and most other Blue moms once they are willing to admit it.

To be honest, 80% of the time Blues moms opt to home school as the ultimate rescue for several different reasons. Your child is not getting enough attention. Your child is not being taught well enough. Other kids pick on your child. He's ignored, she's criticized.

They are talking about sex and drugs in fourth grade. Be very careful. If you are choosing to home school for those kinds of reasons, you're probably rescuing. Don't do it to rescue them from the big bad world. Give yourself permission to lovingly support your kids, and everyone else's kids (they may need you even more) as they struggle and ultimately succeed in the tough, cruel, unfair, corrupt, and seedy world of public school.

IF you plunge ahead and do home school, you gotta do it for the right reasons, not to rescue. And you CANNOT be a Blue mom while you are doing it. You need to become an **alien**. Blue mom's, even Blue-Golds, often stink at holding kids to a schedule, they struggle with naturally holding kids accountable, they tend to rescue, and they go easy on their kids because they are sympathetic. Blue moms also take things to heart, they hate being mean, and they second guess themselves the minute they have to be firm. All that, at the right time, is a good thing, but not when it comes to grading a bad writing assignment, chances are you'll just let them slide because it's just too much red ink and it might hurt their feelings. Or you'll let them slough their way out of doing all those stupid math problems because they understand the concept and after all it's such a pretty day outside. Now before you hate me, be honest. Don't those thoughts go through your mind? That's all I'm saying. They go through my mind, and I'm a parenting expert! I know better and I'm *still* totally guilty! But I'm also a Blue mom.

If you are truly disgusted with your local schools, AND you can see the wisdom in what I'm saying, here's a better solution for you and your child: **Go** and **Fight** *for* your child *with* the schools. Don't increase the stress in your home one hundred fold because you feel like you should home school. If it's not for you, or you've tried and you've found it to be as stressful as I've explained, let yourself bow out gracefully. Instead, be your child's advocate within the school. Educate yourself. Don't put all that home school pressure on yourself and your home. Unless you can truly transform into a tough, detached Extroverted Gold-Green with ship-shape schedules, great discipline on a beautiful day, a separate space to have as the school room, a love of red ink, and an immunity to tears, sidetracks, and the "you're a mean mom" button, I suggest you pass on the home school idea.

Instead, courageously embrace your Blue mom gifts, tell guilt to take a hike and support your kids while they learn about values from YOU, not the school. Have your home be the safe haven they run too, not a prison they want to run from. Help them handle real life situations and spread their wings in appropriate ways. Be their advocate. Speak up for your child and all the kids in public school whose parents don't give a flying flip about them.

If you are determined to home school do it in ways that turn your Blue mom traits into assets. Join a home school co-op and don't be the lone ranger. Have another mom grade the papers and no matter what let them be tough and do that job. You be the Co-op art director, Career Counselor, Music or History teacher. Please just consider the home school question honestly. If you have a Green spouse who's a good guy, and he loves you and the kids, and he has any hesitation, listen to him.

Okay, all that said, don't hate me, and don't send me an email saying it works for you. You are probably that other 20% that make it work and that can transform into the right personality during school hours. If so, I cannot tell you in words how happy I am for you, truly. But think of the 80% of your fellow Blue moms who are trying to live up to you. Do you really want to make other Blue moms feel inferior? I didn't think so because you don't have a mean bone in your body! Instead, we will just support each other and cheer each other on in whatever capacity that needs to be.

BLUE Parents: A Last Word or Two

Just the Gospel according to Shannon ;-)

Blue moms and dads make my job easy. So I hope I can make your job easier, too. Being a Blue parent is the best job in the world; but it can also be the most challenging. I know that you are up for the challenge. You can do it and you will do it well. Don't become "weary in well doing." Take care of yourself as you take care of others. Balance is one of the Blue's greatest values but can often seem elusive and difficult to achieve—especially when you are chasing toddlers, negotiating bedtimes with 3-graders, driving pre-teens to boy/girl parties, and turning over the car keys to teens who just yesterday were the toddlers you chased. Remember my dear Blue moms and dads that someone (I wish I knew who) once wisely said, "Parenting is the art of letting go." I hope that this book and the books I have yet to write will help you with that quest.

Parenting by PERSONALITY

Part Two

Kid's COLORS

This section will help you...

1. Discover your Kid's Colors
2. Understand your Kid's Colors
3. Figure out what to do with your Kid's Colors (that's the Parenting Stuff)

Parenting by PERSONALITY

Kid's COLORS

Discover Your Kid's Colors

This first chapter helps you discover your child's Interaction Style.
Are they an Introvert or an Extrovert?

Next you will determine what are your child's first and second color.

Kid's COLORS!
Some Basic Instructions
For determining YOUR child's colors

The Quick Answer...

To discover your child's COLORS you will go through the same kind of process you did to find your COLORS.

For children 2 to 8 or so: You will have to read the Kid's Color Descriptions and take some time to observe their behavior. As you work to determine your child's COLORS, be careful NOT to be "prejudiced" by your own COLORS. Take your time. Don't get frustrated. With some children you will determine their COLORS right away, with others it can take several days of observations.

For mature pre-teens and teens: read pages 148 to 150 for instructions.

Now, you can either jump right in or read the next few pages for additional information on determining your Kid's COLORS .

To jump in: First, look at The Kid's Introvert and Extrovert Descriptions on pages 154 to 155. Then, read the Kid's Color Descriptions on pages 158 to 165. Finally, use pages 168 to 176 to validate your idea of your child's COLOR combination. Don't skip to the validation process, you'll go crazy, there's 16 combos!

For more information: Read the "The Simple Truth" in the next few pages and then go to the color descriptions on pages 152 to 166 as discussed above.

The Simple Truth...

Determining Your Child's Colors:
For toddlers to pre-teens

To determine your child's colors you will go through a process much like you did to discover your own colors. Since young children, ages 2 to 7 or 8, don't have the maturity to look at a list of characteristics and traits, or stressors and stress behaviors in order to determine their own colors, you must do this for them. So, as their parents, read the descriptions on the next several pages and in just a short time you will be able to discover your child's personality type. If your child is 8 or so and pretty mature, read the Kid's Color Descriptions with them and make it a fun activity.

BASIC INSTRUCTIONS

First take a stab at determining your child's Interaction Style of Introvert or Extrovert.

The Introvert and Extrovert Color Descriptions are found on pages 154 and 155. See which one seems most like your child most of the time. As you are looking for your child's Interaction Style, be careful not to be prejudice by your own Interaction Style. Compare the descriptions on the Introvert/Extrovert description to what you observe as you watch your child's interactions with others, with you, and how they "think" through new information or how they approach a new situation. See them for who they are, not for who you are. There's a 50/50 chance that they have an opposite Interaction Style from you.

If determining whether your child is an Introvert or an Extrovert is not easy to do then put that step on hold for a while and move on to figuring out their first color.

For our purposes here... which is to learn a better way to parent your child... knowing their first color is the most important part. Knowing Introvert or Extrovert, and their second color, helps as they get older and helps in understanding how to teach them to make better decisions, so if you are not sure at first it's alright. 90% of your new parenting efforts will be greatly improved by just understanding their first color. Determining your child's Interaction Style can wait for them to get a little older and for you to be a little more confident in understanding personality types.

Next, go to the Kid's Color Descriptions on pages 158 to 165

Whether you were able to determine that your child is an Introvert or an Extrovert, or you decided to skip it for now, follow the instructions on pages 156 and 157. **Read all four Color Descriptions.** Get a good feel for the differences between the four colors. You may know right away that your child is definitely one color or another or you may not have a clue at first. Either way, **take the time to observe your child's behavior for a few days. Compare what you see in their behavior to the descriptions on the four color pages.** Especially watch what they do when they are upset. What are their most common everyday actions? What are their regular stress behaviors, or in other words, what do they do when they are upset or misbehaving? **Match those behaviors, good and not so good, to ONLY ONE of the color descriptions and you will have a good idea about your child's first color.** A few rules: first, your child does not have two first colors, and second, depending on their first color, there are only two choices, not the other three for their second color (I'll explain all that in a second).

To discover your child's second color follow the directions on the bottom of your child's first color description.

You will be directed to go to two other color pages. For first color GOLDS and ORANGES, their second color can only be Blue or Green. For first color BLUES and GREENS, only Gold or Orange can be their second color. This is because of the way our personalities develop.

Here's the short story (now you might read this in other places in this book, first it's worth repeating, and second, not everyone will read every word so I've got you catch you when I have you), our personalities, according to Jung (1979) and others are made up of four basic dimensions or continuums. I detail only three in this book for our purposes. The fourth is complicated and doesn't really help with parenting... remember I'm trying to keep this simple.

So back to why your child can only have one of two specific second colors depending on their first color... Gold and Orange are opposites on the "how we organize our world" continuum, and Blue and Green are opposites on the "how we make our decisions" continuum of our personality make-up. This will all make more sense as you read about your kid's colors. I actually talk a lot about this stuff later. So bottom line, we can only *naturally* have one "color" from each continuum. One is naturally more dominate... our first color, and one is less dominant but important... our second color. (For more information on this see, Jung, 1979; Murphy,1992; Tieger and Barron-Teiger, 1997, in the bibliography, or take my word for it... it's a lot of very dry reading.)

Because of all this, the younger your child is, say from 2 to 5 or 6, you may first see Orange or Gold as your child's first color. Then when they are about 5 or 6, all of sudden they seem to change into a first color Blue or Green. Never fear! Things are as they should be. Often true first color Blue and Green children seem to be first color Gold or Orange when they are very young. That's only because it's easier to see how a child organizes their world in their behaviors then it is to see their decision making process when they are so small. They have not changed colors, they have just developed to the point where their "decision-making" processes are more obvious. Don't worry about any of this, though! Here's the beauty of all of this... if you have a little pre-school Gold or Orange on your hands that's how you will parent them. If later, say when your child hits about 5 or 6, you see a significant change to Blue or Green then you start parenting them with that in mind and it will work just as wonderfully as parenting them as a Gold or Orange did as when they were a pre-schooler. In my experience, this only happens about 10% of the time but I had to mention it at some point. This was that point.

What if you can't see their second color? No problem. Again, it's their first color that matters most for right now.

Often you can see a second color the first time you read the descriptions. If so that's awesome! If not, remember that for now, it's their first color that is the most important thing to know to start parenting them according to their personality type .

Determining Your Child's Colors: For Mature Pre-teens and Teens ages 13 to 18

For mature pre-teens and teens, follow the same path as outlined above but use the Adults & Teens Color descriptions found on pages 22 to 46.

Look at their Interaction Style first, then look for their first and second colors using the Four Color Adult Description on pages 36 to 39. I suggest that you create a fun time to work together on discovering their colors. Be prepared to help your pre-teens and less mature teens with definitions and examples of the descriptions as they apply to your family and their lives. Don't force them to do this or lead them toward what you think first.

As you go through the process with your teen or pre-teen make it fun and emotionally safe.

In other words, do not argue about what they perceive about themselves, instead embrace their assessment of who they are. If you disagree about what color they think they are, keep it to yourself for now. Ask questions about *their* colors choice, don't ask them questions leading them into *your* color choice for them. That's very manipulative. Instead, focus on their story, learn why they think or feel a certain way about what they think their colors are. On your own take the time to watch their behavior to see whose perspective is closer to reality. Of course, be mindful of possible bias on your part. I've often had parents convinced they know their child better then the teen knew themselves, only to discover that they teen was right and the parent had judged wrong. On the other hand, I had parents see the teen's true personality right away and the teen had such low self-esteem that they choose a color for themselves that sounded far cooler than their real colors. These teens often want to be Orange. Either way, there is a reason for the misunderstanding. For now, create a supportive environment as you do this activity together. Over time, and with a gentle, supportive approach, I've seen every, and I mean every, situation like this come around to where both the parent and teen see eye to eye.

What if you have a very private, quiet thinker teen who wants to look at the colors alone?

That's fine. Let them mull it over on their own. No harm done, unless you are a very excited and involved Extroverted Blue mom, then you will feel a little rejected and pushed away, especially when this seems so therapeutic to you. That's very normal for a Blue. But here's the scoop on your quiet teen for any color parent... it will be healing and therapeutic to them as they think it through. You need to let the process be the most natural for *their* personality, not for yours. Then later get together and have a positive discussion about your colors and their colors. Talk later, and have a good chuckle, about how their stress behaviors may be your stressors and vise versa. Again, if you don't agree with their assessment of their personality, do not make it into a conflict. Remember that you can use the **16 Color Combination Descriptions** on pages 168 to 176 to further narrow down your guesses and theirs. In the end, remember that their assessment of their color is their perspective and is just as valid as your perspective of your own color. You probably would not like your teen to argue that you've got your colors wrong so please don't do that to them. You'd be surprised how often I've seen this kind of silly conflict happen. Instead, just agree to disagree and then follow my next suggestion.

> **If you don't see eye to eye with your teen on what their colors are, how do you know what colors to use to parent them with?**

It's really very simple. In the sections on Kid's Colors read both chapters, their idea of their colors, and read the one that corresponds to what you think their colors are. Then, use the parenting hints and tips from the chapter you think will work the best and see if it works. Here's the magic of **Parenting by PERSONALITY** (or

"**Parenting by COLORS**" as our courses are known by), if the parenting strategy works, you have their color spot on. If the parenting strategy for that color doesn't work, you've got their color wrong. It's not rocket science but the hints and tips really do work when you have their colors right. And don't worry, the only one who will need therapy through this process is you, your teen will be just fine.

A Few Final Words...

The biggest mistake parents make while discovering their child's colors is that they don't get out of their own way. In other words, take the time to be sure that you are truly "seeing" your children and teens for who they really are and that you are not "seeing" them through your own colors. It's a natural bias that we all can be guilty of. Just take the time to set aside the natural traits of your own color so you can see the traits of theirs. Here's a few examples.

First, let's say we have a Gold parent and an Orange child. Often I see Gold parents who swear their child loves and needs a schedule and therefore the parent determines that their child is a Gold... "just like me." But upon further observation, and when the child doesn't always seem like a Gold, let's say they seem to be pretty easygoing when things change, then the parent comes to discover that their child is actually an Orange who keeps to the Gold parent's schedule in order to get their freedom needs met. In this case the Gold parents need to set aside their natural Gold bias to "see" the true Orange traits in their very Orange child.

Our second example is that you are a Blue and your spouse is a Green, what's going on if you see both "feeler" and "thinker" traits in your child or teen? One very common explanation is that your child or teen has the *natural* qualities of one of your colors and has, at a very young age, developed the outward appearances of the other color's traits because you or your spouse's personality is rubbing off on them. Don't be alarmed by this explanation, it is very clever of your child to be so adaptable and it's very normal. Just be aware that it's **impossible** for your child to **naturally** possess both Blue and Green or both Gold and Orange. At the same time, it's totally **possible** that they've **developed** those traits as you've rubbed off on your kids. The remedy is simple, watch your child or teen for a week or so with new eyes and their true colors will shine through.

INTROVERT or EXTROVERT?

Discover Your Child's Interaction Style

The Quick Answer...

To be honest, there is not a "Quick Answer" for this chapter either. If you want to find out what your child's colors are, you will have to take the time to read all the stuff in this section and in the next section.

The next few pages are to be used by parents to determine your child's Interaction Style of either Introvert or Extrovert, and their first and second colors.

The first set of descriptions describe children's Introvert or Extrovert characteristics.

The Simple Truth...

In the next few pages you will find in-depth descriptions about INTROVERTS and EXTROVERTS for children. Below are the steps you need to follow to determine your child's **Interaction Style**. Here's how...

1. Put aside any ideas you have about your child being "shy" or "outgoing," so you are unbiased as you read these descriptions.

2. Read the descriptions and stressors for INTROVERTS on page 155 and then for EXTROVERTS on page 154. Decide which description and list of stressors seem most like your child, most of the time. Don't think in terms of what you want them to be. This will make the outcome inaccurate. Instead, focus on which one describes your child the best. Be honest with yourself about who they really are.

3. If you get stuck, don't worry; watch their behavior for clues. Think about what happens when your child is upset or tired. Do they tend to withdraw or do they want to talk your ears off. Those behaviors might lead you more toward seeing a true INTROVERT or a true EXTROVERT.

4. Most of all have fun. After you've looked at the next few pages, ask your spouse, friends, older children, and family what they think your child might be. Ask for details.

5. Most of all, remember that for children, first color is more important for now. If you get really stuck, put it on the back burner for a few weeks and move on to their first color and to reading about that.

6. Jump in! Is your child an INTROVERT or an EXTROVERT?

EXTROVERT Kids

EXTROVERTED children seem to focus more
on things around them, on other people, and what's
going on outside their skin.

They are usually talkative and as a parent
you often know what they are thinking or feeling
because they will tell you. They tend to ask lots of
questions, sometimes it seems, just to hear themselves talk.

They don't usually like to be totally alone.
They would rather be with others and often "come alive" or
get a "second wind" being with friends or family.

A "long day" to an EXTROVERT is a lot of time alone
or being quiet, lots of "thinking" or personal
studying without discussion or a chance to talk to others.

Extrovert's need:

- Interactions with others, especially at the end of
  an "alone day"
- To be accepted by the group
- Physical contact
- Ability to think out loud with someone they trust
- To be listened to

Extrovert STRESSORS:

- When I am expected to give short answers without being
  allowed to share all the details that matter or that
  complete the story.
- When other people don't talk or when there are
  uncomfortable lulls in conversations.
- When I have to guess what someone is thinking.
- People who don't share their stuff.
- Being quiet and/or still for long periods of time.
- People who are stand-offish or stiffen when I hug them.
- When someone wants me to "think it through" on my own
  when I really need to "talk it out."
- When I have a problem to solve and there is no one to
  talk to about it.
- Long periods of time alone.

INTROVERT Kids

INTROVERTED children focus more on their own thoughts and feelings. Even as a parent you might not know what they are thinking or feeling unless you ask. When you ask they might tell you or they might seem to ignore you at first?

Teachers often describe them as quiet and may say that they don't participate. As the parent you know that they are listening but just not talking out loud. They're busy thinking!

They are re-energized by a little time alone, some time with you, or a chance to zone out in front of the TV.

A "long day" to an INTROVERT is a very interactive day with lots of people at school, at the daycare, or at home. INTROVERTS become drained when they have to "perform" on the spur of the moment for others.

Introvert's need:
- Time to be alone
- Time to process and to think
- Down time at the end of a busy or "people focused" day
- Respect for their not being huggy or touchy
- Respect for their belongings and space
- Extra sleep time especially during stressful times

Introvert STRESSORS:
- People who talk a lot but don't really say anything important or repeat the same thing over and over.
- Real "huggy" people; especially if I don't know them very well or I'm in the middle of doing something.
- People who stand real close to me or talk real loud.
- Having my stuff touched, taken, or rearranged.
- Lots of loud noise for extended periods of time.
- A room full of people I don't know, where I am expected to talk and be friendly.
- Being expected to give quick answers OR having someone else say my answers are not long enough or detailed enough.
- Having people ask me, "What are you thinking?", "What's the matter?", or "Are you okay?" all the time.

What Are Your Kid's Colors?

Are they a... GOLD, ORANGE, GREEN, or BLUE?

The Simple COLORS Truth...

In the next few pages you will find in-depth descriptions for each color child: **GOLD, ORANGE, GREEN,** and **BLUE.** Below are the steps to follow to determine your child's first and second color. You already know the drill. It's a lot like finding your own colors.

1. Put aside any ideas you have about your child being a specific color, especially any thoughts that they are a mini-you. Maybe they are but go at this with new eyes so to speak.

2. Read the descriptions of qualities and stressors for **GOLD, ORANGE, GREEN,** and **BLUE** children on the following pages. Again, decide which description seems most like your child most of the time, not what you want them to be, or what you feel they ought to be, or ought not to be (yes sadly, that HAS happened, I've had a handful of parents dread the idea that they might have an Orange or a Blue child - I kept my cool but just barely).

3. If you get stuck, don't worry. Put the book down and just watch your kid's behavior for a few days, then come back and try again. You'll see their color better then. It works every time! Never fear, trust the process. I do!

4. Again, you might find that more than one color seems to fit. That's okay. When that happens study the list of <u>stressors</u> for

those two colors. Whichever list of stressors and stress behaviors fits your child's triggers and wig-outs best is probably their first color. Go with that color for now. You can adjust your guesses later.

5. To determine their second color follow the directions at the bottom of the second page of their first color descriptions. Remember, certain combinations for their first and second color are not naturally possible (see pages 173). Just as a refresher, if they are a **BLUE** or **GREEN** first color, their second can only be Gold or Orange. If they are a **GOLD** or **ORANGE** first color their second can only be Blue or Green.

6. Again, as with discovering your colors, there are two ways to approach this: 1) "Go with your gut" as you read the color descriptions on the next few pages. If you are the more analytical type, underline the qualities that describe your child in each color and do some kind of informal tally thingy and see which color describes most of their traits. Remember, if you get stuck, walk away, watch their actions for a few days, and come back to all of this. Then wah-lah, their color will manifest itself if you don't over think this. Some parents are sure of their child's color and then even six weeks later they realize they are another color. What changed? Not the child! It was the parent's understanding of the colors that became more precise. So...

7. Most of all, HAVE FUN! Then ask your spouse, older children, and even the child themselves in fun, age appropriate ways.

8. Turn the page, jump in, and get started. Let's find out what your child's colors are!

Order-Maker GOLD

This child <u>creates order</u> from what they see as chaos, even if you don't need their help to do it. They may be bossy, even bossing you occasionally. They need consistency and structure. They are comfortable with rules, things that stay the same, and having things settled and controlled. They prefer to have a set schedule and don't handle change very well. They have a strong sense of what is right or wrong, either through their "feelings" or based on some sort of logical structure. They don't really like surprises and are usually obedient.

> INTROVERT GOLDS who create order will usually like a set way to do things over and over, and quietly set out to do each task each day. They may be impatient, and may tattle on others who make wrong choices or break the rules. They don't like to get into trouble and may pout or withdrawal when disciplined. They tend to be homebodies, have a small circle of friends, and shy away from crowds or new activities. They are quietly service-oriented. They will also shy away from conflict because it feels chaotic or because it's stupid.

> EXTROVERT GOLDS who create order may be very out spoken about what they are doing right, especially when you haven't noticed. They use the word "should" a lot and will often tell you, and others what to do. When upset, they blame others, justify their choices, and tattle. They will be more likely to participate in new activities after they have formed some expectations in their mind. They will have many friends and will be the leader in their group no matter how young they are.

GOLD Child STRESSORS:

Chaos and inconsistency
Unclear rules
Lack of structure
Feeling powerless, out of control
Too much change
Doing something different
Family members who are late
People who don't do what's right
Lack of appreciation
Too much responsibility
Not enough time to finish a task
Broken promises

GOLD Child STRESS BEHAVIORS:

- Resistant to change, may argue, or spout rules
- May be moody or pessimistic about the future
- Becomes very controlling of people, time, things
- Becomes guarded, appears secretive, or compulsive
- May become stubborn - they want what they want and they think they deserve it so they may do anything to get it
- Blames others and will boldly justify their own actions, may say, "But what about him, he's not..."
- Very critical of others, siblings, or teachers
- Adopts a very narrow focus often on the negative
- Becomes concerned about ownership, refuses to share, may grab toys away, or push others away
- Creates rules for everyone else and creates "exceptions" for themselves, "mothers" everyone else including parents
- May become highly controlling and tells others what to do, appears bossy, very opinionated

If you have a first color GOLD, next go to the
Blue and Green descriptions.
One of these will be their natural second color.

Freedom Fighter ORANGE

This child needs <u>flexibility</u> from you but may seem very stubborn. They crave <u>freedom</u> to be and room to act. They are good at handling change if it "feels" right or seems "logical" to them. If that change takes them away from the fun, they don't like it at all and will fight you on it. They are risk takers and love adventures. They prefer hands-on learning with lots of action. This child is great at keeping their options open and creative negotiating. They get things done, but usually at the last minute, and when the reward is worth it.

INTROVERT ORANGES are Freedom Fighters who will often like, and be, quiet. They are often homebodies. They conserve their energy showing only a low level of activity until it's important to *them* to move, usually waiting until the last minute. Then they will move quickly and may take some surprising risks. They may quietly defy the rules. They often seem "sneaky" as they quietly fly under the radar and go about doing whatever they want, when they want it. They can be very funny, even outgoing when it suits hem.

EXTROVERT ORANGES are Freedom Fighters who crave flexibility and fun. They're playful and say just about anything. They have endless energy and short attention spans. They drive adults crazy with their constant talk and endless activity, but they are good in a crisis and are usually great athletes. They can also be funny, clever, and can negotiate their way out of anything. They will probably have a difficult time with school unless you are there for them.

ORANGE Child STRESSORS:

Lack of freedom
Limits or restrictions
Unnecessary routines
Waiting or having nothing to do
Lack of options or choices
Too much structure
Strict "how to's"
Doing things over and over
Lots of paperwork/worksheets
Bossy people
Lack of fun and no rewards
Slow decision making

ORANGE Child STRESS BEHAVIORS:

- Becomes very impatient, wants immediate results
- Seems frustrated, acting like a caged animal if they can't DO something right NOW
- Appears bossy, demanding, and pushy
- <u>Extroverts</u> may attack first with overly dramatic or exaggerated words, then becomes more physical
- <u>Introverts</u> withdraw and become sneaky, quietly doing what they want to anyway
- Jumps from activity to activity, not finishing any
- Takes unusual risks and becomes impulsive
- Focuses on the wrong task to get out of doing something else that is un-fun or a freedom threat
- Becomes careless with details and refuses to wait
- Pushes for quick decisions, goes around the rules
- <u>Extroverts</u> become overly active, shouts, throws tantrums, procrastinates
- <u>Introverts</u> become quietly distracted, gets lost doing the wrong task, appears sneaky, may over-sleep, procrastinates

If you have a first color ORANGE, next go to the
Blue and Green descriptions.
One of these will be their natural second color.

Serious-Minded Thinker GREEN

This child is very logical in their thinking but may seem very *illogical*, stubborn, and unreasonable at times. This is because their "logic system" is immature and probably won't match yours. They rarely worry about what others think unless they have a lot of respect for that person. They can be impatient with their own very deep feelings and the feelings of others. They have very little sense of time and often dawdle, procrastinate, and daydream. They need lots of information, especially when you change plans on them. They play with toys in unusual, creative ways and like experimenting. They enjoy open-ended projects and get frustrated with specific "how-to" instructions. They are very creative and love solving problems. Green girls are very nurturing and you may wonder if they are Blue but they really are very logical when you see how they process.

> INTROVERT GREENS are the <u>ultimate introverts</u> and are usually very involved in their own thoughts. They may appear withdrawn, always thinking or, at times, even spacey. They keep their feelings and ideas to themselves and tend to get overly upset, even violent, if things go wrong or they feel stupid.

> EXTROVERT GREENS will still appear quiet and thought-full, like an introvert. At the same time they will ask lots of "why" questions and talk your ear off about what they've just learned. They will challenge you, your information, your perspective, and your logic. They may appear to be argumentative, know-it-alls.

GREEN Child STRESSORS:

People being stupid
Doing something really dumb themselves
Not being able to learn or try something new *when they want to.*
Illogical rules and restrictions
No time to think about new info, a new plan, or a new activity
Being forced into a quick decision or performing without practice
Lack of appreciation for their competency or for being smart
Ignored ideas or too many unsolvable problems
Too much "touchy-feely" stuff   Other people being emotional

GREEN Child STRESS BEHAVIORS:

- Becomes extremely uncompromising and stubborn
- Wants things a very specific way, picky
- Tries to get what they want through intellectual debate, sidetracking, and hurtful comments
- Not interested in feelings, advice, or ideas of others, especially when they are not listened to
- Experiences "analysis paralysis," may be slow to decide/act but can't turn their brain off at night
- Immobilized by the fear of failure but acts out with defensiveness, arguing, or being very spacey
- Demands to know more details but seems illogical to parents; very argumentative
- Asks "why" over and over again; argues with answers
- May become highly critical of self and others
- Thinks things or people are "stupid"
- Becomes aloof, withdrawn, has "checked-out"
- Quietly refuses to act, appears lazy, un-focused
- Tries to impose big, lofty plans on others
- May be suddenly physical or violent, throws, hits, or destroys things

If you have a first color **GREEN**, go back to the
Gold and **Orange** descriptions.
One of these will be their natural second color.

Intuitive Feeler BLUE

This child is very sensitive to the needs, feelings, and values of others. They often worry about what others think and about the way their choices affect the people they care about. This child can become overwhelmed in emotionally charged situations or during conflict. They are kind, caring, intuitive, and the self-appointed "fixers" of people problems. They often take the blame for conflict. They can seem overly dramatic, needy, or clingy when they are stressed. Their play is very imaginative but usually people focused. They want to be close to you physically and emotionally. They like to help, they usually obey, and they can tell when you are upset. They can be whiney when they are tired and may be overly fearful. Blue boys often display Green qualities but are really more emotional than logical when you really observe them.

> INTROVERT BLUES will be very tender-hearted but they will not readily share their deep feelings or values. They may appear withdrawn and pre-occupied. They become moody and emotional when tired, stressed, or upset. They will take on the cares of the world without you knowing if you are not observant.

> EXTROVERT BLUES will be very tender-hearted AND openly share feelings, concerns, worries and values unless their feelings are dismissed by insensitive adults. They may often appear emotional or overly dramatic at times. They can be bossy or a party animal depending on their second color.

BLUE Child STRESSORS:

People fighting, mean people
Insincerity, inauthenticity
Repetitive work and competition
Personal rejection, lots of mean criticism
Being ignored, ridiculed, or the center of negative attention
Being the middle of an emotionally charged situation
Loud, negative remarks - yelling
People who lie or who act fake
Trying to please too many people, including fighting parents
Bossy, controlling people, including siblings and teachers
Feelings of confusion, not knowing who or how to please

BLUE Child STRESS BEHAVIORS:

- Tries to please everyone but may focus on pleasing friends before family
- Can't seem to get moving, becomes "immobilized"
- Doesn't know where to start a project, report, or big job; wants to work with you on chores
- Becomes highly reactive or emotional, exaggerates details and their feelings if you are not listening
- Can't seem to make a decision; seems afraid to hurt other's feelings or that they've made someone mad
- Seems okay, calm and kind then just loses it
- Extremely disorganized, may live in a mess
- Undisciplined with time, acts "spacey," unfocused
- Let's others "walk all over them," can't say "no"
- Not firm with self or others, inappropriately self-sacrificing; always trying to solve people problems
- Becomes too helpful, tends to rescue, becomes the peacemaker even as a toddler
- Worried about what others will think about them
- Becomes whiney, "blue," down or over-whelmed

If you have a first color BLUE, go back to the
Gold and Orange descriptions.
One of these will be their natural second color.

Okay, so what are your child's colors?
Gold, **Orange**, **Green**, or **Blue** ?

Today's date _____

Child's Name: _____ is an

_____, _____, _____
(Introvert or Extrovert)   (First color)   (Second color)

Child's Name: _____ is an

_____, _____, _____
(Introvert or Extrovert)   (First color)   (Second color)

Child's Name: _____ is an

_____, _____, _____
(Introvert or Extrovert)   (First color)   (Second color)

Child's Name: _____ is an

_____, _____, _____
(Introvert or Extrovert)   (First color)   (Second color)

Child's Name: _____ is an

_____, _____, _____
(Introvert or Extrovert)   (First color)   (Second color)

Child's Name: _____ is an

_____, _____, _____
(Introvert or Extrovert)   (First color)   (Second color)

Gold

Orange

Green

Blue

Understanding Kid's Colors
3 Simple Truths

The Quick Answer...

There are **3 Simple Truths** you need
to know about Kid's Colors

1. There are 16 Color Combinations and they can help you understand a great deal about why your child do what they do.
2. There are a few Color combinations that are not possible such as: Blue/Green and Gold/Orange.
3. What do you do if you are still not sure what your child's first color really is?

Read these 3 Simple Truths if you like or skip them if you prefer. Either way...

While reading your Kid's Colors keep in mind...
Why do your kids do what they do?
To get their unmet needs...met.

And why does that drive you crazy?
*Because their bad behavior is most
likely one of your STRESSORS!*

Simple Truth #1

There are 16 Color Combinations and they will help you understand your child.

As I explained earlier in the adult colors section, each color combination has a unique set of **NEEDS, VALUES, MOTIVES,** **STRESSORS,** and **STRESS BEHAVIORS**. Even for kids and teens, when you combine one interaction style, with two of the four colors there are 16 personality types or sets of color combinations that describe a specific, and scientifically observed, set of needs, values, stressors, and stress behaviors (Tieger, 1997).

Understanding your child's unique color combination will provide you with valuable insight into why they are doing what they are doing and what's the best way to handle it or teach them to change it. This will also help you know how best to teach them your values, coach them through learning new behaviors, and how to praise them for a job well done.

In the 16 descriptions below you will see common phrases and ideas as you read through these descriptions. I did that on purpose so that you could get a sense of what each color combination has in common and how they are different. The phrases I use illustrates how each of the 16 combinations break down into three of their basic dimensions based on the research behind personality types. The three dimensions described here include how Introvert and Extrovert are on opposite ends of a continuum that describes how we INTERACT with our world. Gold and Orange are on opposite ends of a continuum that describes how we ORGANIZE our world. Blue and Green are on opposite ends of a continuum that describes how we MAKE DECISIONS about our world through the filter of either a logical standard (first or second color Greens) or through the filter of emotions and their personal value system (first or second color Blues). The phrases and descriptions I use here are based on showing you how each color combination approaches these three dimensions of our personality (Jung, 1979; Murphy, 1992; Tieger, 1997). Basically these descriptions outline how each color combination is hard wired and how they think but these descriptions are not necessarily a snapshot of their behavior. Those snapshots of behavior are found in the following Kid's Colors Chapters starting on page 179 with the Gold Child. The 16 type combinations are listed here with their Myers-Briggs Type Indicator format.

The Four GOLD Combinations are:

Extrovert Gold-Blue (ESFJ)   "Let's all work together."
This child is COOPERATIVE.
They focus on the world outside their skin and process information externally. They live in the moment and organize that moment with structure. Their decision-making process is secondary to acting in a structured way in that moment and is based on their feelings and values. Chaos, change, and mean people are their biggest stressors.

Introvert Gold-Blue (ISFJ)   "You can depend on me."
This child is TRUSTWORTHY.
They focus on the world inside their heart and head, and process information internally. They live in the moment and organize that moment with structure. Their decision-making process is secondary to acting in a structured way in the moment and is based on their feelings and values. Chaos, change, and mean people are their biggest stressors.

Extrovert Gold-Green (ESTJ)
"Quiet on the set, aaaaaand ACTION!"
This child is a LEADER.
They focus on the world outside their skin and process information externally. They live in the moment and organize that moment with structure. Their decision-making process is secondary to acting in a structured way in the moment and is based on their own brand of logic. Chaos, change, and lack of logic are their biggest stressors.

Introvert Gold-Green (ISTJ)   "Let's think this through."
This child is DECISIVE.
They focus on the world inside their head and process information internally. They live in the moment and organize that moment with structure. Their decision-making process is secondary to acting in a structured way in the moment and is based on their own brand of logic. Chaos, change, and lack of logic are their biggest stressors.

The Four ORANGE Combinations are:

Extrovert Orange-Blue (ESFP) "Let's TALK!"
This child is ANIMATED.
They focus on the world outside their skin and process information externally. They live in the moment and organize that moment with freedom in mind. Their decision-making process is secondary to being free in the moment and is based on their feelings and values. A lack of freedom and mean people are their biggest stressors.

Introvert Orange-Blue (ISFP) "Dreamer Child"
This child is GENTLE.
They focus on the world inside their heart and head, and process information internally. They live in the moment and organize that moment with freedom in mind. Their decision-making process is secondary to being free in the moment and is based on their feelings and values. A lack of freedom and mean people are their biggest stressors.

Extrovert Orange-Green (ESTP) "Higher, Faster, Louder!"
This child is ADVENTEROUS.
They focus on the world outside their skin and process information externally. They live in the moment and organize that moment with freedom in mind. Their decision-making process is secondary to being free in the moment and is based on their own brand of logic. A lack of freedom and illogical restrictions are their biggest stressors.

Introvert Orange-Green (ISTP) "What would happen if I..."
This child is COURIOUS.
They focus on the world inside their head, and process information internally. They live in the moment and organize that moment with freedom in mind. Their decision-making process is secondary to being free in the moment and is based on their own brand of logic. A lack of freedom and illogical restrictions are their biggest stressors.

The Four GREEN Combinations are:

Extrovert Green-Gold (ENTJ)
"I've got the final word on that."
This child is DETERMINED.
They focus on the world outside their skin, and process information externally. They are continuously taking in raw data and making decisions about how to apply it based on their own brand of logic. They live in the world of possibilities and organize that world with structure and order. A lack of information, logic, and order are their biggest stressors.

Introvert Green-Gold (INTJ) "In the Pursuit of Knowledge."

This child is METHODICAL.

They focus on the world inside their head, and process information internally. They are continuously taking in raw data and making decisions about how to apply it based on their own brand of logic. They live in the world of possibilities and organize that world with structure and order. A lack of information, logic, and order are their biggest stressors.

Extrovert Green-Orange (ENTP) "I've Got a GREAT Idea!"

This child is CREATIVE.

They focus on the world outside their skin, and process information externally. They are continuously taking in raw data and making decisions about how to apply it based on their own brand of logic. They live in the world of possibilities and organize that world with freedom and flexibility. A lack of information, logic, and freedom are their biggest stressors.

Introvert Green-Orange (INTP)
"Quietly Working to Make Your No, My Yes."

This child is INTRIGUING.

They focus on the world inside their own head, and process information internally. They are continuously taking in raw data and making decisions about how to apply it based on their own brand of logic. They live in the world of possibilities and organize that world with freedom and flexibility. A lack of information, logic, and freedom to carry out their own activities are their biggest stressors.

The Four BLUE Combinations are:

Extrovert Blue-Gold (ENFJ) "Off on a Noble Quest."

This child is ENTHUSIASTIC.

They focus on the world outside their skin, and process emotions externally. They intuitively pick up on the raw emotions around them and continuously make decisions based on their values as to what they should do with all those emotions. They live in the world of ideals and organize that world with their own sense of structure. Conflict and disharmony are their biggest stressors.

Introvert Blue-Gold (INFJ) "The Secret Keeper."

This child is CONSIDERATE.

They focus on the world inside their own feelings, and process emotions internally. They intuitively pick up on the raw emotions around them and continuously make decisions based on their values as to what they should do with all those emotions. They live in the world of ideals and organize that world with their own sense of structure. Conflict and disharmony are their biggest stressors.

Extrovert Blue-Orange (ENFP) "Life is Good."

This child is GENEROUS.

They focus on the world outside their skin, and process emotions externally. They intuitively pick up on the raw emotions around them and continuously make decisions based on their values as to what they should do with all those emotions. They live in the world of ideals and organize that world with their own sense of freedom and authenticity. Conflict, disharmony, and lack of freedom are their biggest stressors.

Introvert Blue-Orange (INFP) "My Heart's on My Sleeve."

This child is SENSITIVE.

They focus on the world inside their own feelings, and process emotions internally. They intuitively pick up on the raw emotions around them and continuously make decisions based on their values as to what they should do with all those emotions. They live in the world of ideals and organize that world with their own sense of freedom and authenticity. Conflict, disharmony, and lack of freedom are their biggest stressors.

Simple Truth #2

There are a few color combinations that are just not possible... according to the science behind personality types or color.

These are the impossible combinations: Blue-Green, Green-Blue, Gold-Orange, or Orange-Gold. Okay, hold on to your head, Fred! Here comes some psycho babble... if that's not fun for you or you could care less... move on and skip this section. I'm just saying.

Up to this point I think I've addressed a few times how there are several dimensions to our personality. Each dimension represents a set of opposite preferences that Jung (1979) identified as being part of our natural personality. For example, the two opposites on the "how we relate to our world" continuum, or dimension, are **Introvert** and **Extrovert**. Understanding that our **Interaction Style** is not about being outgoing or shy, but about how we process information and how we recharge when we are drained, I'm sure you can see how we can't *naturally* be both at the same time. We might be close to the middle, say 51% Extrovert and 49% Introvert, but we can't be exactly both. Jung, and others (too many to name here - see my reference list), suggested that instead we have a natural preference for one end or the other end of each dimension of our personality. Over time, hopefully, as we become more balanced we slide closer to the middle of some, or all, of those continuums but we still have a natural preference for one end or the other and that doesn't change. Even as we become more balanced, our preferences usually come out when we are stressed.

So the point of all this is that, **Gold** and **Orange** are on opposite ends of the "how we organize our world" dimension, and **Blue** and **Green** are on opposite ends of the "decision-making" dimension. And since we cannot occupy two places at once, we can't *naturally* be both Gold AND Orange, or Blue AND Green. So we can't have a Gold-Orange kid, or an Orange-Gold child, or a Blue-Green teen, or a Green-Blue tween. According to more than a century's worth of social science, it just ain't gunna happen.

Whew! Glad that's done. I was almost putting myself to sleep! I hope most of you Oranges skipped that whole thing. If not, my hats off to you!

Now, having said all that, what if you really thought your child or teens was one of those impossible combinations, what do you do next? The easy answer is to just go read the first six to eight pages of each of the color chapters you thought your child was. Just doing that will most likely help you figure out which color they really are.

Second, here's a hint based only on my experience (meaning no scientific proof), if you have a boy and you are stuck between Blue and Green, he's probably a Blue boy and he's sorta rare. If you have a girl and you are stuck between Green and Blue, she's probably a sorta rare Green girl. Try that first. If you are stuck between Orange and Gold the boy/girl thing is irrelevant. Instead it has more to do with them probably being YOUR opposite. If you are Gold and you see your child as an Orange-Gold or Gold-Orange, I betcha your child is an Orange and they've just gotten really good at mimicking your Goldness to get their freedom needs meet, so I'd start with the Orange chapter. Oranges are the ultimate chameleons.

Simple Truth #3

What do you do if you are still not sure what your child's first color really is?

What if you are stuck between the "allowable switch-a-roos," as I call them. For example, you are stuck between thinking your child is a Green-Orange or an Orange-Green, or let's say you can't tell if you daughter is a Gold-Blue or a Blue-Gold? In that case, read the first six to eight pages of each of those Kid's Colors chapters. One color or the other will emerge as the right one pretty quick. Actually the "switch-a-roos" are most often the easiest to validate because their motivations and needs are very different even if some of their stress behaviors at first seem to be pretty much the same.

Soooo... what if you don't see eye to eye with your spouse on what your child's colors are? It's really very simple. In the Kid's Colors chapters, read **TOGETHER** whatever two chapters correspond closest to what you and your spouse think are your child's colors. Then, *with a UNITED plan*, use the parenting hints and tips from one chapter at a time and see what works best. Whatever color set of suggestions works best that's probably your child's color. And no "I told you so's" allowed. No competition, no winner, no loser. It's a celebration that you've come to an understanding of your child's colors, together, end of story.

Now here's the beauty of **Parenting by PERSONALITY** or **Parenting by COLORS** (as we usually call it)... WHEN, not IF, the parenting strategies for a specific color works, you have their color spot on. If the parenting strategies for a specific color (the color you thought that was your child's color) doesn't work, you've got the color wrong. In other words, you've got your child's color right when the set of parenting strategies for that color works. Believe me, you will know in just a few days, maybe in a few hours if you are wrong. If it's right you will know, most likely the first time you try it. No joke! If you don't believe me read the testimonials on our *www.parentingbycolors.com* web site. The proof is in the pudding! And don't worry about testing different parenting strategies for different colors on your kids. Your kids will be fine. You, however, may need therapy before it's all over. (Just kidding... sort of. ;-)

Okay, now that that's all out of the way... let's learn about your child's colors, why they do what they do, and what in the world you can do about it!

Parenting by PERSONALITY

Kid's COLORS

Parenting YOUR Kids By THEIR Colors... Really Works!

This section discusses each of the four Kid's Colors in detail.

Then teaches you how to work effectively as parent with each color child or teen.

GOLD Kids

Structure, Consistency, Expectations

The Quick Answer To GOLD KIDS

Need STRUCTURE
Structure, order, and plans that make sense, dependability from others.

Value CONSISTENCY
Respects things that stay the same, rules, order, conformity, and tradition. Change is very stressful. Needs time to adjust.

Best Discipline Do EXPECTATIONS
Learns best by understanding specifically what is expected from them before they have committed to, or completed, a task.

The Simple GOLD KIDS Truth

Gold children are very practical, realistic, organized, and comfortable with rules. These children will be (for the most part) obedient and respectful of authority. They enjoy belonging to a group, including the family, and love to serve/help out. They have an internal drive to do what is right and follow the rules. They are most comfortable following clear instructions and love to complete tasks. Gold children will work hard and play according to the rules.

They are not usually risk-takers and are generally very conservative in their dress, actions, and talk. They approach life with an unusual degree of caution and will hang back when new activities or people are presented to them. They are usually reliable, dependable, trustworthy, and responsible—traits that the other temperaments don't develop until much later in life. Gold children are every parents dream!

First and foremost, parents of Gold children need to know that they are very grounded in the here-and-now. This is their overarching approach to the world. Gold children have a hard time understanding the future or comprehending "big picture" ideals. They need, not want, but NEED concrete examples, solid reasoning, and lots of proof of anything and everything...rules, your love, why their teacher is smart, why an art project is valuable. They need to see "it" with their eyes. To Gold children and teens, "seeing is believing." Anything lofty, hard to explain, idealistic, "fluffy," creative, freeform, or over-emotional is very hard for Gold children to get their minds around. This approach to the world can be frustrating for Blue-Orange or Green-Orange parents. The Gold child is not usually overly emotional unless they are extremely frustrated or stressed. They are very detail-oriented when it comes to what they see, hear, touch, taste, and smell but not detailed about dreams, stories, creative endeavors, or make-believe. They don't have a lot of faith in the future or in the promises of others and therefore can be somewhat pessimistic and at times moody. Trust is not easily granted by a Gold child or teen. Because they are so grounded in-the-moment, concepts like "trust," "faith," and "hope" are lofty ideals that focus on future events and are hard for Gold children to understand. The most important thing to understand about Gold children is their firm stand in the present. Most of their childhood fears and stresses (if you look a little deeper) comes from this difficulty with believing in the future.

The second most important thing to understand about Gold

children is their inherent need for structure, consistency, tradition, and organization. Change is very difficult for Gold children, especially when they are not prepared for it. Change to a Gold seems like inconsistency and a threat to the structure that makes them feel safe. Orange and Blue-Orange parents will find this characteristic of Gold children very frustrating as they are not very structured themselves. To build the trust of a Gold child, parents need to be very structured with their Gold child's time schedule. Parents of Gold children also need to be consistent in their discipline methods and in their explanations for why certain behavior is acceptable or not. The older a Gold child gets the more they need to be in on the rule-making process with their parents. This helps them feel some appropriate control over the structure in their life. Gold teenagers rebel when they feel powerless. Giving a Gold teen some power and control over their participation in rulemaking can be really important to them. As Gold teens feel less and less in control of other aspects of their life, they may act-out inappropriately toward friends, parents, and siblings. They may become overly critical and controlling. Parents of stressed Gold teens need to address these inappropriate choices immediately. Give them appropriate ways to exercise control and give them choices, responsibility, and your trust whenever possible and appropriate. Gold kids and teens need to be taught that the world is rarely consistent or fair but that they can be personally consistent and fair with themselves and others.

Gold children are particularly hampered by "control issues." They can seem bossy and unbending. This comes from the combination of their focus on the here-and-now and their need for structure and consistency. When their sense of consistency and structure is threatened they can be very controlling, demanding, and stubborn. A wise, Color Works parent will understand that this behavior in a Gold child comes from some sort of stress they are experiencing when their needs for structure, order, fairness (from their perspective), or consistency are going unmet. They may become very controlling about their toys, food choices, schedule, or become uncooperative. When Gold children become stubborn and unbending, look at life from their perspective and find what seems to be out of control for them.

A GOLD'S Greatest Need: STRUCTURE

STRUCTURE to a Gold is comforting, provides safety, and lowers their stress. When structure is provided for a Gold they are usually even-tempered and easy to get along with.

- Golds need structure to bring order to their world and need structure the way the rest of us need air. A sense of structure is woven through every fiber of their being.

- When *their* idea of structure is threatened they will become stubborn, hard to reason with, and most likely be very difficult to handle if they are young, and frustrating or disrespectful if they are older.

- Structure for a Gold comes in the form of schedules, rules, and consistent actions from parents and other adults. As you can see right away, these things are not always possible in a family and therefore will cause stress for Gold children and teens of all ages.

- Daily schedules provide the most basic of structures for your Gold and they depend upon them. If you change the schedule, it can be very stressful for them.

- The younger your Gold the more concrete your schedule needs to be. Use color-coded calendars, write-on/wipe-off boards, magnetized boards where they move the magnet as they complete the items on their schedule. You can't just "talk" the schedule, they need to see it every moment.

- Older Golds will have their own structure in mind. If you want or need something different than they had expected, you may be in for a fight or at least a rolling of the eyes, an exasperated sign, or some other non-verbal expression of frustration. You've just upset their apple cart and they are not happy about it.

- Another form of structure for Golds are rules. Gold kids need to know and understand the rules of anything—games, sports, social situations, bedtimes, or anything new or unexpected. Many Golds will hang back and observe the situation before jumping in or trying anything new or different if they don't know the "rules" or what is expected of them.

- As parents of Golds, be sure to structure in some sort of recognition system for their completed jobs and their positive efforts along the way. Gold kids and teens want to be productive in-the-moment and then be recognized for it after they've worked hard. They don't want some sort of reward like a prize, they want you to appreciate their efforts and hard work. They like charts, stickers, grades, money, and tokens. Also, compliments, certificates, public thanks, and giving them more responsibility are good forms of recognition.

- Usefulness is highly valued by Golds and they want to show their ability to be responsible. This is their own way of showing their ability to be structured.

- Last but not least, your structure building efforts needs to allow time for them to complete assigned tasks. They may do some things really fast and other things will take awhile. You may not see a pattern but there is one. It has to do with rules and expectations. For example:
  - ⇒ If your Gold feels, or thinks, that they have clear directions, rules, or expectations for completing an assignment, they will accomplish it quickly and be expecting some form of recognition.

⇒ If your Gold child or teen doesn't perceive they have a clear understanding of what's to be done and how to do it, they will dawdle, hesitate, or argue with you about doing it in one way or another. They will feel, or think, that the details for how to be responsible and success-ful are elusive, inconsistent, or constantly changing.

- For a Gold child or teen, a lack of structure through a lack of understanding the rules and expectations for an assignment, job, chore is very stressful but can be easily remedied. Parents of Gold can lower this stress by firming up as many details as possible and realistic for the project, chore, assignment, or job. Include the plan, how to's, and what you want or expect. All of this detail will help your Gold child or teen do their best.

- If the lack of structure is out of your control to fix, like a vague school assignment—well, good luck with that. Take a deep breath, be encouraging and use it as a teaching moment for your Gold. Teach that vague directions are not the end of the world and that it's a chance to build their own structure. It's also the time to teach that your child or teen has the responsibility to respectfully try to get more details from the teacher (if that is possible and age-appropriate). If it's a touchy-feely art project with lots of wiggle room to be "creative," be ready for a bumpy ride. It will probably drive your Gold crazy until they acquire the maturity to understand that "no structure" is the structure. Yeah, I know. This too shall pass!

A GOLD'S Strongest Value:
CONSISTENCY

A Gold's need for structure includes order and "order" is the outward manifestation of CONSISTENCY. A Gold's strongest value is that of CONSISTENCY.

- Your Golds will prefer to have the same order to the same

events of each day, everyday. They want to have everyone act the same, be the same, and do the same as they think they should. This sense of consistency is their strongest value.

- They need to have their things in the same place they left them. They may not leave things in the same place, but everybody else had better do it!

- They want you to discipline everyone in the house the same too, regardless of age, skill level, gender, hair color, and shoe size (or offense). If you don't, they will most likely tell you about it or they will silently keep score with you losing more and more points as times goes by.

- They will demand consistency in other things too. They will be consistently put-out with you if you don't hop to it and "make it so" with whatever "it" is. Yes, reality will teach them over time that life is different. And guess who gets to help them learn that? You! ;-)

- Golds think that if day after day they do a set of actions in the same sequence and one day you try to change the order; it's the end of their world. If you always put their t-shirts in the second drawer and then change it to the top drawer one day it could be melt-down city.

- Keeping promises are a sign of consistency for a Gold. Golds need to be able to depend on you for their psychological safety. They will feel safe when they know that you will keep your promises, do what you say you will do, and be where you say you will be. When this doesn't happen, and all families have moments when things need to be more fluid and flexible, talk about the changes that need to take place as early as possible.

- Listen to your Gold's concerns when things change or when you "seem" inconsistent to them. Have your Gold, no matter how young, be involved in the planning actions as much as is appropriate. Discuss their feelings and let them vent, briefly, when things are not how they think they should be. Then switch to problem-solving as soon as possible.

- When things change, communicate to your Gold that your love and support is a **constant** and can be depended on. Explain that they have great control over their reactions to things that change even if they have no control over the events.

- Gold children and teens rely on you for stability and security. These conditions are established as you build some structure for them and are consistent in following that structure or else talk about it when you can't. They need to know that even when things change, and they will, that you will be there to depend on, love them, and help them through the perceived chaos with understanding and a safe plan.

- Gold kids and teens need to know that they have some sort of appropriate control. They also need to know that you are in control, too. During times of change, keep your emotions in check but continue to openly talk about how you are feeling and what you are thinking. Don't shelter them, but provide emotional safety and security.

- Gold children and teens also value cooperation, commitment, integrity, loyalty, dependability, accountability, responsibility, fairness, following the rules, and diligence or having a stick-to-it-'til-it's-done attitude.

The BIG Discipline Strategy for GOLDS: Clear EXPECTATIONS

Gold children and teens need to have clear EXPECTATIONS for their behavior. EXPECTATIONS provide structure to the Gold's choices and allow them to be dependable.

- Providing clear expectations help Golds know exactly what to do, how to do it, and provide structure to them by giving them an idea of how to be good.

- Continually let them know what is expected of them (without nagging). Be concrete and detailed in your requests, teach them what is right and don't assume they know. Remember, they want to succeed, obey, and be responsible. They will experience stress if you keep them guessing about what you want.

- Provide clear expectations before situations occur if possible. This will help them choose appropriate behavior and sidestep the negative consequences of inappropriate behavior. Doing what's right is fun!

- Provide an appropriate amount of time to complete tasks as expected. Golds have a natural desire to complete tasks the right way, on time, but they can get stressed about completing a task if they don't have a CONCRETE understanding of what is expected and what "complete" looks like.

- Gold kids appreciate clear directions on *how* to do something, too. However, as Golds get older ask if they need more direction before you volunteer it. Gold teens have very specific ideas of how things should be accomplished. As long as their way is in line with family values, this is one area where parents can give Gold teens appropriate control. Gold teens will rebel if parents are too detailed in their "how to" direction because it takes away their control and assumes that the teen is stupid—this is insulting and over-controlling to the Gold teen.

- Prepare Gold kids and teens for change whenever possible by sharing clear expectations of what is going to happen when possible, what they can control, and how to act as they face changes. Teach coping skills and expect a healthy acceptance of change. Let them know that it is a sign of being grown up or a sign of maturity for them to be able to handle unforeseen change.

- Teach Gold kids that the reason they may have a hard time having faith in people and in the future is because they don't know what to expect. At the same time teach them that to overcome this by remembering times in the past that turned out alright. This helps them "see" evidence from the past as proof for the possibility of a good future. This builds their faith in the future and other people. They see that people can be trusted.

- Golds can build their faith in the future and in others by consistently remembering how something good in the here-and-now is connected to a past event, choice, or action of another person, even when things did not go as expected.

- Be aware of your Gold's expectations of you. As you are consistent in your rules, schedule, discipline, communication, and emotional responses you will create safety for your Gold child, fulfill their expectations, and build your "trustworthiness" in their eyes. Let teens be in on the process by talking about their expectations of you and whether those expectations are fair or realistic. Openly discuss any differences that come up between your Gold teen and you.

- Be careful not to have expectations that are too high, too old, or unrealistic for their color, age, or circumstances.

Influence of Introvert or Extrovert and a GOLD'S Second Color on their Behavior and Choices

Gold's are always focused on keeping things STRUCTURED and CONSISTENT but their interaction style and their second color will influence their need for both.

Extroverted Gold-Blues, while tender-hearted, are

mostly focused on adding structure to the people around them. This means that they can be bossy and demanding with their communication when the Gold feel someone should be doing something other than what they are doing. Because they are Extroverts, they won't hesitate to share with you what they expect everyone, including you, should do. For the most part they will be very obedient and usually want to please you. They love to be of service, especially at a young age. Don't count them out of doing things just because you think they are too young. Teach them how to do things and then let them do it; they tend to follow through and complete their assignments.

They may become stubborn, and argumentative about what they feel is right and about defending their choices—even their wrong choices. Extrovert Gold-Blues won't hesitate to tell you why they did what they did. All Golds want so desperately to do what's right and being wrong is so abhorrent to them that they all have a very difficult time admitting they are wrong. Extrovert Gold-Blues will verbally fight—not admitting it because not only did they really feel they were doing what's right as all Gold's do, but they feel compelled to TELL you their point-of-view (Extrovert) and their second color Blue wants you desperately to understand them. If you can accept *why* they are being argumentative, even if you don't understand it, you will have an easier time teaching them where they went wrong, what they need to do differently next time, and why. Let them get it all out, then say, "I believe that you felt you were doing the right thing. However, I need to teach you a better way to..."

If you will listen first, then let them get it all out (as long as they are being respectful) they can clear their head of their excuses and explanations and be more open to learning a better way. If you stand there and argue, they will eventually become disrespectful. Then you have a whole new set of problems on your hands. When you argue with them you are just teaching by example that arguing and escalating a misunderstanding is acceptable. If you listen, then calmly teach a better way (with maybe a consequence or two) you are more expertly fitting into their *structure, or expectation,* of what a parent *should* be like. They will follow your example and become better at sharing their point-of-view without all the argumentativeness and drama. For a Gold, any Gold, you have to be the example, in-the-moment, of what you want them to do.

At the same time, Gold-*Blues* will have an easier time than Gold-*Greens* admitting they've done something wrong and feeling bad about it, once they can see that they've disappointed you. This is because of their second color Blue and their secondary need to please you and gain your approval. *Extrovert* Gold-Blues will most likely need to talk it out (thus the defensiveness) and will probably want to fix it and move on. Give them a chance to fix whatever they did wrong and to make amends. This allows for them to swallow their pride and learn a lesson but with their self-worth still intact. When they get bossy or commanding help them tap into their second color by asking them how they think other's feel when they are being bossy.

Extrovert Gold-Blues are very sensitive to friends, people, and the emotions of others. They will make natural leaders and probably direct the play of their friends even at a young age. They will want to be teacher's pet even in pre-school and up through grade school. In middle school and beyond they will most likely be the kids who are interested in student government and be the kids in the advanced classes. Extroverted Gold-Blues will likely be on the Prom committee and have a large group of friends. Again, they will most likely only get into trouble by being too bossy.

Introverted Gold-Blues are also very sensitive but quiet. They will seem very Blue and emotional. Because they are Introverts they will "extrovert" or show their Blue side more often than their Gold motivations, but their Gold motivators are still their primary drivers. As second color Blues, they will crave interaction but because they are an Introvert they will also be worn out by it. They are gentle and need lots of affection from parents. They will quietly go around being good and will often go unnoticed if there are other children or teens in the family that require more of their parents' time and attention. They will, however, privately "keep score" if their parents are unfair, ask them to do more than the other kids in the family, or discipline differently. They will quietly grow to resent their parents' inattention and lack of fairness. They are usually quiet, calm and focused on their own interests unless they become highly interested in how unfairly they are being treated by you or others. Then their attention will be turned outward activating the mental score card and they'll start taking mental note of what everyone *should* be doing, including their parents. If they are unhappy they won't communicate it much and instead seem withdrawn. They won't be too argumentative unless they are really backed into a corner and then might lash out unexpectedly with more venom than you thought possible (because all that "score keeping" really added up). If they suddenly explode after months or years of calm, be calm yourself and hear them out and realize that you have some relationship repairing to do.

One idea for building a better relationship with your Introvert Gold-Blue is to give them a journal that they can write in. Doing this usually helps. You may find it therapeutic and healing to have a special journal or notebook that you and your Introvert Gold-Blue privately pass back and forth to share thoughts and feelings about situations and about each other. Let them know they are safe to say anything. For your part be honest, accepting, and positive in it. It may be the only "conversation" you can create. One truly insightful Orange mom and her Gold daughter have a journal that they write "notes" back and forth to each other about any topic, especially ones that the daughter may have a difficult time discussing face-to-face. The Gold daughter can even bring up times when she is upset with her mom and feels safe enough to write about it in the "pass" journal. It keeps the line of communication open and builds trust. As this particular Gold daughter is reaching her teen years, she is much more comfortable talking to her mom about anything face-to-face because they established trust through the "pass" journal.

Introvert Gold-Blues will *feel* defensive if their actions or motives are questioned, but won't likely *act* defensive unless attacked. All Golds want so desperately to do what's right and being wrong is so abhorrent to them that they all have a very difficult time admitting they are wrong. Introvert Gold-Blues will fight admitting their wrongdoing in their mind but will only outwardly communicate their frustration with you through body language such as standing with their arms folded, clenching their fists, expressing an angry pout, rolling their eyes, squinting an angry glare, turning on their heels, or a thousand other actions that express, "you don't have a clue and I really hate you right now." This all happens because not only did they really feel they were doing what's right as all Gold's do, but they also feel compelled to tell you their point-of-view without saying a word because they are an Introvert and because of their second color Blue—they desperately want you to understand them.

If you can accept *why* they are acting so defiant without speaking a word, even if you don't understand it, you will have an easier time teaching them where they went wrong, what they need to do differently next time, and why. Ask them to tell you what's upsetting them when you see this frustrated body language. They really want you to notice and they really want you to hear them out. Let them talk out all their frustrations, then say, "I believe that you felt you were doing the right thing. However, I need to teach you a better way that..." If you will ask them first to talk and then let them get it all out (as long as they are being respectful), they can clear their head of their excuses and explanations and be more open to learning a better way. If you stand there and lecture through a one-sided argument they will eventually become disrespectful and distrustful of you and then you have a whole new set of problems on your hands. When you lecture them without asking for their perspective you are just teaching by example that lecturing and escalating a misunderstanding is acceptable. If you listen and then calmly teach a better way, with maybe a consequence or two, you are more expertly fitting into their *structure and their expectations* of what a parent *should* be like. They will follow your example and become better at sharing their point-of-view without all the silence and drama. For a Gold, any Gold, you have to be the example, in-the-moment, of what you want them to do.

Introvert Gold-Blues are very sensitive to friends, people, and the emotions of others but they will have a very difficult time expressing their feelings, thoughts, and concerns out loud. They will keep it all bottled up inside. Try to earn their trust and their confidence. Listen to them whenever they do talk. They will be natural doers and probably will go along with the leadership of more Extroverted friends. But don't be lulled into a fearful sense that they won't stand up for themselves and do what's right. They absolutely will! They are really pretty tough little buggers. They are only *second* color Blue—Gold comes first and so does doing what they feel is right.

Introvert Gold-Blues are the secret "givers." These are the ones who quietly sidle up to mom to whisper in her ear when she is usually talking to another adult or an older child. The "secret" is usually about what their brothers or sisters are doing that they shouldn't, or it's focused on asking for something that they want but don't want to say it out loud. They will want the teacher's approval even in pre-school. They may try to quietly tattle on the other kids by trying to whisper their "secret" to the teacher at the wrong time.

These kids will also be completely frustrated by the middle school meanness and will want to come home and complain about it. These are the quiet kids who get the good grades and don't participate in "groupy" things. They will usually participate in band, choir, art, track, cross country, or other activities where they can be a team player but sort of hide in the group, too. They won't go for the limelight or the attention.

For the most part your Introvert Gold-Blue will be very obedient and usually want to please you. Teach them how to do things and then let them do it. They tend to follow through and complete their assignments without a lot of fanfare. They really just need you to notice what they are doing right. They appreciate any public kudos from you so it's good to remember to reward them for their completed assignments and service. At the same time, don't forget that they will be expecting you to keep things equal, and if you can't you need to see it and admit it to them.

Introverted Gold-Blues, like all Golds, will have very high expectations of themselves and others. Be mindful of your Introvert Gold-Blues because they won't often communicate their expectations, or the stress they experience when someone, or something, lets them down. They need lots of structure and love. Give your Introverted Gold-Blue a bit of both and you will have a quiet, obedient child and teen. At the same time, watch their facial expressions and body language—they communicate a lot. It may be your only clue that something is up with your Introvert Gold-Blue.

Extroverted Gold-Greens are very logical and make the ultimate manager or leader. Think of a successful business manager only as a child or teen without the much needed communication or stress management skills and you've got an Extroverted Gold-Green child. They could truly run the world at 10. And they'll try! At least, they will try to run YOUR world.

They are the more serious logical thinkers who will talk about what should be done or how things *are* according to *their* logic. They may also be outspoken and frustrated with people's lack of organization and their blatant stupidity. They are, in a nutshell, a combination of structure, logic, information, and outspokenness. They will, at times, be unreasonable and stubborn, and at other times they will be very hardworking, industrious, and trustworthy. They will most likely be great students as long as they don't think their teachers are idiots. Boys will enjoy scouting, student government, and may start neighborhood "all boys" clubs because girls are "stupid." Girls will find a million different ways to be leaders, too, from telling you that you need to hurry to organizing a lemonade stand to playing school with strict grades and detailed assignments.

They may become stubborn and argumentative about what they feel is right and about defending their choices—even their wrong choices. Extrovert Gold-Greens won't hesitate to tell you why they did what they did and how stupid not doing it would have been if they are SURE that they are right. At the same time, if they have respect for you and you are really presenting a logical case for their wrongdoing, they will be more likely to hear you out and put their defensiveness on hold. Remember that all Golds want so desperately to do what's right that being wrong, is completely abhorrent to them. All Golds have a very difficult time admitting they are wrong especially a Gold-Green whose logic is telling them that they are really right.

Extrovert Gold-Greens will verbally fight admitting that they are wrong for several reasons, all hinging on their being an Extrovert Gold-Green. Not only did they really think they were doing what's right (as all Golds do) but they also think they need to tell you their point-of-view because obviously YOU need the information and being an Extrovert they have no problem sharing it. Understanding *why* they are being argumentative (internal stress) will help you deal with it in a calmer and unemotional way. You need to hear them out just long enough to have them settle down, then teach them where they went wrong, what they need to do differently next time, and why. Let them get it all out, then say, "I believe that you think (don't say "feel" - Gold-Greens don't understand "feel") you were doing the right thing, however I need to teach you a better way." If you will listen first and let them get it all out (as long as they are being respectful), then they can clear their head of their faulty logic and be more open to learning a better way. If you stand there and argue it will just escalate into a power struggle and they will eventually become disrespectful and you will have a whole new set of problems on your hands. When you argue you are teaching by example that arguing and escalating a misunderstanding is acceptable. You will also teach them that basing a decision solely on logic, even faulty logic, is okay and that family values are irrelevant. If you listen and then calmly teach a better way, teach values and maybe administer a consequence or two, you are more expertly fitting into their *structure, or expectation,* of what a parent *should* logically do. They will follow your example and become better at sharing their point-of-view without all the arguments and drama. For any Gold, you have to be the example in-the-moment of what you want them to do.

As Extrovert Gold-Greens admit their wrongdoing, suffer the consequences, and grow new behaviors, they will most likely need to talk it out and share later what they've learned as part of the process. They will probably want to fix the problem and move on. Give them a chance to fix whatever they did wrong and make amends. This allows them to swallow their pride and learn a lesson but with their self-esteem still intact. When they get bossy or commanding help them tap into their second color by asking them how they think others feel when they are being bossy or if it is logical to thing that they will get what they want by offending others with their bossiness.

Extrovert Gold-Greens are very good at creating plans, structures, rules, and procedures. They are also good at seeing things that make sense and things that don't, solving problems, and organizing friends, people, and activities. They have a very difficult time with their own emotions and the feelings of others. They are natural organizers and project managers but will struggle with being sensitive. They usually direct the play of their friends, even at a young age, but will struggle with being nice or tactful. They want to be the teacher's helper and will try to keep everyone on task and in line from pre-school through grade school.

In middle school and beyond they usually are the kids who are interested in student government and in the advanced classes. They may like writing and reading, math and science. They take on the role of group leader and enjoy planning the family vacation. Extroverted Gold-Greens may like being on the Prom committee, service club leadership, or planning committees in high school and will have a large group of friends who will drive them crazy if there is any friend drama (they just won't get it). They most likely only get into trouble by being too bossy or doing something that seems logical to them but is not in line with family values like compassion, forgiveness, sensitivity to the feelings of others, or patience.

Introverted Gold-Greens are the quiet version of the manager. They will seem very Green. They need logic from everyone around them but may not always reason logically themselves. They are more focused on structure and need others to be dependable. They appear to do whatever the heck they want but do it very quietly and fly under the radar. They are quiet, reserved, serious, and often headstrong.

Most of the time they will quietly go around being good and will do what seems logical to them. They can often go unnoticed if there are other children or teens in the family that require more time and attention from you as a parent. However, they will privately "keep score" if their parents are unfair, ask them to do more than the other kids in the family, or discipline differently. They will quietly grow to resent their parent's inattention and lack of fairness.

They are usually quiet, calm, and focused on their own interests unless they become highly interested in how stupid someone is acting or how unfairly they are being treated by you or others. Then their attention will be turned outward, the mental score card is activated, and they start taking mental note of what everyone *should* be doing, including their parents. If they are unhappy they won't communicate it much and instead will seem withdrawn, sulky, moody, grumpy, and quietly defiant. They will also think everything is stupid and if they communicate anything, that's what they will tell you.

Introverted Gold-Greens are very good at creating plans, structures, rules, and procedures but they may have a hard time communicating or sharing them. Teach them how to get things out of their heads and into the hands of others in positive ways.

They are also good at seeing things that make sense (and things that don't), solving problems, and organizing projects, people, and activities. They have a very difficult time with their own emotions and the feelings of others. While they are natural organizers and project managers, they will struggle with being sensitive to people. They will probably hang back and observe the actions of others or prefer to play, or be, by themselves. Even at a young age they will struggle with participating in groups, school, or being nice or tactful. They will want to be teacher's helper because they are service minded but they don't want the limelight or the ridicule. If they are left in charge they will try to keep everyone on task and in line, even in pre-school and then up through grade school.

In middle school and beyond they will most likely be the kids who are interested in student government and will be the kids in the advanced classes and may like writing and reading, even some math and science. They will take on the role of group leader when forced to because of the lack of leadership of anyone else but they won't enjoy it and they will have a hard time communicating as effectively as a group leader needs to. They will assume that other's will just do their part and then will be very frustrated with those who don't live up to their expectations. They may quietly enjoy planning the family vacation but you will need to really communicate everyone's expectations because your Introvert will not naturally seek them out.

Introverted Gold-Greens may like being on the Prom committee, in the service club, playing on the team, or planning committees in high school but will not want to serve in a leadership position. They may or may not have a large group of friends but at some point people, and their silly high school antics, will wear them out and drive them crazy, especially if their friends let them down. These kids may especially be drawn to Extroverted Orange friends who are fun like they want to be but just can't be. At the same time Extroverted Orange friends will often ask your Introvert Gold to do things that they know they shouldn't do and will therefore cause stress. Or their Orange friends will be flighty and *seem* to make commitments to your child that they, as an Orange, really didn't think they were making. When there is any friend drama, your Gold-Green just won't get it.

Introverted Gold-Greens need lots of guidance and special attention in their thought processes to help lead them toward structure and logic that is aligned with your family's values. As an Introvert they will keep their thoughts and motives to themselves unless you ask to them to share their thoughts and feelings with you. As the parent, you need to pay attention to what's going on in their heads so that you correct immature logic and unrealistic expectations as they grow up. When your Introvert Gold-Green does something inappropriate be sure to not only correct the behavior but to also teach your family's values so that over time their logic structure will be based on what's right rather than what seems logical for their age.

Introverted Gold-Greens will *think* defensively (even if they don't argue defensively out loud) if their actions or motives are questioned. Remember all Golds want desperately to do what's right so admitting they are wrong is tough. Introverted Gold-Greens will fight admitting their wrongdoing in their mind and only outwardly communicate their frustration with you through their facial expressions and body language. At these times they may stand with their arms folded, clench their fists, express an angry pout, roll their eyes, squint an angry glare that I call the "stink eye" and turn on their heels, and a thousand other actions that express, "you don't have a clue because YOU are an idiot."

All this negative body language gets "spoken" loud and clear for a few different reasons with your Introvert Gold-Green. First of all, being Gold they really think they were doing what's right (as all Golds do) but they are also logically compelled to "tell" you how right they are as a second color Green. But because they are an Introvert their chosen mode of communication is with looks and gestures rather than words. I know it sounds complicated, but if you can understand *why* they are acting so defiant you will have an easier time staying calm and teaching them where they went wrong, what they need to do differently next time, and why.

When you see this type of body language don't react negatively. Stay calm, point out that you see them rolling their eyes at you and that you would like them to tell you *respectfully*, with words, what's upsetting them so much. Then hear them out as long as they are respectful. They really want you to notice that they are upset, that's why all the dramatic body language. They also really want you to hear them out so that THEY can help YOU stop being such an idiot. I know, aren't they precious? But if you stay unemotional and let them talk out all their frustrations you will see where their logic is faulty and then you can have a better tactical position from which to teach them a better way. When they get it all out say, "I believe that you thought you were doing the right thing and I am grateful that you tried. However, I need to teach you a better way." Even a 3-year-old Gold-Green will be easier to handle if you will calmly do this.

Introverted Gold-Greens will become argumentative, however, and resort to mean angry words right out of the gate, when they think you are backing them into a corner. When that happens they might lash out unexpectedly with more logical venom than you thought possible. All that "score keeping" I referred to earlier really has added up and is coming out and so is all the logic they can muster. If they suddenly explode after months or years of calm, be calm yourself and hear them out and realize that you have some relationship repairing to do.

One idea for building a better relationship with your Introverted Gold-Green is to give them a journal that they can write in as suggested for the Introverted Gold-Blues. Doing this will usually help your Gold-Green as long as they don't see it as an illogical exercise of stupidity. As with the Gold-Blues, you both may find it therapeutic and healing to have a special journal or notebook that you and your Introverted Gold-Green privately pass back and forth to share thoughts and feelings about situations and about each other. Let them know they are safe to say anything as long as it is respectful.

For your part, when you write back, be honest, accepting, logical, and as unemotional in it as is possible. Share your thoughts and feelings about things, feel free to provide reasons behind your perspective but don't justify your parenting choices. You are the parent and you don't have to justify yourself to your child. Explain sure but don't justify yourself like you are asking your child or teen permission to stand your ground. Stand your ground and let them accept it or not. If you can't share logical reasons for a parenting decision own that too, don't be bashful to "go with your gut." Say, "I cannot provide you with a logical argument about this but I feel it deeply based on years of experience." Saying it that way to your Gold-Green will be more logical than just being emotional or pleading with them to understand your gut. I'm saying all this especially for Blue parents.

This journal may create the opportunity for some of the best "conversations" you can create. Being positive and hopeful in this journal will help your Introverted Gold-Green be more positive rather than focusing on the negative. One truly insightful Orange-Green mom and her Gold-Green daughter have a journal that they write "notes" back and forth to each other about any topic—especially ones that the daughter may have a difficult time discussing face-to-face. The Gold daughter can even bring up times when she is upset with her mom because she feels safe enough to write respectfully about it in the "pass" journal. It keeps the line of communication open and builds trust. As this particular Gold daughter is reaching her teen years she is much more comfortable talking to her mom about anything face-to-face because they established trust through the "pass" journal.

In the end, your Introverted Gold-Green will most likely be obedient and pretty easy if you help them diffuse any negative emotions as they come up. They will only get into trouble by being too quiet, or too bossy, or by doing something that seems logical, and therefore right to them, but that is not in line with family values such as being compassionate, forgiving, sensitive to the feelings of others, or patient.

How GOLD Children and Teens Behave Badly...

Recognizing <u>GOLD Stress Behaviors</u> helps parents understand that their child is experiencing stress.

When you see these types of misbehaviors, understand that your GOLD is experiencing a lack of STRUCTURE, some form of INCONSISTENCY, or does not understand, or agree with, what's EXPECTED of them.

- Gold's most often become controlling, possessive, and/or demanding with their toys, time, friends, and schedule.

- Becomes very guarded. Appears secretive or like they are holding back information or themselves from you or anyone they perceive is untrustworthy or who has let them down.

- Exaggerated resistance to change OR extreme conformity because they think they "should" do what every one is doing.

- Self-righteousness – Gold's may think, "nobody can do it as right as me" when it comes to chores, schoolwork, even parenting. It's all wrapped up in their need for structure and their expectations of how things "should be" and how others "should act."

- Martyrdom – Gold tweens and teens especially may feel that "nobody cares as much as me, nobody works as hard" and it will show up as a rolling of the eyes, a squinty-eyed look that communicates complete disrespect or disapproval without a word, a huffy turn on their heels, a determined folding of the arms, and huffy answer or sound.

- Narrowly focused on the faults of others or on the negative qualities of a situation, event, or plan.

- Highly opinionated about what others should do. They may especially try to parent you into parenting their siblings.

- Very pessimistic about the future or about other people's ability to do what they promise. They may communicate, outright, a lack of faith in you or someone else or they may just make elaborate plans for every contingency because they distrust your plan or the plan of someone else. They may also become very adamant about having a back-up plan. This, too, shows a lack of faith in the person, or the situation.

- Becomes stubborn, rigid, or bossy – they want things their way because it is the only right way. They may think you are just plain wrong. They may also feel they deserve to have things their way because they've worked it out, or that they've worked hard for it.

- Blames others or the situation for their wrong choices. Gold children or teens often feel so bad when they do something wrong. They know what they shouldn't have done but as a defense mechanism they blame other people or things. They generally try so hard to do what is right that they cannot stand the thought that they actually did something wrong. This self-loathing is so acute that they will blame first, then (hopefully) come to a full acceptance of their wrongdoing. No amount of lecturing, cajoling, demanding an apology, or trying to reason with them will help them see it. It's best to give them their consequence, quickly and without ceremony but with the invitation to hear what they could have done differently, later.

Why GOLD'S Behave Badly...

Understanding <u>GOLD Stressors</u> can help parents figure out WHY their GOLD is experiencing stress and acting out.

GOLD's experience stress when they perceive a lack of STRUCTURE, some form of INCONSISTENCY, or when they do not understand, or agree with, what you EXPECTED of them.

- Gold's misbehave when they perceive a lack of structure or a change in the structure that makes them feel safe. An example, you go shopping but don't go to the stores in the order you told your Gold when you left the house.

- A change in your bedtime routine or when you skip a certain daily activity like saying a prayer before you eat.

- When you change the rules for anything such as driving three houses down the street without a seat belt when you've made it very clear that your Gold is never to ride without a seat belt on.

- The emotional outbursts of others. Gold's see outbursts such as yelling, arguing, or crying as unpredictable and uncontrolled behavior. However, they may become very emotional and do exactly the same thing but don't see it the same way. If YOU do it you are out of control, if THEY do they are justified; most often because YOU made them mad.

- Ambiguity, unclear expectations, unclear messages, lofty idealistic explanations about anything that is not concrete can be very confusing to Golds. They prefer to have clear, concrete, detailed instructions on anything from doing the dishes, to cleaning their room, to completing an art project, to needing to say, "I'm sorry" for something they've done wrong especially when they don't think, or feel, they've done anything wrong.

- Surprises are not fun at all! Think about it: there's no structure, no consistency and no safety in surprises. Leave surprises for the Extroverted Oranges.

- Acceptance of poorly performed tasks – they really don't want to get away with inferior work. They want to do what's right, but they will be very upset with criticism from you. It's best when they see that their work doesn't meet expectations, but when you must point it out, restate the expectations and then ask if they think, or feel, that they've succeeded. If possible, give them a chance to correct the problem and bring their work up to snuff.

- Irresponsibility in themselves and others is very frustrating to a Gold. It creates a lack of structure and inconsistency leading to distrust.

- Chaos – things or people out of control (including themselves) that violate their expectations of control, consistency, and structure. Noisy classrooms with kids running all over the place, a desk with too many unorganized papers, a school assignment that seems to keep changing, friends that are all over the place with their commitments, and parents that break the rules or their promises; all examples of "chaos" in a Gold's life.

- Lack of time to complete a job, do it well, and to work on one thing at a time. This can be confusing, frustrating, and upsetting to a Gold because all 3 Words are violated: Structure, Consistency and Expectations.

- Unclear directions, lack of a concrete example or model for anything and everything. They want you to be their example on how to act. They want the directions for an arts and crafts project to be detailed, clear, preferably with a picture so they can do it exactly like that picture. They want rules to be clear for everyone (except they tend to change the rules to suit THEIR own needs because they are right and deserve their own set of rules).

- They expect you to be exact about assignments: do you want them to clean the kitchen, or to just do the dishes? Believe it or not, to a Gold, there is a BIG difference between cleaning the kitchen and doing the dishes. So, be clear or you will come home to dishes in the dishwasher with the dishwasher never being turned on and it's YOUR fault because *you didn't say to turn on the dishwasher*. (You know exactly what I mean, don't you?)

- Ignored time-lines/deadlines, being late or other's making them late drive Golds crazy! Little Golds, big Golds, and in-between Golds don't ever want to be late if they can help it. I swear, Golds are born with a clock right next to their heart!

- Waiting unnecessarily or doing the work of others completely blows their expectations. It turns their ordered world all topsy-turvy. They don't like waiting because it's not in the plan and they don't like doing what others are supposed to because it's just rude and just wrong.

Signs of LOW SELF-ESTEEM in GOLDS

- Lots of complaining, only seeing the negative in themselves, others, and situations more often then seeing the positive.

- Extremely worried about things, the future, and what others will think they are doing wrong.

- Plays the "victim" by expressing a lack of control over their choices; seems defeated or helpless.

- Extended periods of acting depressed, overly tired, or withdrawn.

- Exhibits phobic (fearful) reactions. Seems to have several "ailments" or illnesses.

- Becomes very controlling, excessively bossy, making malicious judgments, and refuses to be cooperative.

- Blindly follows the crowd or exhibits a "herd mentality."

Like it or not, low self-esteem usually stems from controlling and critical behavior from the parent. When kids or teens demonstrate these extreme behaviors, immediately decrease negative criticism and any overly controlling behavior on your part (see page 394 for Command and Control tactics). Increase your time listening and genuinely praising your child or teen for appropriate right choices.

At the same time I am NOT suggesting that you become lax about appropriate discipline; instead, pick your battles and address serious misbehaviors through choices and consequences, never through Command and Control. Don't nit-pick about little annoyances that aren't really hurting anyone or anything. A messy room or mismatched clothes never hurt anyone - let it go and build your child's self-worth when these extreme behaviors are present. If your child or teen continues to demonstrate these behaviors seek additional help from a reputable family counselor or therapist.

Ways to Build SELF-ESTEEM in GOLDS

- Increase a *balance* of appropriate praise and rewards for good choices *with* discipline in the form of clear expectations, choices, and consequences for acting out.

- Listen attentively, with your story on hold, when your, child is upset. This is crucial!

- Eliminate ALL Command and Control tactics from your parenting efforts (see page 394).

- Give them a chance to be a leader at home.

- Give them jobs that they can succeed at then praise even the smallest of successes.

- After you genuinely listen to their concerns, have them start finding just one positive perspective in the situation. Give them time to see it. Don't do the work for them and don't be overly positive yourself; that would be condescending.

- Have them list what they are grateful for.

- Have them help in planning a family outing or activity, then get everyone to join in with a positive attitude.

- Have them keep a "Book of Evidence" where they record good things. Have them refer back to it when they are feeling or thinking negatively. It can be like a writing journal or a scrapbook type.

- Have them perform some sort of meaningful service for someone in the family or for someone who has less than they do.

Best To-Do's For Parents of Gold Kids

**Parenting the GOLD child needs to be full of
STRUCTURE, CONSISTENCY, and
clear EXPECTATIONS of what you want from them.**

- Honor their need for a plan.

- Be somewhat organized and structured around them. This will create safety for them.

- Communicate your expectations of their behavior upfront before they have to make a choice or decision so they can do what's right without guessing what you want from them.

- Be on time when possible.

- Be as fair as possible with your Gold. Be consistent in your day-to-day treatment of your Gold. If they question your discipline tactics for another child of a different color or a different age, respectfully tell your Gold that you are the parent and that it's your responsibility to discipline each child in the family according to who *they* are, meaning for *their* color. This is especially applicable if you have an Orange and you regularly take away their freedoms but you don't take away the freedoms of your Gold because they are generally not as ornery and all over the place as an Orange. Ask them if they really want you to be absolutely fair, meaning the same, or would they rather you be fair in that you treat each according to their own needs? That'll get 'em, believe me!

- Be responsible and follow through on ALL of your promises. If you might not be able to follow through on a promise, don't promise. Remember, Golds are all about consistency and expectations and they consistently expect you to keep your promises, and they consistently expect open-ended situations to be stressful. Make promises only with much seriousness and with much thought.

- Don't change your mind too often. When you do, explain any new details and time frames, even the reasons for the change. Understand that you've just blown their expectations on some level. I don't mean to suggest that you be afraid of changing things on your Gold. Just understand that there is an easy way and a hard way to address change with your Gold. If just a few words of explanation will make things smoother, why not use the words? Seems like a simple no-brainer to me!

- If your Gold is having a melt-down, assume they perceive something's changed or out of order; ask what's wrong and listen, with your own story on hold for a bit. Ferret out the "blown expectation" or the "structure stressor" and you've got 95% of the issue figured out. But you can only discern that if you are listening instead of talking!

- Let them finish one assignment at a time and praise each accomplishment as they finish. As they get older you can add more responsibility. The best way to know is to ask your Gold how many assignments they think, or feel, they can handle at one time. Give them some appropriate control. As you do, they won't need to be in control of *you* so much!

- Too many responsibilities can be overwhelming to them so limit their jobs or assignments by age. Ask them how much they can handle right now.

- Understand that chaos and change is very stressful to them. This is their number one stressor. If *you* are the cause of it, that's even harder for a lot of Gold kids— especially as they get older. Golds often have a hard time *being* frustrated with you. They may feel, or think, that they shouldn't *communicate* their frustration about you, with you, because it's not right to be *that* disrespectful. How's that for a dilemma?

- Do your part, keep your promises, don't be a "slacker" parent. Remember Golds will keep score. They will be very obedient and respectful for years, but if you have been inconsistent, a slacker, a promise breaker, commanding, absent, or dingy, by the time they are teens and bigger then all of a sudden you will have a huge disrespect problem on your hands. The best antidote to this is 1) listen, 2) communicate, and 3) don't lecture. If you will do these three things you will have a wonderful relationship with your Gold.

- Appreciate their consistency and willingness to be prepared, organized, helpful, and responsible. Don't forget to express your gratitude and appreciation with words and with time for their good works.

- Don't be disloyal by talking negatively about them to other parents or sharing their secrets. Brag all you want about their accomplishments, they secretly love that, but don't share anything confidential or even remotely private, especially about their pre-teen and teenage angst, crushes, or mistakes. They will see this as betrayal.

- Be grateful for what they do for you and their service to others. Reward their good works with words of appreciation.

- Don't expect them to take risks until they are much older and after you've taught them to see "risk" as an opportunity to "plan" for the unexpected and to have faith in their ability to handle anything. Teach them to see the positive that can come from doing something that you can't necessarily see all the outcomes for before they must "jump."

- Give them time to figure out what the rules are in any situation when possible. Teach them that when they don't have time to figure out the rules first that they can rely on the principles and family values that you've taught them to always be their safety net. This gives them a sense of intrinsic structure when there is no external structure available.

- Teach them that sometimes the only plan is to be calm and poised and gracious no matter what happens.

- Understand that they will help *you* follow the rules. Be grateful for that.

- Do not tolerate tattle-tales. Redirect their focus to their own behavior. Set up specific rules for being an "informant" such as only if someone is bleeding, if the house is on fire, or they are going to be hit by a truck.

- Give concrete recognition for a job well done, handling changes appropriately, service rendered, being on time, being loyal, and responsible. Expressing appreciation and gratitude for a Gold's positive actions and contributions influence them to repeat the positive behavior.

- Communicate positive recognition emphasizing how their good choices positively affect others and the environment. This has several benefits. First, they learn to see how their choices in the here-and-now influence their future and the future of others for good. Second, they feel an appropriate sense of control, not over others, but over themselves. Thus they are better prepared to handle future stressors by learning to control their own choices rather than acting inappropriately and trying to control others or the situation.

- Provide lots of time to complete tasks whenever possible. Gold kids appreciate clear directions, deadlines, examples, and how to's. As Golds get older however, ask them if they need more direction before you volunteer it. Gold teens have very specific ideas of how things should be accomplished. As long as their "way" is in line with family values, this is one area where parents can give Gold teens appropriate freedoms. Gold teens will rebel if parents are too detailed in their "how to" directions—it seems insulting and over-controlling to the Gold teen.

- Prepare Gold kids and teens for change whenever possible. Teach healthy acceptance and coping skills for them to be able to handle unforeseen change.

- Teach Gold kids to build their faith in the future and others by consistently pointing out how something good in the here-and-now is connected to a past event, choice, or to the action of another person. This helps them "see" evidence from the past as proof for the possibility of a future that is good. In other words, it builds their faith in the future and in other people. They see that people can be trusted. They may want to record the good outcomes in a journal as a "Book of Evidence."

- Be consistent in your rules, schedule, discipline, communication, and emotional responses as often as possible. When it's not possible, talk about the differences. This creates safety for your Gold and builds your "trustworthiness" in their eyes.

- You might want to take a look at the chapter that explains their second color. For your Gold that will either be the Green chapter or the Blue chapter.

- If they are second color Green remember that while they are first and foremost structured, strive for consistency, and have very specific and high expectations, their second color Green will also seek for information and logic when it comes to making judgments and decisions.

- If they are second color Blue remember that while they are first and foremost structured, strive for consistency, and have very specific and high expectations, their second color Blue will seek to build positive relationships and make judgments and decisions based on their feelings and values.

- When your Gold becomes to embroiled in "move, move, move, push, push, control, control" teach them to tap into their second color to STOP and think (Green) or STOP and feel (Blue) what others might be feeling about their controlling pushy behaviors.

- Provide clear expectations before situations occur if possible. Remember they want to succeed, obey, and be responsible. They will experience stress if you keep them guessing about what you want. This will help them choose appropriate behavior and sidestep the negative consequences of inappropriate behavior. Doing what's right is fun for your Gold!

Best Phrases to use with GOLD Kids

"What's your plan for today?" / "Here's (my, our) plan for today."
"How can we put our plans together?"

"Help me schedule our day today. It's a crazy one!"

For tattling or blaming... "Let's focus on your behavior, not someone else's actions."

"Things have to change today, here's what you can control."

"Things have to change today, how can I help you handle it gracefully?"

For complaining or seeing the negative... "You do sound like you had a tough day. Tell me at least three things that you did right or that went right today."

"I can see that you are upset. How did things not go according to your plan today?"

A Last Word about GOLD Kids

Most of all, try to provide as much structure as you can, talk about change when it comes, and give them really, really, REALLY clear expectations about what you want from them—ahead of time if possible. If you can do these things your Golds will be the most helpful children and teens. They want desperately to do what's right and to be recognized for being good. Don't accept blaming, inflexibility, and judging. Help them see the positive in life, others, and you.

The Quick Answer To ORANGE KIDS

Need <u>FREEDOM</u>
Freedom to act and to be themselves. Grateful for the ability to move on.

Value <u>REWARDS</u>
Likes immediate, positive feedback. Prefers action over words. Enjoys new freedoms and fun.

Best Discipline Do <u>BOUNDARIES</u>
Learns by doing. Needs clear boundaries (rules you can see) explained BEFORE they make a choice, if possible. Focus on rewards for good behavior, not punishment for bad choices.

The Simple Truth about ORANGE KIDS

The Orange child is perhaps the most misunderstood of the four personality types, yet they can be the most fun of all the temperaments. Oranges are VERY present in-the-moment and order their world through flexibility, although you may not think so. I'll explain more about this in a minute. These two qualities, being in-the-moment and their inherent desire for flexibility, when combined, are a recipe for what many so called experts determine is hyperactive and lacking the ability to focus. For parents of Oranges, the combination of these two traits do bring some unique parenting challenges but Oranges are not any more difficult to parent than each of the other colors. They are just unique and a bit counter-intuitive, especially if you are a Gold parent. I often tell the parents in my classes that Orange children and teens, while they *seem* challenging, are actually the easiest of the four colors to parent once you know how they tick. Not sure about that? Read on and I'll explain.

First and foremost, parents of all Orange children need to understand the two very important traits I mentioned just a minute ago. Oranges are very grounded in the here-and-now. You absolutely need to remember this if you want some peace between you and your Orange. They truly live moment-to-moment. This is their overarching approach to the world: the here and *right* now. It's how it is and it's not going to change no matter how you try to train it out of them. I always say in my classes when a parent can't understand why their "teaching" hasn't taken hold, or why they have to repeat things to their Oranges, I say, "They've BLINKED since then." What do I mean by that?

Orange kids and teens are so in-the-moment that they don't naturally connect moment-to-moment, or a rule in this moment to a similar, but slightly different behavior in the next moment, let alone to the next day or next week. They've BLINKED since then. *Please understand, I'm not making excuses for bad behavior here.* I'm just helping you understand how Oranges are wired so that you can teach them a more balanced way. If you are a Gold or a Green parent this may be especially hard for you to swallow and I can completely understand that. But for any color parent with an Orange child or teen you can either embrace this idea and work with it to grow mature, healthy, focused, and balanced Oranges, or you can fight it, deny it, and continue to go crazy parenting your Orange. It's your choice, but I can show you a quicker, simpler way.

Orange children, who are by nature living in-the-moment, have a hard time understanding the future or comprehending "big picture" ideals because those things are not in the here-and-now to them. Because they don't have a natural thought for the future or have an easy time with big picture principles they tend to seem rather impulsive, in-the-moment, and highly distracted or at the very least unfocused. Remember, they've BLINKED since then. But there is a simple remedy to overcome their natural tendency to only focus on what they want in-the-moment. I will show you how to help them "tap into" their second color in-the-moment to make better choices for the next moment, next day and the future. For now, though, I need to continue to explain how they think.

The second most important thing to understand about Orange children is their inherent ability to be very flexible about what they want, in-the-moment. But you need to read between the lines here… they are flexible about what THEY want, not necessarily about what YOU want… unless what you want *is* what they want. In other words, they can be very stubborn about what YOU want and still adamantly want what THEY want when they want it, but then change what they want in the next moment depending on what changes in that moment. Do you need to go back and read that a few times? Go ahead. I'll wait. ;-)

That's how they are "flexible." Sort of. They live moment-to-moment and they can be flexible about moving from moment-to-moment depending on what's happening in that moment. You can begin to see why this combination of in-the-moment and the Orange brand of "flexible" in that moment can lead to many Oranges being labeled as having no focus and being all over the place.

When Oranges can't have what they want when they want it they don't seem flexible at all. Instead they can be completely unreasonable, they may often repeat their demands over and over again no matter what you say. They may pitch such a fit that leaves you ready to give them away to the lowest bidder. So how can I even begin to use the word flexible with that kind of Orange behavior lurking in your near past? It's all in the fact that they can go from happy and cooperative one moment to stubborn and unreasonable the next. Sort of Jekyll and Hyde like. Well, that seems pretty flexible if you ask me, it's just not positive. We are not equating Orange "flexible" with easygoing. I'm defining Orange flexible as in highly changeable.

What that means in a nutshell is that at times your Orange will be way easygoing, and other times they won't, maybe even about the same thing though the timing will be different. As the parent, you will likely not know when they will be easy and when they will be stubborn and crazy, thus creating a recipe for you to be crazy. I call it the Orange trait of "stubborn flexibility." Again, they want what they want when they want it and there may be no apparent pattern to what they want right now compared to ten minutes, or even ten seconds ago. My suggestion to you is don't try to find a pattern; just use the parenting suggestions that follow.

I will teach you in this chapter to parent Oranges in-the-moment, for that moment, based on their behavior right then. It will work better for you, anyway. Since they are so in-the-moment, I will show you how to give them the choice to either act better in the next moment which will bring some sort of worthy appropriate reward, or suffer a consequence in the next moment that will curtail their freedom and be minus any reward. In other words, you will have their ability to be flexible work for you instead of against you.

When your Orange is showing signs of "stubborn flexibility," don't get upset, frustrated, or controlling. None of that stuff is going to work for you, anyway. Oranges don't really care, especially Orange-Greens. Oranges will, and do, change on a dime so we will use that trait to teach them how to focus, be balanced, and how to develop self-discipline. I'll show you how to do this after I explain more about Orange kids and teens. Read on. We are almost done.

Having this "stubborn flexibility" thing is why Oranges seem to lack any self-discipline or self-control in-the-moment. Without the right skills, taught to them by you, they will drift from one focus to another, one activity to another, one want to another. They will seem to change in a second, from second to second. That's why they are so misunderstood. That's why they are often labeled ADD or ADHD.

That's why they need YOU to be the boundary giver, the fence at the cliff's edge, their safety line through their young life. We must do this for them as they develop the skills to eventually do it for themselves because they are not naturally wired to do it for themselves like the other three colors. They *can't* do it for themselves and it's unfair, even cruel, to expect Oranges to do it for themselves until YOU teach them how to. You may not agree, but it doesn't change the fact that it is true.

Here's the good and bad of it: it may take you all of the eighteen years that you have them to teach them how to make better decisions and not be distracted. But how cool is it that you have eighteen years? What if you don't have 18 years? What if you are reading this and your Orange is a 16 or 14-year-old and you only have two to four years? No problem. These suggestions and ideas will still work, you just need to be a little tougher and a little more focused but you too will succeed. Absolutely!

Another interesting trait about Oranges is their unique way of communicating. It's based on being in-the-moment and on being action oriented. Oranges use verbs. Lots of verbs. The other colors don't use verbs to the extent that Oranges do. Oranges use verbs to communicate everything: their feelings, needs, and values. Everything is in terms of what they did, are doing, or are going to do. This Orange characteristic of using verbs to communicate everything is subtle, but once you know what to look for it's so obvious and they do it all the time.

For example, a young Orange who is mad might have trouble saying, "I'm mad." but they can easily say, "I going to hit you." or

"I hate you!" because these phrases are focused on an action, a verb. They may say, with a verb, "I can't stop crying." but they can't communicate feelings by saying, "I'm really sad right now." A frustrated, caged-in, Orange teenager who is overwhelmed with a barrage of several different feelings and is experiencing tons of stress may never say, "I'm feeling overwhelmed and stressed and I need some help, not criticism, but help from you my dear, wise parent. What should I do?" Instead they will grab the keys and their backpack and yell, "You never get me. I am SO outta here!" Verbs and action.

When you *see* abrupt, sneaky, or even risky behavior or "actions," while *hearing* a lot of grumpy, negative, pessimistic verbs, you've got a stressed Orange. Here's what you do: 1) Stop all criticism, and listen. 2) Put your story on hold. 3) Think of them as skirting the cliff edge with a blindfold on. They need you. They need you to understand. They need you to help. They need you to "see" their freedom threat and somehow, with compassion in your heart, and in your voice and words, reach out to them. Help them "see" that they are safe, that they have control of some choice, and that they can do whatever needs to be done. Once they calm down, they need to have appropriate boundaries spelled out and agreed upon. That will "rescue" your Orange child, pre-teen and teen from the cliff edge. It will keep them coming back to you for more. It's true. You may be the only one who can ever really reach your Orange. You're the only one who loves them as much as you do!

In the end, by combining the traits of being in-the-moment and the innate ability to organize their world with flexibility gives you what I call "Orange Freedom Fighters." Remember that your Orange Freedom Fighters want what they want in-the-moment and they will be very creative in trying to get it. If you stand in the way of getting what they want, they will most likely see *you* as a freedom threat. Remember, these Orange Freedom Fighters can be easily distracted by whatever captures their attention in-the-moment. They follow suit with flexible behavior choices that seem random and undisciplined. Also, remember they are not as all over the place as they seem. They are just following what grabs their attention in-the-moment. So we have to help them follow appropriate "attention grabbers" in-the-moment that are stronger than the passing fancy.

Now comes the part you've been waiting for. How do we do this? How do you parent an Orange? While it's simple, it may not always be easy. You will have to repeat the process over and over again, a bazillion times, as they grow to maturity. *Here it is, the key to parenting happy healthy balanced Oranges...*

Artfully Balance appropriate FREEDOM and REWARDS with concrete BOUNDARIES.

Now repeat that three times: I must *artfully balance appropriate freedom and rewards with concrete boundaries;* I must *artfully balance appropriate freedom and rewards with concrete boundaries;* I must *artfully balance appropriate freedom and rewards with concrete boundaries.* Okay you got it, now let's break it down.

Artfully Balance... Freedom, Rewards, & Boundaries

- The number one challenge for parents of Orange children and teens is allowing freedom within boundaries. Let the child's or teen's own maturity and willingness to make good choices be your guide to balancing these two elements. As an Orange makes good choices, reward them with a bit more freedom to play, to be silly, to have friends over, to go see a movie, etc.

- To balance freedom and boundaries, be creative and fun for your Orange. Be practical about giving freedoms that are age-appropriate but that don't take away from anyone else's rights or needs, including yours.

- Don't give a freedom that you can't live with, like "more time on the PlayStation." To an Orange, they hear unlimited time on the PlayStation, while you may mean ten extra minutes. Be sure to communicate clear, specific limits. For more on this, read the Boundaries section.

- Think about what seems like a freedom or a reward to your ORANGE and be careful not to think about this through YOUR color. Freedom and rewards will not be the same to both of you, even if you are both Oranges because you are an old Orange and your child or teen is a young Orange. If you are Green-Gold, Gold, or Blue-Gold... forget it... your idea of freedom and rewards will never match theirs.

- Don't be afraid to dangle a reward in front of your Orange or create a challenge for them. Your Orange is up for it even when you are not. Just be ready to follow through. First of all, your Orange will likely succeed no matter how tough you make the challenge. Secondly, if you don't deliver on the reward or freedom you promise, you've lost all your leverage for getting your Orange to focus on doing what's right in-the-moment, instead of doing what they want.

- When you get stuck and need more ideas on balancing freedoms with boundaries, reread this chapter to get your bearings and I promise you, fresh ideas will fill your mind.

- The simple solution to balance the freedom needs of an Orange and your need to get them to obey, help out, and act in appropriate ways is three-fold:
    1. Always give choices. It's best to give two good choices, like maybe the choice to do something now or at a later time, say in ten minutes or an hour. Even if you are forced to have one of the choices be the consequence

for making a wrong choice, your Orange will still see it as a better option than just being told what to do, NOW. Be careful to not always have your choices be the right one or a consequence. Doing that over and over will feel like a freedom threat.

2. Focus more on giving freedoms, however small, with rewards, however simple, for good choices while minimizing your focus on negative consequences and punishment. If you are a "glass half empty" person you are going to have to learn to focus on the positive for your Orange. They need you to.

3. Communicate clear, concrete BOUNDARIES. Read, reread, absorb, digest, and then live and breathe the section on BOUNDARIES. Without boundaries think of your wonderful, fun, full of life Orange walking along a cliff edge with no fence and a blindfold on. You'd never let that happen! An Orange without firm, clear boundaries, from you, *before* they make a choice (as often as possible) IS blindfolded on the cliff edge. Be their safety line. Stop doing "Command and Control" and start balancing FREEDOM within BOUNDARIES.

An ORANGE'S Greatest Need: Appropriate FREEDOM

FREEDOM to an Orange is life-giving, provides them with energy, and lowers their stress. When boundaries are provided to balance their FREEDOM, Oranges are even-tempered, fun, focused, and easy to get along with.

- Oranges need freedom the way the rest of us need air. A sense of freedom, or lack thereof, is woven through every fiber of their being and is as unconscious to them as breathing. While your Orange is wired to be in-the-moment and "flexible," it's this idea of FREEDOM that is their primary motivator. Freedom, for your Orange, is the key to everything. That's why I say they truly are the easiest of all the colors to parent.

- For an Orange it's ALWAYS about FREEDOM. You don't have to guess or wonder—it's ALWAYS about freedom. That's why they are easy. They're upset? It's because they want more freedom. Being sneaky? They're feeling a freedom threat so they are going to get it… their way… quietly… and behind your back. Toddler having a tantrum? It's a freedom thing. They want out, they want in, they want gum, they want to play. It's freedom they really want. Have a 10-year-old who is a world class negotiator? It's their need for freedom—always keeping their options open. For an Orange, it's ALWAYS about freedom.

- When *their* idea of freedom is threatened they will become stubborn, hard to reason with, and will most likely be very difficult to handle if they are young, and will be frustrating, demanding, or sneaky about getting what they want as they grow.

- Freedom for an Orange comes in the form of choices, opportunities, open ended challenges, and sometimes competition.

- When an Orange perceives that they have no choice, or no freedom, they will experience great stress, as if they are being strangled and will act out in order to get out from under the freedom threat. They will often panic, then DO almost anything to get their freedom back. They will do whatever it takes to get what they want until they gain the skills and maturity to see that 98% of their perceived freedom threats are not real. When they see that the threat is not real they can learn to make better choices.

- Daily, even hourly, choices can provide the most basic of freedoms for your Orange and they thrive on them. Here's an example, let's say you need your Orange to set the table for dinner. Don't ask them *if they will* set the table, instead say, "You have a choice. Would you like the freedom to set the table now (it's 4:00) or right before dinner, no later than 5:15, so we can be ready to eat at 5:30 (clear boundary)?" If you word every, and I really do mean every, request like that you will get much farther with your Orange.

- What if they say they don't want to help set the table and won't make a choice? That's simple too. Stay calm and first try, "That's not one of your choices. Do you want to set it now or at 5:15? I need a decision." If they still refuse, stay calm and say, "Since you've chosen not to help, then I will not be serving you any dinner. I know that tomorrow when I ask you will make a better choice." Then no matter what, don't feed them dinner this one time. Don't fall prey to their negotiation skills, even if they escalate to throwing and pitching a fit. Deal with all that as best as you can. You are teaching a bigger lesson here. Going hungry one night will not kill your Orange and they will learn to make a better choice the next day for two reasons. First, they would rather have their freedom tomorrow and be stubbornly flexible in the direction that YOU want, instead of in the direction THEY want. Secondly, they would rather have the reward of eating than the consequence of being hungry. They learned that you were really serious and not just making an idle threat.

- When they do make the right choice, you are not through! Reward their appropriate use of freedom to set the table with big fanfare! Maybe a big hug, a surprise chocolate peanut butter cup, a surprise chance for ten extra minutes on the Wii. See the next section for more on this. With a surprise reward when the good choice happens you will reinforce to the in-the-moment Orange that they would rather use their freedom moments for good choices than for dumb, stubborn ones.

- When an Orange is misbehaving or acting out use this idea of freedom to understand the reason for their stress. If you remember this one word—freedom—and look for it as the underlying motivator for everything they do, you will always understand why your Orange is doing what they are doing.

- When your Orange is upset ask yourself, "What freedom do they think is being taken away?," or ask, "What do they see as a freedom threat right now?" Answering one of those questions will lead you right to their freedom threat.

- Just because you recognize their freedom threat does not mean that you always have to alleviate it. Understanding it will help you know best how to deal with it but it may not always be appropriate to allow your Orange the freedom that they are seeking. Please don't think that I am in any way suggesting that they should have every freedom. Some freedoms are not allowed, such as hitting a brother with a 2x4. I'm sure you agree that just because we can do something, doesn't always mean that we should do something. This is a lesson that all Oranges, and some Green-Oranges, need to learn.

- Freedom for an Orange also means freedom to move. They live an action-oriented life. They are go, go, go, especially if they are an Extrovert. For any Orange, physical restrictions in the way of boring chores, tight formal clothing, and standing in lines are just a few examples of ways that Orange will experience a lack of physical freedom. Not only do they want emotional freedom but they also crave physical freedom.

- Oranges who sense their freedom needs are being met are usually lovable, can be very funny, and pretty happy-go-lucky. Again, this doesn't mean that we let them run amuck without a care or a boundary in sight. In fact, quite the opposite.

- Oranges need and want freedom, but that freedom needs to be balanced with concrete, clear limits, or boundaries. For more on this, see the section after Rewards that focuses on Boundaries.

- A final note about freedom: The older an Orange child gets the more freedom they need. If they prove themselves worthy of your trust and show (remember they are all about action) that they can make choices within the established boundaries, by all means give them more freedom. Remember, they WANT freedom and will surprise you by being responsible so that they can keep their new freedoms. Have faith in them and work to assume the best in them. You may be the only one who will give them the chance to succeed.

An ORANGE'S Strongest Value: Appropriate REWARDS

An ORANGE'S need for Freedom is always coupled with REWARDS, whether we like it or not. Using appropriate rewards for good choices can steer your Orange toward making more choices that are right and healthy.

- Your Orange is all about the rewards. If your 5-year-old Orange hits your 3-year-old after you've warned him not to, guess what's influencing your Orange's behavior? The REWARD of hearing his sister yelp. That reward is well worth the price of listening to your scolding. For an Orange teen, the reward of ditching school is well worth the price of a possible detention *if* she gets caught—and she already knows she might not. Your 3-year-old Orange escape artist who slips out the back door over and over again sees the reward of the freedom outside until you find him well worth the price of a five minute time out. Get the picture?

- Oranges WILL work for REWARDS, no matter what you want, so why not use REWARDS in your favor rather than try to pretend your Orange doesn't operate their own reward system?

- Never fear. Rewards do not have to escalate over time until you are forced to reward your 16-year-old with a BMW just for getting up in the morning. Actually, quite the opposite.

- The main thing to remember with Orange children is to shape their behavior by REWARDING their good choices, give choices whenever possible, and redirect their inappropriate ones as soon as possible with as little fanfare, talking, or big deal making as possible.

- If you are currently in the habit of only giving your Orange attention when they are doing what's wrong and you make a big deal out of the time out, the punishment, or your lecture, your Orange will continue to misbehave to get their "reward." For an Orange who is craving any sort of attention, they would rather get negative attention from you, which is in some way a reward, than no attention, and therefore no reward at all. To turn things around, start rewarding even the smallest good action, and their behavior will do a 180° turn from bad to good. Oranges value rewards. Period. Reward the good, and you'll get more good.

- Start by using simple physical rewards with toddlers like clapping, cheering, "Yeah!," or giving a sudden excited hug. Then graduate to "time" rewards of reading or playing with young children. Eventually move onto freedom based or "doesn't that make you feel good" rewards for pre-teens and teens. If you do this you will eventually teach your Oranges, over time, to work, and to do what's right, for just the intrinsic rewards of doing what's right. I know this to be true. I have an amazing Orange grown-up daughter who does what's right because it's what's right and she now sees that doing what's right opens doors, a.k.a. REAL FREEDOM!

- Only give out rewards you can live with. For example, don't promise a trip to the zoo or the movies if you don't plan on delivering or if a good movie won't be out for three weeks. Oranges need immediate rewards for the rewards to be learning tools. That's why rewards don't have to be big or expensive. They do need to be concrete, immediate, fun, or freedom enhancing, and seem like a reward to the child, not to you.

- Make the reward proportional to the work. Don't be stingy, or overindulgent, neither one will get you the results you want.

- If you are a parent that either because of your color, or your upbringing, cannot get your head around the idea of rewarding a child or teen for just doing what they should, I understand. At the same time, you are denying the fact that you *do* operate on a reward system, too. Everyone does. Golds are rewarded by titles, appropriate control, and checking off a to do list. Blues are rewarded by acceptance, recognition, hugs, and kind words. Greens are rewarded by knowing that they've solved a problem no one else could, or by being smarter than the problem, or by have the coolest tech "toys" around. So, admit your need for rewards and get over yourself. Your Oranges will behave and eventually learn to do what's right because it's right if they can see the reward in it. Is that really so bad?

- The best rewards for your Orange will be very individual. A good reward for your Orange is one that adds to their experiencing more freedom, more fun, more action, and more time to do what they want. At the same time, keep it age appropriate and proportional to the good choice. It would be impossible for me to make a list of rewards. Instead think of what would seem like a little bit of extra fun, freedom, or special "kudo" for your child or teen. Always use your best judgment and communicate the link between their reward and their good choice so that it is appreciated and motivates continued good choices.

- If you are not sure what a good reward would be for your

Orange, ask them. You might be surprised. Even a 2-year-old knows that they would pick up all their books for a popsicle. A 13-year-old might keep their room clean for the next six weeks if they got a new Wii game out of the deal. It will probably not be as outlandish as you are afraid it might be. If it is, just clarify that you have veto power when you ask for suggestions.

- A caution about rewards: if your Orange is using your idea for a reward to negotiate... meaning they say, "Well, what will you give me if..." shut down negotiations right then and there. At that point, they've become a terrorist, and you DO NOT negotiate with terrorists. Give them a choice to change their attitude and their tactics, immediately, or all bets are off. End of negotiation. Guess what? I'll bet they will do a 180°. They DO NOT want to lose their reward of freedom. You need to stand tough. No waffling or you'll completely lose your leverage.

- Never feel trapped into giving a reward. Rewards are *earned* after good behaviors and good choices. If you give a reward *before* the good behavior or *before* the good choice, it's a bribe and we do not do bribes! Ever.

- If the rewards you give are not building gratitude in your child or teen, then tell them that instant that you are suspending all rewards and freedoms until they are grateful again. Guess what happens. They get grateful in about two seconds, no joke. That's fine. Don't institute some long punishment period, unless they don't change their attitude. If they change on the spot give them back the rewards on the spot. Remember, your Oranges really do change on a dime, so let them. They've BLINKED since then. Long punishments only cause an Orange to forget what you wanted them to do in the first place or gives them time to plot your demise.

- Having said that, if ingratitude is a RECURRING concern (as with any bad habit or attitude) then by all means, insist on a change of attitude and have the rewards come after the change of attitude is longer lasting. I'd start with a few days, a week or two, depending on the child's maturity and what degree of in- gratitude they are displaying. For an "I just forget" slipup, I'd have the "no rewards, but you still do the work" period be a few days after they start to display the right attitude. If it's a more serious "I deserve this because I'm me" sort of display of ingrat- itude from say a 13-year-old, then I might make the lack of rewards be more severe like two weeks from when they start acting better. Either way, I'd institute a one minute, nighttime "check in" system where you evaluate their daily "gratitude" pro- gress. Look for small things during the day that you can compli- ment them on so they don't get discouraged and share that dur- ing this one minute progress report. It's sort of a mini reward system, but they don't need to know that. Keep these chats focused on the positive with as little criticism as possible. This provides immediate feedback while they are learning something that is NOT at all concrete and therefore hard to get their head around. Use this process with almost any value that you are trying to instill in your Orange.

- Use a calendar as a concrete reward system to mark right ac- tions, completed subtasks of a bigger project, or "good days" leading to a bigger change in attitude or a bad habit. Build in smaller rewards at specific intervals, with possibly a bigger re- ward at the "end" of the process.

- Give Oranges concrete recognition for task performance; not for perfection. Adults often fail to remember that all children, even teens, and especially Oranges, are a work in progress. Even if the whole job is not completed, or they fight a change but later accept it, or they think through the consequences of their choices AFTER the choice, you should still reward these efforts to an appropriate degree.

- Oranges need you to focus on their progress—not their imperfection. The rest of the world will do that well enough for your Orange. You need to give them encouragement to progress—not excuses for settling for some label or diagnosis. By rewarding progress you get greater progress; not a termination of effort.

- Reward Oranges for respecting boundaries, people, things, and rules. REWARDS teach Oranges far better than consequences. This is your best tool!

- As Oranges get older, make SOME of the rewards more and more abstract and a little farther out in the future. This will help them strive for things not in the here-and-now. It will effectively teach them the value of intrinsic rewards. It gets Oranges away from the need for "immediate gratification" and that it feels good just to do what's right.

- Provide lots of opportunity for action, service, and fun. These can be seen as rewards if you sincerely talk about them in fun and positive ways.

- Reward tasks that are completed immediately. That way you will get more and more things done right away.

- For Orange children, food is typically a GOOD reward unless they have a weight issue. Oranges typically don't have weight problems and don't normally associate food with comfort. Blue children (and some Gold-Blues) do that. Oranges are usually thin with a very active metabolism, so food rewards do not typically turn into unhealthy habits. It's usually only Blue children, teens, and adults who associate food with comfort, acceptance, and stress relief. Oranges usually see food as fuel.

- If you are concerned about using food as a reward, then it's really simple: don't. Instead have a "Prize Jar" or use pennies that add up over time to a trip to the dollar store. Using food as a reward only works for toddlers and younger children, anyway.

- Money as a reward? Go for it! Oranges love it. But I would suggest that there are certain chores or responsibilities that your Orange does not get paid for. Those things must be done first and done correctly with the right care. If your Orange starts to put too much emphasis on money, have a brief "coaching" session explaining that your family values are focused on work, service, responsibility, and dependability. Let them know you'll give them a few days to change their focus and attitude about work or the whole pay plan is gone—while maintaining their assigned chores. I guarantee, they will sing a different tune very quickly and learn by experience to do something for the right reason.

- Remember that using rewards for an Orange to change their behavior in-the-moment is only a means to an end and is used to teach the Orange the value of doing the right thing. You want them to experience the good feelings associated with doing what's right. Using rewards early and often gives you the time you need to teach your Orange through repetition that it's better to do what's right and that it brings greater freedoms and real happiness in the future. It's actually very cool!

The BIG Discipline Strategy for ORANGES:
Concrete BOUNDARIES

ORANGE children and teens need to have clear BOUNDARIES set as limits for their behavior. BOUNDARIES provide a safety net for an ORANGE that they think they don't want, but that they really need to be happy.

- Boundaries are rules you can see. A fence, a timer, a gas gauge, a speed limit sign, a door, a step, a sidewalk, a clock, a check list, a picture of a clean room, a yell, the first "stop it" that a sibling utters, a temperature, your Orange's fist touching the skin of another person, a chalk line, a wall, the street light in front of your house, your teenage son's girlfriend's bra and panties or at least where they should be. All of these things are things that you and your Orange can see (or at least imagine, in the case of the girlfriend's unders). And they can all serve as a BOUNDARY that must not be crossed for your in-the-moment Freedom Fighter.

- The more concrete the better. If you leave it open for negotiation, they will negotiate. Don't be afraid to say, "This is not open for negotiation." Blue moms will have a hard time with that—but don't. Most Oranges will know you mean business and stop. If they don't, it's time for a consequence and then walk away. Mean what you say or your actions will communicate you ARE open to negotiation.

- Providing clear boundaries helps your Orange know exactly where the limits are so they can enjoy all the freedom in between. It helps them know where the line is so they don't have to lose any precious freedoms or possibilities for rewards. They like that!

- Boundaries continually let Oranges know what is expected of them (without nagging). Be concrete and detailed in your requests, teach them what is right, and don't ever assume they know. Remember they want to succeed, obey, and be responsible. They will experience stress if you keep them guessing about what you want.

- They need, not want, but NEED concrete examples, solid reasons, clear expectations, and understandable boundaries. They need to see with their eyes because "seeing is believing." They understand better if they can experience it, whatever "it" is.

- Any boundary that's lofty, hard to explain, idealistic, "fluffy," free form or overemotional is very hard for Orange children to get their minds around. Something like, "You need to be nice; you're hurting her feelings." is idealistic, overemotional, and it's hard to see "nice." Instead say, "We don't say that she smells. It's mean. And we don't walk away from someone when they are talking." This is much more concrete. This approach can be frustrating for Blue or Green parents because they are naturally intuitive and know better. Oranges are just NOT.

- Boundaries help Oranges be good and do what's right. No boundaries force an Orange to guess in-the-moment what is right and good and they may not have the maturity to get it right. Don't set them up to fail. Give them the boundaries ahead of time whenever possible.

- What if you don't give a boundary because you didn't even see that a boundary would be needed? Oh my goodness! This happened to me all the time with my Orange. Through trial and error I learned to give my sweet, well meaning, and good hearted Orange the benefit of the doubt and for those times she got one "Freebie." After each boundary "oops," I clearly outlined the new boundary (for future reference) and the Freebie was over. If she crossed the now known boundary there would be an immediate, and freedom taking, consequence.

- Parents of Orange children and teens should use consequences to teach when boundaries are violated, but ONLY AFTER you have clearly and pointedly communicated what those boundaries and expectations are *beforehand*. Because your Orange is so in-the-moment, they don't have a lot of natural "common sense." They have to learn it from you in the form of concrete boundaries. To punish without teaching is harsh and breeds rebellion, not trust. Teach first. Give choices with boundaries. Then, expect your Orange to live WITHIN the boundaries. Most of the time they will. When they don't, and you've clearly outlined the boundary beforehand, it's time for a consequence—immediately and without hesitation.

- The one exception to giving a Freebie when you've not had the chance to clearly communicate a boundary *before* a choice is if your Orange surprises you with a wrong choice that is danger-ous, hurtful, or illegal. In this case your Orange should not catch a break. NO Freebies for dangerous or risky behavior! Just consequences, right away!

- Okay, so back to Freebies for a "missed" boundary. There are several amazing positives. Here's how and why...

    1. For your Orange, they don't get in trouble for some-thing neither one of you saw coming. This teaches mercy and builds trust. In the future, your Orange will know that they can come to you about anything, and that's what we want.

    2. Oranges learn they can trust you to be understanding with them about genuine poor judgment while they learn to have better judgment.

    3. You will get better at seeing how your Orange thinks and better at anticipating needed boundaries before they are needed.

    4. Your Orange will learn more and more about creating their own boundaries as they mature by seeing when there *should have been* a boundary and *when they needed* one. They feel like a genuine idiot for having hindsight but not foresight—especially Orange-Greens. It helps them grow that "common sense" and not repeat something dumb. Don't add to their feeling like an idiot with "I told you so" but do let that feeling work for *their* advantage. Remember—that's the whole point of this parenting thing, to help your Orange create and live by their own boundaries.

5. The Freebie system only works for first offences that completely blindside both you and your Orange. If you give a Freebie for something that you have discussed and created a boundary for, you are negating the whole point. Give your Orange choices, but they only get ONE chance to do what's right, one Freebie for a specific action. Otherwise your actions will say, "I didn't really mean that boundary was a real line not to cross. It's more of a suggestion." That's the kind of parenting that lands Orange teens in jail. They need boundaries, not second chances. Freebies are not second chances, they are learning opportunities.

- What kind of things are non-negotiable first offences and never worthy of a Freebie? Those are the big things you've probably already set boundaries for and don't realize it, such as, "don't do drugs." In our home, for teens a few examples were, "don't commit to an activity until you check the family calendar", "we don't volunteer each other for anything (like promising mom will make sixty dozen cookies)," and "assuming you have free reign of the car." For a younger child it might be "no hitting," "no calling people stupid," or "no going outside without asking." You may want to make the boundary clearer, more concrete, or more specific now that you are reading this. Freebies are only for those things you didn't see coming until after the fact. Oranges will provide you hundreds of Freebie opportunities.

- A Shannon Story. A first offence at our house that we never saw coming was drag racing. We didn't see that one coming at all for our blond, petite, Introverted Orange-Green dancer daughter who drove the family Z71 four-wheel drive truck. She was mortified after she drag raced one night and put her truck in a ditch. It could have killed her. She realized that right away. She got a ticket and had to attend an eight hour aggressive driving class with scary people. Yup, lesson learned. After that, she drove like a grandma and created her own boundaries based on "the seven bad decisions I made that landed me in that ditch." She also came to us on her own and wanted to fix the damage to the yard of the man whose house was by the ditch. Yeah, a Freebie was in order. A harsh consequence issued by us would not have taught her the lesson that she learned giving herself some consequences once she had a day or two to use that hindsight that was not foresight. Several people at our church were actually critical that we didn't ground her from driving. But they didn't see the growth that we did. Don't let other parents try to tell you how to parent your Orange, especially when they don't have an Orange. You have in your hands the best information on parenting Oranges that you ever need!

- Just to be clear, Freebies are not rescues. I didn't rescue my daughter from the consequences of drag racing; I just didn't add any more punishment onto the natural occurring freedom zappers and non-rewards that came with the crime. A Freebie for not planning better on a school project is that you don't get mad, lecture, or make things harder for them. Do let them get the bad grade. Don't rescue or help but don't add to their stress. Believe me, to an Orange, that's a Freebie. Then, after the project is done and the crazy moment has settled, institute a new, clear boundary that you expect them to plan better and that low grades in the future will be further freedom zappers and acceptable grades will bring appropriate rewards.

- Most parents of Oranges find that they experience tons of first time Freebies that spark new boundaries. They also see, much to their amazement, that those newly established boundaries were rarely tested. 95% of the time as your Orange matures and as you give age-appropriate choices and age-appropriate freedoms, rarely do they cross a new boundary with a second offence. But, I'll be honest, our Orange sure was good at coming up with minor things I never saw coming! I bet yours will too.

- If you already have a pre-teen or teenager you want to start using the Freebie System with, sit down together and in as few words as possible explain what you are going to do and how it works. Also, let them know that a Freebie is NOT a "get out of jail free" card. It's not a rescue and it's not a second chance. It's a first chance to learn to make better choices when they are honest, open, not sneaky, and really sorry for the dumb choice. Explain that if they choose to take advantage of the Freebie System, tell them the Freebie System goes away, pronto. YOU, not them, are in charge of WHEN a Freebie is in order.

- As your Orange matures, let them show you they can set boundaries for themselves. Reward them appropriately. Let them be free to be themselves within the framework of your family's values. Teach them to do service for others. Keep them busy working toward rewards that are farther and farther out in the future, and more and more based on values and feelings than on physical stuff.

The Influence of Introvert or Extrovert for ORANGES

For Oranges, more than any other color,
Introvert or Extrovert characteristics create
very different personalities in children and adults.

Oranges, both Introverts and Extroverts, as discussed earlier, are a combination of living in-the-moment and are very flexible with that moment. Both have the highest need for freedom, value rewards, and need boundaries. Where Orange Introverts and Orange Extroverts differ is in how they process information, communicate, and in their level of observable movement.

Extroverted Oranges are always on the go and like to make things happen. Introverted Oranges are also action-oriented but not in the same way as Extroverted Oranges. Introverts conserve their energy for action until action is really needed. Then they are very efficient, quick, quiet, and focused. When Introvert Oranges go, they go, but they are stealthy and surprisingly adept. They will wait until the last moment but then when they do what they set out to do, they generally do it without hesitation.

Extroverted Oranges like to not only *have* fun, but they like to *create* fun. Introverted Oranges love to have fun too but they are more likely to watch first, join later, and their "fun" is on the "quietly dare-devilish" side. Introverted Oranges are "go with the flow" types and usually very laid back, where Extroverted Oranges need to be more active and sitting too long will drive them crazy. An Introverted Orange will be able to sit still longer than an Extroverted Orange but the Introvert will have trouble concentrating on one topic for a long time. The Extroverted Orange's body will literally wander while the Introverted Orange's mind will wander. The Introverted Orange will be distracted easily by other interesting thoughts going on in their head and the Extroverted Orange will be distracted too, but not by their own thoughts. They are distracted by things going on around them. This is why "time outs" longer than thirty seconds don't work for either Introverted or Extroverted Oranges.

Both Introverted and Extroverted Oranges are spontaneous and both are always up for a good challenge but they will approach it differently. An Introverted Orange will need time to process and digest the problem. They will take the time to come up with a fast, efficient solution. They may seem indifferent and detached from the issue until all-of-a-sudden you see them move to act. Then, they may not do the wisest thing but they will do what seems fastest and is the quickest way to either freedom or a reward. On the other hand, an Extrovert will jump in and attack the challenge without much forethought or deliberation. This way of addressing challenges may seem more like a bull in a china shop. However, if the challenge seems in any way like a freedom threat or is not attached to a worthy, interesting reward, forget it. Your Orange child or teen will dismiss it as boring and will turn to other distractions.

What if the challenge is part competition? Oranges enjoy many different types of competition - sometimes with themselves, sometimes with others – depending on whether or not they are Introverted or Extroverted. They love to play around, especially outdoors. Extroverts like to be with friends. Introverts do fine by themselves and while they like to be with friends, they may tire of all the interaction. All Oranges love to build things with their hands and are comfortable using any kind of tool. They are usually great athletes as their best "tool" can be their own body. Extroverts are most likely to enjoy team sports and competition with others. Introverts usually prefer individual sports like dance, gymnastics, golf, swimming, and running but may hate competing publicly or against anyone.

Extroverted Oranges usually communicate rather openly and are talkative. Introverted Oranges, on the other hand, may have a very difficult time saying what's on their minds. This happens because they process everything internally and think in terms of actions—so they have a hard time assigning "words" to what they are thinking. When they can't speak fast enough or communicate effectively (remember Oranges are all about doing everything fast), they become very frustrated with themselves and with you. Give them time to talk and figure it out. Understand that they may prefer to give up rather than struggle through trying to get you to understand what they are thinking. Ask if you can help them figure out what they need to say. Use reflective listening, but keep it short and sweet and not too "touchy feely," especially for your Introverted Orange-Greens.

The Orange child is not usually overly emotional unless they are extremely frustrated or stressed. Then they can become very dramatic. Introverts quietly melt-down. Extroverts may explode. All Oranges can be very good workers and always up to a good challenge IF there is a "see-able" reward in the immediate future that is fun and freedom enhancing.

To rein in the seemingly unending flow of energy and action of an Extroverted Orange child or the always present sense of quiet individualism from the Introverted Orange, parents need to be very clear about setting boundaries for what's appropriate action, giving age-appropriate freedoms in the form of choices, consistently rewarding good choices, and redirecting bad choices through consequences and the loss of freedom. Orange children and teens really require a four-sided approach to steer them in the right direction. Parents also need to communicate clear expectations about the Orange child's interactions with others. Extroverted Orange children need to learn to not say everything and anything. Introverted Oranges need to learn that they need to talk to others and let them in on what's going on in their heads and hearts.

Extroverted Oranges are most successful when their parents teach them early how to entertain themselves quietly and appropriately for increasing amounts of time. This coping tool will be very useful to an Orange child as the world does not always appreciate their never-ending stream of action. Introverted Oranges are most successful when their parents teach them communication skills and how to avoid procrastination (which comes from their tendency to conserve energy and put off action until the last minute).

Oranges handle change pretty easily because of their inherent "here-and-now" focus and their flexibility. (The exception to this may be the Introverted Orange-Green.) Both Introverts and Extroverts are pretty good with new situations, especially when those new situations are action oriented. Extroverts will usually jump right in. Introverts will need a little time to watch and then probably give it a try. Both types of Oranges appreciate a "heads up" about change as long as the parent communicates any news quickly and in ten words or less. Change to any Orange is usually an adventure to be experienced and not much of a threat. In fact, Extroverted Oranges often create change just for the fun of it. Gold, Green-Gold, and Blue-Gold parents may find this characteristic of Extroverted Orange children very frustrating as they are very structured themselves and change can be a challenge for them personally. Introverted Oranges may bring about change in quiet, somewhat sneaky ways. They may just go about doing whatever they want and a preoccupied parent may miss it until it's too late. Both Introverted and Extroverted Oranges are risk takers and great negotiators.

Influence of an ORANGE'S Second Color on Their Behavior and Choices

The Power of the Orange's Second Color is the Power to Make Better Choices in-the-moment

By now you've probably wondered how in the world can you teach your Orange to make a better choice in-the-moment. Well, there's actually a simple answer to that. It's all about teaching your Orange how to use the natural characteristics of their SECOND COLOR to help them out of doing a "dumb" in-the-moment.

Let's start with a little theory. Your Orange's natural second color will be either Blue or Green. If you think their second color is Gold, I understand, but remember it's not a natural possibility. If your Orange seems to be second color Gold it's because they've learned a lot of Gold from you, from another Gold parent, or another Gold authority figure who had power over their freedom. An Orange is a natural chameleon and will take on the qualities of any other color who can reward them with freedoms. So to reiterate the point, your Orange's *natural* second color is either Green or Blue; not Gold.

Remember, there are two principles, according to the science of personality types, that will help you understand how an Orange's second color influences their choices. First, remember that Orange and Gold are on opposite ends of the dimension that determines how we organize our world. Second, Blue and Green are on opposite ends of the dimension that determines how we make decisions. That's why Oranges are either Orange-Blues or Orange-Greens.

To add further insult to injury, since the Orange's decision-making dimension is their SECOND color AFTER their "in-the-moment, action-oriented, flexible-in-how-I-organize-my-world" part of their personality is WHY

(... drum roll please...)

Oranges make such dumb choices in-the-moment!

There is your Orange in a nutshell!

This also explains why, when your Orange does something stupid and you say, "What were you thinking?" or "Why did you do that?" and they look at you with that deer-in-the-headlight look and say, "I don't know" it's because they really don't. Here's a big Orange parenting suggestion: don't ask what they were thinking. You won't like the answer. Oranges really don't know. They acted first and may never have thought or felt anything about it.

Here's what you want to do to help your Orange "in-the-moment Go, Go, Go Freedom Fighter" STOP and make a better choice in that moment, you are going to teach them to tap into their second color. To be specific, when they are faced with a choice, we want them to STOP in that moment and if they are Orange-Greens, we want them to STOP and THINK. If they are Orange-Blues, we want them to STOP and FEEL.

Now with that big picture in mind, let's look at each of the four "flavors" of Orange Freedom Fighters to see how they naturally process and make decisions so that you can teach them a smarter, more structured, more feeling way.

246

Extroverted Oranges-Blues, while tender-hearted, they are your original party animals. They love to be around people and have a good time. They are happy-go-lucky, smiley, and cuddly when they have their freedom needs appropriately met. They especially want the freedom to be themselves and experience all the fun they can muster. As Oranges they are particularly focused in-the-moment and because they are Extroverts they are focused in that moment on everything outside their body. Then, because of their second color Blue, they are very concerned with people and what everyone is doing and feeling. They are pretty in tune to their basic feelings of happy, sad, mad, glad, fun, and for sure… freedom. They are somewhat in tune to what their friends and family members are basically feeling.

In a nutshell, Extrovert Orange-Blues are in-the-moment, focused on what's going on around them. They are not at all naturally introspective and will be very concerned about pleasing their friends and their parents. These are the Oranges (especially in their teen years) that will probably make the dumbest choices when they are influenced by dumb friends, but won't be as likely to take a lot of hurtful or personally dangerous risks on their own. When they do see that they've made a mistake, they will generally be very sorry as soon as they realize that you know they've done something dumb.

To help Extrovert Orange-Blues make better decisions, you need to train them to override their Orange. You do this with their intuitive feelings and their sense of what they **really** value. They need to STOP in-the-moment and FEEL how this choice will affect their family and freedom and whether or not it will hurt someone. They need to realize that to do anything hurtful NOW will negatively affect people they love, themselves, or their freedom in the future. Doing just this one thing and learning to follow-up on what they feel to be right will help them do the right thing in-the-moment. Because they are an Extrovert, they will more likely be compulsive about discussing their choice process out loud, giving friends a chance to persuade them away from what's right. Help your Extrovert know that they need to keep this process to themselves. Bottom line: your Extroverted Orange will keep their freedom, and even create more freedoms, if they will STOP and FEEL their way to right choices.

Introverted Orange-Blues are also sensitive but quiet. They seem very Blue because they Introvert (keep private) their first color and Extrovert (show) their second color. They crave interaction with you and some friends but simultaneously be worn out by it. They are gentle and need lots of affection from parents. Because they are highly tactile they like small beautiful objects and soft clothing. They love animals. They are usually calm and highly centered energy conservers. If they feel a freedom threat, they will be illogical and sneaky because they are just "feeling" their way through life in a very private way. They are still very action oriented but their actions will be low-key. They won't normally be big talkers.

As Oranges, they are particularly focused in-the-moment, but because they are Introverts they are focused on what's going on in their heart (and sometimes their head) in that moment. They are not very tuned in to other's feelings, but are pretty focused on their own. They may seem very emotional without being very communicative about their feelings. They are just feeling every feeling as a verb and will act out those verb feelings. I am talking Emmy Award material. They may cry, whine, hurt, and be very dramatic but won't use many words, it's all acted out instead. As they get older, they will be sneaky unless pushed into a fight; then they may fight nasty. Since their second color is Blue, you can help them become more concerned about how their choices affect the ones they love. When they realize the error of their choice, Introverted Orange -Blues are usually very sorry.

In a nutshell, Introverted Orange-Blues are in-the-moment,

focused on what's going on with their own feelings. They are more naturally introspective if they are taught to be. They can quickly learn to be concerned with what other's feel. For the most part they are likely to be genuinely concerned about pleasing you and some of their friends. These are the Oranges (especially in their teen years) that will seem withdrawn, depressed, or sneaky. They won't say much unless pushed, instead they will most likely "put up" with your lectures and then go about doing exactly what they want. They may say something smart like, "Are you done?", just to tick you off and to get you to quit being their freedom suck. They may be influenced by friends who offer fun, escapes, and freedom that they feel they deserve or need. They are more likely to make the dumbest choices when they are influenced by dumb friends, but won't be as likely to take a lot of risks on their own.

To help Introverted Orange-Blues make better decisions, you need to train them to override their Orange. Do this with their intuitive feelings and their sense of what they *really* value. They need to STOP in-the-moment and FEEL how this choice will affect their family and freedom. They need to realize that it's stupid to do anything NOW that will negatively affect their freedom and family in the future. Doing this one thing, and learning to follow up on what they know to be right, will help them do the right thing in-the-moment. Because they are Introverts, they will have an easier time in-the-moment to silently consider their choice. You are going to need to give them time to process through their choice without you nagging them after their wrong decisions. Give them time to process through their mistakes and talk about it all later, after the emotions subside. Keep your discussions short and to the point and let them move on quickly. Don't be afraid to communicate your expectations that they STOP and FEEL their way to a better choice in the future.

Extroverted Orange-Greens are very logical and make

the ultimate fighter pilot. Think of a fighter pilot as a child or teen. They are more serious logical thinkers who will talk a good story (that is probably a *true* story) and want to be flying Mach 10 with their hair on fire. They may be outspoken and frustrated with people's stupidity. They are funny, irreverent, and even at times outrageous.

Extroverted Orange-Greens are in-the-moment, focused on what's going on around them, and may be a bit introspective but usually after the fact. They will be very concerned about their freedom and the stupid ways that others threaten their freedom. These are the Oranges (especially in their teen years) that will probably make the dumbest choices when they are pushed into doing something. They either don't want to seem stupid in front of all their friends, or they think a rule or the logic in NOT doing something is stupid and they want to prove it. When they do see that they've made a mistake they will either fight admitting it or will be so hard on themselves that you won't know what to do to get themselves out of the depths of despair. Because they ARE Oranges, they will change on a dime and get themselves out of their despair. Be prepared for such mood shifts in your Extroverted Orange-Greens. They can change from one moment to the next as explained earlier.

To help Extroverted Orange-Greens make better decisions, you need to train them to override their Orange "let's do this" with their second color Green logical thinking and their sense of what's stupid. They need to STOP in-the-moment and THINK about how this choice will affect their family and their freedom and that it's stupid to do anything NOW that will negatively affect either in the future. Doing this one thing, and learning to follow up on what they *know* (a very Green word) to be right, will help them do the right thing in-the-moment. Because they are Extroverts, you are going to need to help them process through their decisions (probably after the fact) out loud and as briefly as possible. Remember to clarify their boundaries and inform them that they've just used up a

"Freebie" and there won't be another "Freebie" for the same bad choice.

Introverted Orange-Greens are the quiet version of the fighter pilot. They seem very Green because Introverts tend to Extrovert (project) their second color and keep private their first color. They may need logic from you but they may not always reason logically themselves. They often appear to do whatever the heck they want to because the Green in them tends to make them less sensitive to what you may think or feel. They are risk-takers but do it very quietly and fly under the radar. They are quiet, reserved, and often serious although they have the funniest, driest sense of humor. They, too, conserve their energy and find ingenious ways to procrastinate. Once they move into action they are very focused and efficient.

As Oranges, they are particularly focused in-the-moment but because they are Introverts they are very focused in that moment on what's going on inside their own head. They are not tuned into other's feelings, but they are pretty focused on their own ideas and their own sense of what's logical. However, their logic may be skewed because it's secondary to their Orange "let's do this" way of working through their world. They're not very good about dealing with or communicating their feelings. In this way they are very Green. Reading the Green chapter may help you with this. For my Introverted Orange-Green daughter, I had to know as much about dealing with a Green as I did about an Orange. Sorry about that, but it will make your life easier to understand both. One thing about Introverted Orange-Greens is that they are not usually influenced by their friends. They may not have a lot of close friends. Instead they are more influenced by their interesting view of the world and their own logic, in-the-moment. As they get older, they will get better at being sneaky and won't be too confrontational unless pushed into a fight. It's their silence that you might want to be wary of.

Remember, that they can be "Silent but Deadly" in that they can surprise you faster and seem to be sneakier than another color combination because they are quiet, freedom fighters who follow their own brand of independent logic. Love them but watch them like a hawk. Have fun with them but be ready for anything.

To help Introverted Orange-Greens make better decisions, you need to train them to override their Orange "let's do this" with a logical set of values, checks and balances, and non-negotiable boundaries that they can fall back on to influence their sense of what's stupid in-the-moment. They need to STOP in-the-moment and THINK about how this choice will affect their family and freedom and that it's stupid to do anything NOW that will negatively affect either in the future. Doing this one thing, and learning to follow up on what they know to be right, will help them do the right thing in-the-moment. As Introverts they will have an easier time taking a moment to silently consider their choice if they will learn to take that moment. The best way to teach an Introverted Orange-Green to use that moment is to balance teaching them this process (over and over again) with rewards when it works for them and immediate consequences when they fail to use the moment of consideration. Use the following steps and focus on using discussion questions focused on "thinking" processes.

How ORANGE Children and Teens Behave Badly...

Recognizing <u>ORANGE Stress Behaviors</u> helps parents understand that their child is experiencing stress.

When you see these types of misbehaviors, understand that your ORANGE is experiencing a lack of FREEDOM, some form of diminished REWARDS, or does not understand, or agree with, the BOUNDARIES you have for them.

- Extrovert Oranges become argumentative, domineering, demanding, somewhat bossy, and may be on the attack.

- Extrovert Oranges also become open and pushy about what they are going to do. For example, "I'm leaving and you can't do anything about it!" or "I'm going to run away!"

- Introvert Oranges become very sneaky – appears secretive; goes around the rules and does what they want but you don't realize it until it's way too late.

- Introvert Oranges WON'T say what they are going to do, they just do it usually on the sly, when you're not looking. They don't say they are going to run away, they just go to their room and start packing and then head out the door.

- All Oranges push others for quick decisions.

- Becomes overly dramatic in action or talk.

- Jumps from one activity to another.

- Procrastinates, may sleep in, put off doing what you've asked, especially if they don't see a reward.

- May talk loud, become rude, roll their eyes, say, "This is boring." or "This is stupid."

- Seems to not hear you, ignores you.

- Becomes careless about details, unfocused.

- Acts overly impulsive, takes risks.

- Becomes unpredictable.

- Jumps from one activity to the next.

- May lie or make up stories to cover their wrong choices.

- Acts defiantly as they look right at you.

- An Orange-Green may look at you as if to say, "You are just an idiot."

Why ORANGE'S Behave Badly...

Understanding <u>ORANGE Stressors</u> can help parents figure out WHY their ORANGE is experiencing stress and acting out.

ORANGE's experience stress when they perceive a lack of FREEDOM, missing REWARDS, or when they do not know, understand, or agree with the BOUNDARIES they've been given.

- Oranges usually act out because they are experiencing a "Freedom Threat" of some kind. A lack of freedom in any form is their biggest and most common stressor.

- Being forced into a ridged daily routine without any freedom to play, have fun, or control over the schedule.

- Personal restrictions, a lack of freedom to move, restrictive clothing, schedules, directions, or a lack of choices.

- Inability to do what they want when they want without an attractive alternative or reward.

- Unnecessary routines and waiting imposed by an outside source when they want to move, go, be, or stay.

- Lack of resources to do what they want to when they want to (money, time, friends, equipment, toys, etc.).

- Being bogged down with too many rules.

- Being told *how* to do something or *how* to work.

- Lots of details and detailed activities.

- Repetition or rehearsals.

- Activities that lack some sort of challenge, fun, freedom, or reward.

- Being forced to go at a slower pace.

- Slow decision making from parents, teachers, friends, or "the system."

- Inflexibility or the lack of options and choices.

- Being in a rule-bound world, classroom, home, or daycare.

- Long discussions of theory, concepts or philosophy, reading highly theoretical or technical books, instructions.

- Reading programs that make the student read specific stories and require a test before they can move on.

- Any repetitive homework, classwork, assignment, or project that seems like busywork and doesn't allow for any flexibility of choice or individualization.

- Rigid or nonflexible authoritarian behavior from parents, teachers, or friends.

- Rigid time lines; limited opportunity to move ahead.

- Feeling used or unappreciated with no rewards.

- Being forced into doing excessive paperwork, homework, or schoolwork on someone else's time frame.

- The lack of positive recognition of their strength and gifts.

- Rigidly enforced requirements or procedures; too much structure for its own sake.

- Having teachers "tattle" on them and get them in trouble at home without a chance to defend themselves.

- Being completely misunderstood, labeled, and judged to be something they don't think, or feel, they are.

- Getting consequences for something they didn't know was wrong.

Signs of LOW SELF-ESTEEM in ORANGES

- Chronic rudeness, defensiveness, disrespectful comments, actions, and gestures.

- Showing little respect for life, acting out in physically dangerous ways; being overtly hurtful, abusive, or neglectful.

- Acting on impulse in destructive ways with no regard for the feelings of others.

- Ignoring consequences, thinking that consequences don't apply to them, or thinking that something is only wrong if they get caught.

- Dismissing others' needs and their own worth. Justifying their actions with a "nobody cares anyway" attitude.

- Intentionally breaking the rules with very little regard for their own safety or the safety of others.

- Being defiant or sneaky in their efforts to get a thrill, do something risky, or break a rule.

- Lying or denying inappropriate actions or habits when it is clear to everyone else they are participating in such things.

- Use of alcohol, drugs, sex, and the internet to escape from their current situation.

- Overuse of video games to escape reality or hide from building and working on real, face-to-face relationships.

- Any addictive, repetitive habit or actions that undermines their cheerfulness and fun nature.

- Being humble and teachable one moment and then quickly denying their mistake or their need to change the next.

- Resigning or quitting, giving up on themselves, or giving up on activities or friends that used to be fun for them.

- Acting out in ways that are more than just a "dumb, spur of the moment" action. Participating in self-destructive, extremely risky or extremely scary behaviors.

- Verbal confrontations and physical aggressiveness.

Like it or not, low self-esteem usually stems from controlling and critical behavior from the parent. When kids or teens demonstrate these _extreme_ behaviors, immediately decrease negative criticism and any overly controlling behavior on your part (see pages 394 for Command and Control tactics). Increase your time listening and genuinely praising your child or teen for appropriate right choices.

At the same time, I am NOT suggesting that you become lax about appropriate discipline but pick your battles and address serious misbehaviors through choices and consequences never through Command and Control. Don't nit-pick about little annoyances that aren't really hurting anyone or anything. A messy room or mismatched clothes never hurt anyone - let it go and build your child's self-worth when these extreme behaviors are present. If your child or teen continues to demonstrate these behaviors seek additional help from a reputable family counselor or therapist.

Ways to Build SELF-ESTEEM in ORANGES

- Increase a **balance** of appropriate praise and rewards for good choices **with** discipline in the form of clear boundaries, choices, and consequences for acting out.

- Listen attentively, with your story on hold, when your child is upset. This is crucial!

- Eliminate ALL Command and Control tactics from your parenting efforts. (see page 394).

- Give them a chance to act as a leader at home, church, or while doing service for others.

- Give them jobs that they can succeed at, then reward their efforts.

- Recognize them for their prompt action whenever you ask them to do something or when they get to work on an assignment without being asked.

- Let them show off their physical skills, praise their progress, and how easy they make it look.

- Share their ideas, successes, and projects with others.

- Let them use their negotiation skills when appropriate.

- Recognize them for their contributions to the family, their ability to energize or calm others, their action-orientation, and ability to get things done even at the last minute.

- Let them know that you have faith in their ability to accept a challenge and to come out a winner.

- Validate their talents and their sense of humor through rewards and being their Cheerleader.

- Come to their defense when other's are being critical, questioning their ability or talents.

- Be their advocate when they need one, this communicates to them that they are of value and that you won't let them be misunderstood or misjudged.

Best To-Do's For Parents of ORANGE Kids

Parenting the ORANGE child needs to be focused on an artful balance of FREEDOM, REWARDS, and BOUNDARIES.

- Freedom is everything to an Orange. That's what makes them so simple to understand…and SEEM so hard to parent. Once you understand their absolute need for FREEDOM, you will have an easier time parenting your Orange.

- Do four things with your Orange and you've got it.

  1. Give them appropriate freedom when you can,

  2. Reward good choices with more appropriate freedoms,

  3. Take freedom away when they abuse it or make wrong choices, and

4. Teach them how to live within, accept, and even appreciate boundaries as a means to keep their freedom.

- You will get farther by rewarding good choices than punishing bad behavior. Do both but if you spend more time on rewarding good behavior you will get more good behavior. They will do anything for freedom, including be good. As they mature they will learn to do the right thing for the right reason, but while they are young help them get in the habit of doing what's right for freedom's sake and not suffer consequences.

- Oranges think that everything is open for negotiation, so don't be afraid to stand your ground. They need a boundary maker, not a best friend.

- Honor their need for freedom. It's all about the freedom for an Orange! If they are acting out, look for "freedom" clues (or the lack of freedom) for reasons behind their misbehavior or wrong choices. Ask yourself, "How is their freedom being threatened? How are they exercising their need for freedom even though I told them no?" When you start to think like an Orange, who needs freedom above all else, you will start to understand your Orange.

- Give them as many choices and as much freedom as is age appropriate but only one chance to do what's right. Remember, give them all the choices you want at one time, but ONE CHANCE. Too often parents of Oranges, especially Blues, try to coerce, beg, nag, or convince your Orange by giving them more than one chance.

- Here's an example of Choices… not chances: "Hey, Sarah, will you go put on your shoes so we can go to the movies?" Sarah's answer: "Okay, in a second." You: "No, honey, now. We need to go now. You have a choice, shoes on now and we leave, or we won't go. What's your decision?." Sarah's answer is silence so you think that she's getting her shoes while you're preoccupied getting keys and your purse or wallet. Three minutes later you check and Sarah is still playing with her toys. If you say, "Sarah, I asked you to get your shoes on. You're still playing. Come on, honey, let's go" you are now officially begging and giving another chance. Instead, as soon as you see her not getting her shoes on you need to say, "Oh Sarah, I see that you've decided to stay home. There will be no movie for you today." Then either stay home or arrange for everyone else to go without Sarah. If you give in you are only teaching your Orange not to make a good choice but how to play you when others are involved.

- When giving your Orange choices and they procrastinate do not try to convince them to do what's right by giving them chances. Do not back down no matter how many other children are involved, no matter how much your Orange says they are sorry or tries to negotiate. If you want them to learn to obey and make good choices you need to make sure that you either give immediate rewards or immediate consequences.

- The only exception is the need for a Freebie as explained in the "Boundaries" section.

- If you want obedience, use your word choices to your advantage when you talk to your Orange. Don't lecture. Use the "ten words or less" rule, and give choices.

- Understand that like it or not if you use "command and control" language and tactics your Orange will either obey out of fear of losing their freedom or they will rebel. Neither one is an effective outcome and neither outcome will teach your

Orange to grow into a balanced, successful Orange adult (see page 394 for Command and Control Tactics).

- Get to the point when you talk, discipline, or give boundaries. Don't repeat yourself. Instead ask, "Do you hear what I'm saying? I need you to say something or shake your head." Understand that the first time you repeat yourself or restate something you've just said you are lecturing and completely sucking your Orange's freedom and your effectiveness as a parent. Most parents lecture because they are not getting the feedback from their kids they want. Ask for that feedback as explained above.

- Use ten words or less, especially when sharing your feelings, values, rules, boundaries, or expectations. Be clear and succinct. Then give choices and only one chance.

- Keep things fun and moving when possible and explain it when you can't. This addresses their need for freedom when you can't give it or it's not appropriate.

- As you give boundaries you will have to set-up what things are "non-negotiable" like no hitting, no missing church except for illness, driving without a license, dating before a certain age, being disrespectful to you, teachers, or other authority figures.

- When your Orange does something wrong and you ask why and your Orange says, "I don't know" please understand that they really don't. Don't fight it. Instead ask, "What should you have done differently?" You'll get a much better answer. They are so in-the-moment that they really don't think, they just *do*. You have to teach them to "do" the thinking, or feeling (depending on their second color) before they *do* wrong.

- Understand that emotions may be very hard for Oranges to understand and describe, especially if they are second color Green. They generally act out their emotions instead of communicating them. Remember, they don't say, "I'm mad!," they say, "I want to hit something" or "I'm so outta here!" They use verbs to communicate their emotions more often than using "feeling" words.

- Consequences work best if they are administered quickly, with little talking, lots of action, and restrict freedom or rewards.

- Remember, they are all about the action and will get bored by always talking about things first. Set up some ground rules for whatever it is and then let them go.

- When making assignments for chores, jobs, projects, or activities stay focused on the end result and not on strict how to's. The how to's can be where you allow freedom within boundaries.

- Understand that Oranges are likely to procrastinate doing assignments or making commitments because they are keeping their options open and creating freedom where they see none. Teach them that truly successful Oranges get things done right away as a way of not only creating more freedom but as a way of guaranteeing it for later.

- Praise performance for DOING something, anything, appropriately, quickly, and efficiently. Don't just focus on end results until they are much older and more mature.

- Give concrete recognition for task <u>performance</u>, even if the whole job is not completed (especially for younger Oranges), for handling change appropriately, for thinking through the consequences of their choices, and for respecting boundaries, people, things, and rule. REWARDS teach Oranges far better than consequences. This is your best tool!

- As Oranges get older make SOME of the rewards more and more abstract and a little farther out in the future. This way they will learn to strive for things not only in the here-and-now, but also for things that only come to them in the future. As they get older create more and more intrinsic rewards which are rewards that are tied to "feeling" good about making good choices such as hugs and seeing mommy happy or the reward of more time to play games and more responsibility because they can be trusted. This teaches Oranges to get away from the need for instant gratification.

- Listen attentively when they are upset but respect their ability to get it out and move on. Don't belabor communication, negative feelings, regrets, explanations, or lectures…they've already MOVED ON. At the same time, if they go on and on about being hurt and you sense that enough is enough, help them to move on quickly by being kind but bold in your idea of what is really going on. Don't let them wallow.

- Provide lots of opportunity for action, service, and fun. Reward tasks that are completed immediately with bigger rewards, sending the message that fast is even better.

- Quickly reward the show of values such as integrity with choices (meaning making the right choices when no one is looking), being patient without reminding, kindness, unsolicited service and compassion, maturity, and thinking (or feeling) before doing.

- Prepare Extroverted Orange kids for down time or quiet time. Teach coping skills. Give them the opportunity for a little fun after school.

- Prepare Introverted Oranges for lots of interaction. Let them get the extra sleep they need. Let them nap after school but don't let them sleep too long. Teach them how to "power nap."

- Teach healthy acceptance and recognition of the feelings of others, especially of the Blues.

- Teach Oranges to understand that Gold friends can keep them out of doing something dumb and Green friends need information and time to think.

- When they are young use time-outs to reinforce boundaries but keep time-outs short. Disregard the "one minute of time-out for every year of the age of the child" rule. For Oranges it just doesn't work. Instead use a thirty second to one minute interruption of activity but <u>always</u>, in ten words or less, explain why their "action and freedom" was interrupted and give them their choice to change right away. Sometimes their buns only have to touch the chair and they are ready to make a better choice. Let them! It's the parents' hang up that children have to *suffer* through a long time-out.

- If an Orange can change immediately, then why not reinforce that? Oranges-Blues don't need you to make a strong logical link between their action and the consequence. Orange-Greens do. The trick with time-outs for younger Oranges and being grounded for pre-teens and teens is that they are IMMEDI-ATELY not able to do the fun, freedom thing because they crossed a boundary. In the future, they won't cross that line again. They may get right up to it, but they won't cross it again. Follow up on the right choices later with some sort of reward. With this "one-two" approach, you will have a mature, balanced Orange in no time.

- Be consistent, Be Consistent, Be CONSISTENT with your boundaries, rules, and consequences. If you give a short time-out for hitting, you need to do it EVERY time or the Orange child will see the time you don't as the signal that somehow hitting is negotiable at certain times.

- If your consequences don't work it's because you've not hit on the right consequence that is really a true freedom suck for YOUR Orange. Try another consequence but I'd warn them that there will be a new consequence for the same old behavior. If you get the right consequence (meaning that the price to pay outweighs the fun or freedom of the misbehavior) then you may never see the misbehavior again—especially if you've been consistent in the past with following through and they know you mean business.

- Now that you've been told to be consistent, you need to balance that with flexibility. Be willing to bend the rules when the situation warrants it or when the child out-grows a certain boundary...the trick is to communicate very clearly why the change is appropriate. This teaches the Orange child or teen that there are times for appropriate "negotiation" or change. Never waiver on values or principles, but change the rules when it's the right thing to do and ALWAYS explain the difference!

- Let them know what is expected of them and be concrete and detailed in what you want as an end result. Connect your expectations, or boundary keeping, to some reward. Stay focused on end results. Don't give a lot of detailed instruction for "how" they get there. That's where you can give more freedom.

- Here's an example of giving boundaries with end results and not a lot of how-to's, explain what a clean kitchen looks like but don't give them a list in a precise order of what to do when they work to get the kitchen clean. Give them a time frame with some wiggle room and back off. They will do it at the last minute but you will be amazed at how fast they are! When you give this much freedom, you have to give a more strict deadline but at some point they are more likely to respect it if you explain that to them. They want to have fun and be active – let them know they can keep having fun and be active as long as they keep making good choices and stay within the boundaries.

- Remember to include Orange pre-teens and teens in the rule making process. They will respect rules or boundaries they helped establish.

- Be prepared for what seems to be constant negotiations with your Orange. Because of their here-and-now flexible take on life, EVERYTHING is open for negotiation. Teens get to be great negotiators! If there is a loop-hole, depend on an Orange to find it. Don't get upset, just be ready for a "no-go" or a "non-negotiable" stance on things that really matter. Don't assume they know what those things are or that they don't need some reminding.

- Speaking of "non-negotiable" topics, understand that Oranges have a real disconnect between you sharing a value like compassion and seeing how to apply it in this moment from one situation to the next. They will need you to explain the connection over and over again. They are so in-the-moment that they don't see moments as connected to each other or to a vague value or principle until they mature and gain experience. Be patient with your Orange as they learn abstract values and principles and how to apply them.

- Beware the Introverted Orange who negotiates with you in their mind but forgets to let you in on the conversation! They are the ones who say, "Well, you said I could go." And you KNOW that you never said that at all. Stay calm. The first time this happens (or if it's not happened in a long, long time and a lot has changed) then you may want to reiterate the boundary and use a Freebie. If it's a recurring issue then they must suffer consequences right away, no second chances. Explain that they can have their freedom back as soon as they learn to communicate with you better in the future. Be clear that you will not accept their misunderstanding of you, again.

- One strong boundary that I would suggest you institute as soon as your toddler can open a door is that **they** are responsible for getting your permission to leave the house, leave you in a store, to make plans with friends, and other ways that they can *leave*... non-negotiable. The definition of "leaving" will change as they grow. Refine the "permission" boundary as needed and give a Freebie if the change arrives without you noticing the need to refine. Reward their asking with freedom. Consequence their lack of asking the first time and every time with a lack of freedom. This one simple thing can help you grow an Orange that you are not constantly sending out a search-and-rescue team to find.

- Teach your Oranges this one truth as early as you read them their first Dr. Seuss book: <u>Boundaries are your friend and bring you more freedom. Boundaries are not freedom sucks</u>.

- One very important reward to give is for telling the truth, for honesty. While your Orange is young and you are not likely to get misbehaviors that are life threatening, a reward would be that you give a lesser "sentence" or consequence for truth telling. But you have to really communicate that you are giving them a break for their honesty. That way they learn very quickly that honesty brings rewards and lying is a complete and utter freedom suck. This training will serve you well.

- You might want to take a look at the chapter that explains their second color. For your Orange, that will either be the Green chapter or the Blue chapter.

- If your Orange is second color Green, remember, that while they are first and foremost freedom fighters, respond best to rewards, and need clear and specific boundaries, they will also prefer information and logic as it pertains to their freedom or the loss of it.

- If your Orange is second color Blue, remember, while they are first and foremost freedom fighters, respond best to rewards, and need clear and specific boundaries, they will also prefer to use emotions and values as it pertains to their freedom or the lack of it.

- When your Orange experiences a freedom threat and is about to act out in ways that violate boundaries teach them to tap into their second color to STOP and think (Green) or to STOP and feel (Blue) what others might experience or suffer as a result of their inappropriate freedom-seeking choices.

- Enjoy your Orange's fun side and their sense of humor! Living life with a total slant toward freedom is a real kick and they will help you see the world from a new perspective.

- Most of all LOVE YOUR ORANGE. Be their advocate at school where they will be most misunderstood. Always let them know that they are AWESOME kids or teens from your perspective – the world will tell them otherwise. Don't let them believe it!

Best phrases to use with ORANGE Kids

"I've got to tell you something that might sound like I'm taking away your freedom, but I'm not, so will you hear me out?"

To serious Introverted Oranges… "I know that things are frustrating right now but let's name three things that went right."

"We're leaving in five minutes. If you choose not to be ready next time there will be no…"

"You have a choice. You can either … or …
What's your decision?"

"You always have a choice. You can always choose your attitude."

For issuing a consequence… "Since you chose to (state the wrong choice)… I'm going to (state the consequence in terms of what YOU are going to do, not what you will make them do). I know that next time you will make a better choice."

A Last Word about ORANGE Kids

Most of all, try to provide appropriate freedoms for your Orange. Use rewards as a positive teaching tool and don't see them as a manipulation tactic or as something you should be stingy with and only dole out on rare special occasions. The best reward is a hug or your encouragement. Think in terms of boundaries, not rules. Communicate every boundary in concrete, touchable, and real terms. Boundaries are a parent's best friend. Give boundaries to your Orange, don't hold back. Boundaries are your Orange's safety net. They will be calmer with them and crazy without them. Finally, talk with your Orange about flexibility, as in go with the flow, when they need to be better at it. Help them to grow out of their Orange selfishness by learning to think or feel with their second color.

Next, a very opinionated word about Oranges and ADD or ADHD (and I'm not even going to apologize!)...Remember that the Orange characteristics of being action-oriented, in-the-moment, and their "stubborn" flexibility are often perceived as signs that your Orange child or teen has ADD or ADHD. Be very wary of any educator, doctor, or other professional who comes at you with the suggestion that you get your child checked out for ADD or ADHD. Believe me, those professionals are very good at what they do but they don't know about Oranges. Period. Now you do! While the behaviors and list of symptoms for ADD/ADHD are real for a very small group of children, I would boldly suggest that an inappropriate, or overzealous diagnosis of ADD or ADHD, more often than not, is unfair, detrimental, and limiting to your Orange. It often becomes an excuse for bad behavior on the child's part, and an excuse for parents to not teach their Oranges how to embrace their unique characteristics while being required to harness their choices. Each Orange can be successfully guided by loving, firm parents on how to focus, minimize their distractions, and channel all that energy into more positive endeavors. The parenting skills needed to do just that are in this book and in other books I will be writing.

Above all, LOVE your Orange and be their advocate. You might be the only one! Be their cheerleader, boundary giver, and even, at times, their Fun Sucker. Most of all, learn to understand them and parent them with an Orange perspective in mind. Through it all, if you need more help I'm here for you! - Shannon ;-)

GREEN Kids

Information, Logic, Experiences

The Quick Answer To GREEN KIDS

Need INFORMATION
Desires lots of information, data, facts, details, and to know why. Needs consequences and the "big picture" to be explained BEFORE choices, if possible.

Value LOGIC
Information that makes sense. Prefer independence and autonomy. Respects logical communication, non-emotional problem solving.

Best Discipline Do EXPERIENCES
Learns best from personal experience and consequences. Must be allowed to suffer immediate consequences for wrong choices. Listens to respected authority.

The Simple Truth about GREEN KIDS

The Green child or teen values information and has an overwhelming desire to be competent above all else. They have a very difficult time with stupidity in any form. They experience stress when other people are stupid and illogical but have even a harder time when they, themselves, do something stupid. Following their own thoughts, problem-solving, and logic are very important to

Greens. They are very independent and creative and rarely want advice or help from others—especially, it would seem, from their parents. Doing everything the smart way is what makes Green kids and teens tick; at least, doing things the smart way according to their own logic.

They are intuitive problem solvers. They see everything around them in terms of logic-webs. They see things in terms of being logical or illogical. Stuff that makes sense to them and stuff that does not. Everything is either smart or stupid. It's really that simple to a Green. Things are logical, smart, and competent, or they don't make sense and are stupid. Greens use the word "stupid" to describe everything and everyone that doesn't make sense to them. To a Green, things are either cool, okay, or stupid. That's about the extent of their superlatives, or describing words.

Greens need information the way everyone else needs air. Green children and teens are easy to recognize as they are always asking, "Why?" They love to learn. They are big human data collectors. Data in, data out. They want to know everything including where you or they are going, why plans changed, what's the big deal about wearing a coat, and who said what. They even have questions, queries for information, hidden in statements such as "This is such a stupid assignment!" What they are really saying or asking is, "This assignment makes no sense to me, why do we have to do this?" Or it means, "What are we going to learn from this? I just can't see where this is going to make sense." Whenever a Green talks, they are either asking a question or implying a question. If you will start to see *all* their "questions" in both forms and provide as much information as possible, even if you know they won't like it, you will have a much easier time with your Green right away. They are truly all about information in any form.

A Green's ability to conceptualize the future is a gift to the rest of the world. The can see the future. They can see how to build it. They can mold it. These are our visionaries. They are our "big picture" thinkers, our logical problem solvers. At times Greens seem difficult to approach and somewhat distant but they are probably just thinking about something interesting to them. They even have to "think" their emotions. Green children and teens feel their emotions deeply and often have a hard time putting their feelings into words because even their emotions are tied up in their thoughts. If you ask them how they "feel" about something, they will have to think about it before they can give you an answer. Give them that time. Better yet, don't ask them, "How do you feel?" Ask, "What do you think?" You will get the "feeling" response that you were looking for in the first place, it will just be in terms of how they think they feel. You just need to ask about their feeling in a way that makes sense to a Green child or teen.

To really be able to understand the mind (and therefore the heart) of a Green child or teen you first and foremost need to understand the two overarching traits or characteristics that make up the Green. First, they are very focused on the future and the potential it carries. Second, they base all of their decisions, processing, and thinking on a logical set of sense-making parameters.

Let's talk about their future focus. This is their overarching approach to the world and it makes the Greens appear sort of aloof and distant. Green children can sometimes have a hard time staying focused on things or people in the here-and-now because they are always thinking about something in the future. They procrastinate doing things right now because they think they will get it done later—they have other important stuff to consider now. They also put things off because they don't think they know enough about it to do it "expertly" right now. They need more information, first. They *need* to focus on getting more information now so they can perform more expertly in the future. They can't do it now (whatever it is) because they see themselves doing it competently later. That's in the future, not the now. So they will gather more and more information now until they, not you, are satisfied that they can do it smartly. The interesting thing is that when they finally get to doing it, they are pretty dang good at it the first time. It's absolutely infuriating to a parent but it's true—especially when, as their parent, you know that they could have been fine trying it earlier. The problem comes when they want to gather information, and we know they need to just jump in and do their best. This is just one dilemma that parents of Greens face.

Green children and teens often suffer from "analysis paralysis", especially under stress. They are thinking so hard about something and trying to gather so much information about it that they lose track of time or don't think that they have enough information to proceed competently. This feeling then stops them dead in their tracks. Orange, Gold, and Blue parents have a real difficult time understanding this. Interestingly, Green parents, while they may understand it, may push their same color children to just jump in because they realize they wasted a lot of time as children or teens waiting until they could do things competently. These Green parents don't want to see their Green children make the same stupid mistake. Overall, Green children and teens need to be taught to do the best they can <u>in the time allowed</u> by every color parent. If all you teach your Green is that they need to do the best they can, without the "in the time allowed" they will continue to be frustrated (and be frustrating) with their "analysis paralysis" behaviors. Greens who learn to do the best they can in the time allowed are much happier and much less stressed throughout their whole life.

Greens will hold back with "analysis paralysis" behaviors while they study a new situation, are given an assignment that seems bigger than anything they've ever done before, are faced with uncomfortable social situations, or must deal with emotions. Instead of jumping in they want to think about it, process, gather intel, AND want to do it alone and on their terms. Green kids usually stay aloof when faced with these types of stressors until they have time to think through all the angles of what is going on and what's their smartest move.

Greens will want to leave their options open—not for a Freedom Fighter thing like an Orange, but for a "stupid move" escape plan. Greens can't stand to do something stupid, so when they are stressed by a new situation and given little time to process through it they will waffle or make choices that keep an escape route open to them. Think about your Green. How might they do this when faced with a new situation, dilemma, or problem? My Green would become quite the negotiator, which made him seem very Orange. He was second color Orange, but it was his Green "I can't look stupid so I have to leave an out" that was doing the negotiating. When he started a new sport he would always try to get details up front from us about options for quitting, leaving himself an out if he really bombed. As a Blue, I really felt bad for him and would try to leave him an out, but his father, my Green husband, would say, "No way, no out, he'll be fine." I bet that gives you an interesting look into our life about a decade ago. There are times I'm still trying to leave my twenty-something Green son an out. Now he just smiles and hugs me and does the brave thing in spite of my attempt at "out" giving. I really could have damaged him if not for my wise Green husband. Blue moms: beware of coddling your Greens kids!

For Green children work is play and play is work. Even in sports they play very "intellectual" games. They will study all the right moves, wait until they can be almost sure they can execute the actions perfectly, and only then will they physically engage in the game. Once they do physically enter the game, they are usually very good at what they do. However competently they perform, they will still pick apart their performance, only focusing on what they did that was less than perfect. Greens are perfectionists. They care a great deal about competency.

One of the most important things to understand about Green children and teens is that they are logical, intuitive "thinkers."

They gather information about the people and things around them by determining how those people or things make sense to them according to some logical structure. Now what that logical structure is based on is really the bigger concern here. If their logic is based on immaturity and selfishness, then their decisions and their sense-making structure will lead them to immature and selfish actions. On the other hand, if you teach them your family's values and expect them to do what's right, then their decisions and logic structure will lead them to the right things. If you come from a background that may have been void of worthy values there are several I might suggest, including honesty, integrity, compassion, gratitude, responsibility, accountability, and the value of selfless service and worthy work.

As you strive to teach your Greens to have these values as the basis to their logic, you will find that their intuitive, logical thought processes are usually right on target. If their logical framework is based on worthy truths and values, then their logical choices and assessments should not be dismissed or belittled by you or others who approach the world from another frame of reference. They are instinctually tuned into the "big picture" and how things logically connect. They explore alternatives, ideas, thoughts, and solutions in an effort to have everything fit into a logical order that makes sense to them. Hopefully that is grounded in everlasting values.

The biggest source of frustration for parents of Greens will most likely be when your Green is operating under their own logic and their logic does not match yours. At these times you are likely to find yourself arguing with your Green. When this happens you have two choices. Continue to argue or back off the argument and try another tactic. I suggest you back off and either listen first then present your point-of-view, or just go right into giving a choice while explaining the consequence for non-compliance. Wait a few seconds for their decision. Whatever you do, don't argue with your

Green child or teen. It gets too emotional too quickly and you won't win. It's not that you *can't* win; you can but at what cost? Nobody wins with conflict. You *won't* win that kind of power struggle. You need to be calm to build your parent-child relationship.

When your Green is unreasonable, stop trying to *make* your point. They don't care and don't hear it. That's what "unreasonable" means. You can't successfully reason with them. It's best to either do as I described above with choices and consequences if you need them to do something now, or do something very different and stop and hear them out. You don't have to agree with them, but if you take the time to understand them by listening you may get some new information or insight AND you get them to calm down. Once they calm down and think that you understand, they will be more reasonable, more likely to hear YOU out, and more likely to do what you need them to.

Greens rarely concern themselves with what others think of them, unless the Green child or teen has a great deal of respect for the other person. That's why sometimes they seem to not give a flying flip about what you might think or feel, especially if you often act overly emotional, illogical, or are highly controlling of your Green child or teen. They may humor you for years but they will very quickly have little respect for you.

You can tell they've lost respect for you if they do what you want them to do but you get a lot of arguing from them before they do it. If you see more and more arguing from them you can be sure that they are acting under some inaccurate assumptions about your competency as a parent. Nothing you say will change their perspective of you. You can only change their perspective of you by being a competent parent. They will see you as incompetent if you're acting overly emotional, illogical, or you've been consistently commanding to them.

Some parents reading that may say, "So what?! I'm the parent. Why do I give a flying flip what my Green thinks of me and my parenting?" I can understand that perspective, but what's the cost to you, your child, and your relationship? I'd answer your, "So what?" with another question, do you want to have eighteen years of escalating conflict, defiance, and eventually huge problems with your Green boy or girl as a teen or as a young adult? Then go ahead. Be stubborn and overly commanding or emotional and overly compliant and see where that gets you with your Green. I'd suggest that you take my suggestions and help your Greens grow into the amazing, funny, smart, cooperative, and creative teens and adults that will probably solve the problems of this world.

Now that you can see the logic in working with your Green, let's go on. During conflict, upset, or when your Green is arguing with you, if you refuse to hear them out time and time again when they are trying to tell you something they will first start to be argumentative, then they will eventually get to the point where they will constantly question or challenge what you say. Later they will come to the point where they will totally ignore you, or stare at you when you are talking and do completely the opposite behind your back. Eventually they will become out and out defiant, combative, even violent, and disobey your requests (or commands) right in front of you. They will seem completely out of control at this point. But here's a tough pill to swallow: you most likely created your own monster. This upsetting progression of negative behavior can be completely avoided by keeping your own emotions under control, refusing to argue with them, and by listening to your Green's point-of-view. You don't have to agree, just hear them out.

Here's how it works, Greens are all about <u>information</u> and arguing is not arguing to them. That's why they say, "I'm not arguing!" They don't think they are. They are just trying to provide you with information they deem really important and assume you don't already have. From their logical point-of-view, given the information they have at the present moment, they assume their logic is sound and that YOU are the one missing something. They try to supply their information to you by getting louder and talking faster, which seems like arguing to you. They are actually trying to do the right thing by providing that information to you from their point-of-view.

If you will really look back at what happened first, you will see that they didn't start out arguing. They started out just trying to tell you something. YOU, with your behavior, somehow sent the message that you were not interested in what they had to say; that what they had to say was irrelevant to you or that their perspective was stupid. I'm sure you don't *mean* to convey that message to your Green but that's what they hear when you refuse to listen to the information that they are so desperately trying to convey. This pattern can become a problem whether your Green is 3 or 13 or 23.

For Greens, this progression of negative behavior from mild arguing to defensiveness to being outright combative is not a control issue as many parents would assume. Instead it's all about the information. It may also be about their inability to quickly and accurately process their own feelings, frustration with being so misunderstood, possibly their (wrong) assumption that you think they are stupid, or they think you are stupid. You have to listen to them as soon as you can and as often as you can. Here's why...

Greens are such human computers (data in, data out) and they get overloaded. They think that they are being logical given the information they have right then. When they are upset and trying to tell you something, they are trying to get you the information they assume you don't have. But here's the rub, you have information they don't have and that's what you are fighting to tell them. So we have two people, one a child or teen and one a parent, both insisting that the other one listen first.

The Green child or teen will most likely change their perspective when they are given more information from you but you've got to get them to accept the new data by dumping the old first. The younger your Green is the harder it is for them to do a "data dump" of what they are trying to get out before they can accept "data in."

They just can't. You are the only one who can help them do a "data out" by listening to them first. If you can help them do the "data dump" by letting them get everything out through your listening to them, then they will calm down. Once they are calmer, they will listen to you and your information because they can. They now have empty RAM memory and can process the new data from you.

Another element that will lead to less conflict is understanding that Greens need to know that what they are being told comes from a reliable source. A reliable source to a Green is someone who, as explained earlier, is non-emotional, logical, who listens, and presents loads of information as often as possible. At the same time, you live in the real world and there is not always enough time to share everything you know with your Green. At times like these, the wise parent can say, "I can't give you all the information I have right now but I will as soon as I can. I need you to just trust me right now, and hop in the van. Will you do that?" You are providing the information that you can't provide the information, but that you will later. Then you <u>must</u> follow-through and when the moment settles down divulge everything you can, including why you couldn't give the information at the time.

It seems tiring at first but it's so worth it because doing this eliminates all the arguing, debating, and conflict. What's more tiring—conflict or a few words of preventative maintenance? If you will do this more consistently than engaging in a debate or in doing Command and Control (see page 394), then they will really trust you and go along with what you need because you have become a reliable source to them. The coolest result of this approach is that the earlier you start this the faster you help your Greens see you as a reliable source and as the BEST source of information in their lives. This means you end up with really fun, trustworthy Green teens who really don't do much to drive you crazy.

Another helpful phrase when trying to provide logic to your Green or share other information with them is, "I understand all that." (Referring to the data dump that you just facilitated through listening) "Here's a different perspective." Share with them what you need to say, calmly, succinctly, and with confidence (for the Blue mom). This phrase helped me with my Green. It got him ready to hear something I knew he would not really like. It was very PC (politically correct) of me to use this phrase (he tells me now that he's in his twenties). It made him open his mind to another point-of-view without being Command or Control. He conceded that providing another perspective often convinced him I was right because my perspective was logical. Using that phrase also gave him a way to change his mind without feeling stupid or defiant. Then I had one great, easygoing Green on my hands. It was heaven for this Blue-Orange mom who hated conflict!

A final thought to express about the Green child or teen, he most stressful thing for a Green is to feel stupid or have their thought processes questioned in any way. They have very little patience for things they see as "stupid" or illogical. Greens use the label "stupid" to refer to anything or anyone they see as illogical or not making sense to them. I'm sorry to say, they will even use the term to refer to people, including but not limited to people with little common sense, those who take unnecessary risks, people who become overly emotional (and to many Greens ANY show of emotion may be too much), or label people who boast of skills they can't follow up on.

Please don't misunderstand – Greens are <u>very</u> sympathetic with people who have a limited capacity for learning. What they can't handle is immature, controlling people who choose to do things that seem illogical. Now, using this label of "stupid" for people was not okay in our home. How I handled that (and you can and must do what seems right to you) was to explain that our Greens could use the word stupid as long as it didn't refer to people. As they (our Green-Orange boy and our Orange-Green girl) got older they could use the word to refer to people's choices, actions, and behaviors but never to refer to people themselves. It worked because I pointed out that they would not want anyone to say they were stupid, ever.

If they slipped I would give them a gentle reminder and they would recant their "stupid" people assessment and find another way to say what they were thinking. They take stupidity very seriously and will protect their ability to use the word "stupid" appropriately because it really sums up how they "feel" better than any other word. If you make using the word "stupid" the right way a privilege, they won't abuse it. It's uncanny but it's true. If you choose to make the word "stupid" taboo in your house for all your Greens, that's your right, but just realize that you are cutting off their ability to explain almost anything frustrating to them, especially when they are very young.

When it come to Greens and school there are some unique points for me to share with you. Greens love and hate school. Since Greens are future focused, information-gathering, logical thinkers they are highly interested in learning, the latest technology, and in how things work. They love and crave new information. Greens are often good students and are really good at science and technology classes. They are good at math if they have Green teachers. They are pretty good at taking multiple choice tests but essay questions will be much harder for them. They like creative projects and assignments that make sense. They hate illogical, artsy, feeling projects and strict deadlines. They have little patience for repetitive units or assignments and will prefer to move on as quickly as they learn a topic with little interest in reviewing it.

If they get bored they will switch from learning mode to creative problem-solving mode to figure out how to get out of the busy work. Case in point, in 3rd grade our Green son hated his math worksheets. He was a smart bugger and totally "got it." Bored with repetitive work he'd raise his hand and say, "Teacher, I don't get it." The teacher would come and do his work for him eventually completing almost all the problems on the worksheet. It backfired on him when I got a call from the teacher suggesting he needed Special Ed. It took a while for me to figure out what was really going on, but not until we went through all the Special Ed testing and he scored gifted. The question was, gifted at what? Pulling one over on his teacher, that's what! Those Greens crack me up! ;-)

Greens are generally rewarded in the school system in the United States for their intelligent thinking. On the other hand, they may be highly dissatisfied with being IN school because of the routine work, the rule-driven environment and because of the seemingly "stupid" things other people say and do. School is a mixed bag. Greens may be pretty good at being homeschooled but be sure you have the structure to do it. See the section in the appendix on homeschooling, especially if you are Blue mom. Greens are sometimes seen as "loners" at school especially Introverted Green-Golds. Introverted Green-Oranges are pretty good at school if they can tap into their second color Orange to see the "game" in things that don't make sense to them. Introverted Greens are highly independent and usually deep in thought and mostly aloof from the social aspect of school. Extroverted Greens tend to be more social but their dry sense of humor and tendency to be outspoken, in general, and about their smarts specifically, may get them in trouble.

The main thing to remember with Green children is their focus on the future, ability to sense the logical or illogical way things are connected, and that they rarely turn off their minds. Understand that Greens are very intuitive and are usually very sensible in their thinking. They are often very hard on themselves and struggle with self-esteem issues until they learn that time is not their enemy and they don't have to be perfect. They are constantly searching for more information. Teach them to balance their thought processes with feelings. Help them to understand the feelings of others and that it's "smart" to accept the emotions of friends and family members as real. Teach your Greens to do the best they can within time limits.

Be aware that Green girls and Green young women have it really tough in our society. They are not "allowed" to be logical, smart thinkers or techno-nerds. Let home be a safe haven for them to show their real selves and teach them skills for balancing the emotional girl stuff with being an "intuitive thinker."

Help your Greens identify, understand, and communicate their deep feelings. Give your Greens lots of information about everything and watch them develop into awesome, balanced, intellectual giants who will teach you loads!

A GREEN'S Greatest Need: Accurate INFORMATION

INFORMATION to a Green is life-giving; providing them with the data they need to make sense of their world and make logical decisions. This lowers their stress. When enough INFORMATION is provided to your Green, they are generally even-tempered and easy to get along with.

- Greens need INFORMATION the way the rest of us need air. Their need to continually process data that can make sense of the things around them, or the lack thereof, is woven through out every fiber of their being and is as unconscious to them as breathing.

- A Green child or teen assumes that the information they have is accurate and logical. This is why they seem so stubborn about what they think.

- You must hear them out when they are trying to tell you some-thing if you want them to calm down and listen to you. They are not being as stubborn as they seem, they are just highly in-vested in giving you their information and will be adamant about it. The more you don't listen, the more they will insist you hear them out. On the other hand, the faster you hear them out, the faster they will be open to new information you need to share with them.

- Give a Green the information (TELL THEM) you can't give them all the information they need at the present moment, so they understand they need to trust you and you will tell all you can as soon as you can.

- The kind of information that Greens appreciate are time tables and big picture end results when given an assignment or chore. They want details about who needs to go where and when and want to know why things are the way they are.

- If you need to change plans inform your Green of as many of the details as you can so they can change along with you. They will have questions. Let those questions lead you to the information they need to hear.

- If a Green is misbehaving or acting out in annoying ways or throwing a temper tantrum understand they are acting on faulty information. If you can get them to tell you what's upsetting them (and you really listen) they will mostly likely calm down. Then say, "I need to share some new information. Will you listen to me now?" When they say, "Yes," share what you need them to understand. Most Greens from 3 to 23 will calm down. Parents won't believe me when I talk about it being this easy until they try it. Then they are amazed.

- When you give a Green child or teen a job, assignment, or chore, give your Green an end result, big picture goal to keep in mind instead of a step-by-step, task list. The independent problem solver Green would rather creatively solve the "how-to's" for getting to the goal on their own.

- Greens can be very literal with information, so your end result, big pictures need to be exact—especially when it serves their purpose. A Shannon Story: when our Green-Orange son was about 11 or 12 I asked him to "do the dishes." When I came back a few hours later I was really disappointed to find that he only put the dishes in the dishwasher. He didn't hand wash the pots and pans. He didn't sweep the floor, clean out the sink, take out the garbage, or any of the other little details that makes the kitchen clean. When I got upset with him for not doing what I asked he said, "I did the dishes. That's what you said to do." He was right. I did say "do the dishes" even though what I meant was "clean the kitchen." He only got to use that once. After that, I realized how literal I needed to be with my "end results" descriptions.

- When assigning your Greens chores, they usually do better with the information of what "end results" things you want done and a time frame. If you can, let them decide on what seems like the logical order to do the tasks and the specific "how-to's" for each task.

- Greens will do better with a paper list of things to do than being used as a "go-fer" with just one assignment at a time going for "this and that" kind of Command and Control tactic. The list of seven things they need to do provides information and time to decide how they want to do it. The "go-fer" method provides no information and they may see some of the tasks as overlapping. They will get frustrated with what they perceive as illogical back-and-forth tasks and retracing their steps. Your Green will start to misbehave and may become defiant, argumentative, and unhelpful. You can solve the problem by giving them a list on paper instead of having them "go-fer" for you.

- Bottom line: If your Green is misbehaving and generally driving you crazy try the "information" angle. Think about what information might be missing from his or her point-of-view. Try to determine what they are thinking or what their perspective is by listening. Then calmly, logically provide alternative information that will help them understand what needs to happen.

A GREEN'S Strongest Value: LOGIC

Greens value LOGIC. They prefer LOGICAL information, communication, even LOGICAL feelings. They are always LOGICAL, its just that their logic may not match yours.

- Your Greens are naturally logical and really appreciate logical information, answers, and conversation from everyone around them.

- Part of the reason that logic is so important to your Green child or teen is because they are born with an instinctual need to be competent, smart, intelligent, and eventually wise. This competence thing, for a Green, and even second color Greens, runs so deep that the rest of us can't quite understand it. But understand it or not, being competent is a HUGE motivating factor for every Green from 3 to 93.

- With Greens, you can often get them to adopt better behaviors by teaching them that whatever is the "right" thing to do is also the *competent* thing to do. I helped all my Greens, from my Green husband to our Green son to our second color Green daughter change their attitude about accepting other's "dumb" feelings (especially mine) was the competent way to be a good husband or son. With my daughter, who generally "got me" better then the guys, this approach helped her logically put up with all the illogical (stupid, in her words) girl drama in high school. I shared with her that while I understood that it didn't make any sense to her as an Orange-Green, that to be a competent friend she could at least "act" kind and understanding in-the-moment. It wasn't too long and she was actually "feeling" kind and understanding—even though all the drama never did make any sense to her. Such is the life of a Green, even a second color Green. ;-)

- Teaching your Green competent behaviors in social situations seems like a "well duh" kind of thing to many parents, especially Blues and Golds who tend to have an instinct about social norms. But Greens, boys and girls, tend to be lost or even awkward, when it comes to acting right in social settings. Social settings and social norms are probably the most illogical thing your Green will ever face.

- Teach your Green as you can how to act with people (especially peers of the opposite sex) and adults in power positions (like teachers, bosses, etc.). Just the other day, I needed to share with my wonderful, talented, smart, and successful, but single 26-year-old Green son how to interpret the "girl hints" he encountered on a really encouraging and fun date. Greens are never too old for information on how to be socially competent. Whether or not they apply it communicates just how competent, or how stupid, they REALLY are.

- Since they are always thinking, seeking information, and problem solving, it's best to only ask your Green child or teen smart questions. Don't question their smarts if possible; it won't help you get through to them. Don't be afraid of your Green—they are the child and you are the adult. If you see they have mud on their shoes, don't ask them if they've been out in the mud. You will either get a smart-arty answer, or you will get a lie that they will suddenly adamantly defend and believe themselves. Instead say, "I see that you've been out in the mud in your nice school gym shoes. What do you think is the consequence for that choice?" Nine times out of ten, they'll already know the logical consequence AND secretly expect you to enforce it.

- If a Green lies to you, back up and see what stupid question you asked in the first place. I'm not excusing a lie, but the Greens really will back themselves in a corner with a really illogical lie when they are caught doing something stupid just to save their "competent" face, even at the risk of being stupid. I'm a Blue, so I don't really get this trait, but that doesn't make it any less true or real. Greens will come up with quite the lie when their smarts are questioned.

- To avoid this whole Green lying thing, don't ask a dumb question, just address the issue in a logical way. For example, in the middle of the night when you wake up to go to the bathroom you see a faint light coming from your Green's bedroom. She's still awake and you guessed it: she's reading. Most parents would say something like, "Are you really still up reading at 3:00 am?," when you can clearly see that they are. Because your Green thinks, "Duh," you will get some whopper of a lie/story that you can't believe she will possibly think you believe like, "Uh, well the tv (that you turned off at 11:30) was so loud that it kept me awake, so I was trying to get sleepy again by reading." You think, "Really? That's what you are going with?" You might launch into some form of arguing trying to get your Green to see how dumb that really sounds only to reap defensiveness from her. You can short circuit that whole scene by starting instead with, "I can see that you are still up reading at 3:00 in the morning and you know that's not okay. The logical consequence for that is I am going to take your book away now and you will not get it back for three days. You will also have to get up and do your chores at the regular time. Give me your book." Believe it or not, they will most likely hand it over for several different reasons. First, you stayed calm. Second, you assumed she was smart enough to know she should not have been up reading. You didn't ask an obviously dumb question. Third, you gave her the consequence without a lecture.

- In the end, when you are logical with your Green they will be logical and take the consequence without much ado. You might get the stink-eye, but you don't get much of an argument. The stink-eye you can handle. Arguments from an unreasonable and illogical Green who becomes way too invested in their version of the truth are no fun. They don't learn, they don't change, and you don't get what you need, either.

- Always assume that your Green is smart, even if they are being really immature and they think they are above YOUR stupid rules. Don't argue that your rules are not stupid, just enforce them. Following through is the best way to teach them mature logic.

- Understand that when things don't make sense to them and when things, people, situations, and rules "feel" stupid and illogical to them, they will experience great stress. This is when you are likely to see the Green child or teen version of what I call a Wookiee rage. Turn to page 90 in the Green adult chapter for more on Wookiee rages.

- Again, be logical and keep your emotions under control as a parent. Doing this is the best way to be a good example of someone to be listened to, respected, and honored.

- If you do get emotional, calm down, then go back and communicate in a calm, logical tone why you were really upset. If you stretch the truth about what you were really feeling, sugarcoat, or downplay your seemingly "irrational" behavior, words, or reactions, they will see right through it. Their "bull-honky-o-meter" will go off and they will, in their mind, dismiss you and your feelings. It's better to own up to your outbursts or emotional ups and downs. Here's an important point, if you can own up, they will too—a.k.a. less Green child Wookiee rages.

- Be ready for their logic to be totally illogical. It's a maturity thing. It's all based on the information they have at the time. What 3-year-old doesn't have faulty information based on the perspective of *being* a 3-year-old. So don't get upset with your 3-year-old, 7-year-old, or 15-year-old Green who's not much more logical than a 3-year-old, sometimes. When your Green is being illogical, follow the next bullet point.

- To undo a Wookiee rage, stay calm and use this trick: First, hear them out either in-the-moment, or after you've separated them to calm down and they come back calmer. Second, don't argue. You won't win, so don't try. You are the parent, though, so you do have leverage and information. Third, give them a choice saying "you can either experience an immediate consequence for your over the top fit/temper tantrum/rude behavior Wookiee rage, OR you can stay calm and listen to my alternative perspective. What's your decision?"

- Now, here's the cool thing—when you approach their Wookiee rage in this way, nine times out of ten they will be onboard to hear YOU out. They are very curious about the information you say you have that they don't have. That's what usually gets them. Once you get the chance to share that alternative point-of-view they will often change their logic based on the new information supplied by you.

- Here's a few hints for when you do share information with your Green. Keep it logical. Don't repeat yourself. Stop and ask if they understood you. (Most of the time when you repeat yourself it's because you are not getting the feedback from the child or teen that you've been heard. Don't repeat or lecture. Ask for the feedback you seek.) If you "feel" strongly about something, explain that. You can even explain that you can't explain it; you just "feel" it and that you need them to honor your "feeling" even if they don't understand feelings. Then I usually add something like, "Honoring my feelings is the smart way to be a competent son (daughter) even if they don't make sense to you."

- Don't expect your Green to naturally understand their own

feelings, you'll have to teach them how. The best way to do this, believe it or not, is to really listen to them when they are upset. Listening is the key. As you are listening put your story on hold and really tune into the information that your Green is trying to share. They help them express their feelings by identifying the emotions they can't. Then give them time to process that information. Only share your feelings, frustrations, and your story once they calm down. They won't listen to you until they are not so upset.

- Be logical with your communication, they will respect you more. If you can't be logical, communicate that. They can't really argue with how you feel about something. They may think your feelings are stupid. If they are disrespectful about your feelings, then it's time for a consequence. They will eventually learn to be respectful about your feelings. Then you can take it to the next level as discussed in the next two bullet points.

- Teach your Green that when they are disrespectful of your feelings, intuition, and wisdom, they are really communicating their incompetence and immaturity and the consequence is not being allowed to do things that require maturity. Teach that when they are respectful, they are communicating their maturity and will be more likely to win your approval for what they want to do.

- If you don't "feel" right about something your Green wants to do and your Green is respectful as you talk it over, be open to their perspective. Don't be afraid to trust them and their confidence that they can do something before you think it's "age-appropriate." Be open to compromise. But hold firm to your concerns if warranted, just communicate clearly that you know that your only evidence of "danger" is your feelings, then stand firm. See the next section for more on this. Greens are old souls and can do things competently much sooner than you may be ready for them to do it.

The BIG Discipline Strategy for GREENS:
LEARNING EXPERIENCES

*Green's are all about LEARNING EXPERIENCES,
either through consequences or through
trying new things when they are ready.*

- Greens learn best by personal experience and through consequences. Period.

- They won't learn to change their behavior with you telling them
  the virtues of doing something different. They won't buy it. They
  are too "scientific." They need proof, not just your word for it.
  Use the two-sided approach below to help your young Green
  gain experience and learn by experience that you *do* know
  what you are talking about.

  ⇒ ONE: Allow them to try new things when they ask or
  when they seem interested—even if you think they are
  too young. Don't undermine their courage and confidence by telling them they are "too young" to do something. If you can keep them relatively safe through the
  experience, let them do it. You will be astonished! They
  will succeed 99.9% of the time, even at a young age for
  the activity. This will build their self-esteem. This will
  also build their respect for you causing them to be more
  likely to heed your advice later on.

  ⇒ TWO: Greens must also be allowed to suffer consequences for wrong choices immediately. And suffer
  they will. If you are a Blue parent, so will you. If you
  don't let them learn by experience through consequences for wrong choices as a way to make a better
  choice the next time, all they learn is how to get away
  with wrong choices. They learn that consequences

don't really apply to them, they know better, or they can out-smart the outcomes. Then you have a very smart little psychopath on your hands and that's just messy!

- Don't lecture, argue, or try to convince your little Greens to do what's right. They will tune you out. The way to change your Green is to let them try things before their age says they should and issue and follow through on *logical* consequences for wrong, mean, disrespectful, and/or insensitive actions.

- A word here on logical consequences: the best consequences must be logically connected to the crime (at least in the mind of the Green) to really fit the bill as a learning and changing experience for a Green. It's mostly about how you communicate the consequence, provide the INFORMATION that what they did was wrong, and that what they are about to suffer are logically connected.

- Some examples of logical and illogical consequences. If your Green hits, take them out of arms length from hitting again, preferably someplace away from any fun. Don't make them say I'm sorry right away—that's not logical to them in-the-moment (because they aren't sorry); do that later. Certainly don't hit or spank them while you are yelling, "We don't hit people." If your Green rides their bicycle out of bounds, take the bike away. Don't make them do dishes for a week. If your Green gets argumentative, tell them you are done listening until they can calm down. Don't argue that you are not going to argue. If your Green is unkind about what you are serving for dinner, calmly excuse them from the table and inform them they will be not eating again until the next meal is served. Hope that gives you a few ideas. The consequence needs to be as opposite to what they want as possible. Ride a bike too far = no bike to ride. Opposites. Get argumentative to be heard = all hearing is cut off. Opposites. Hit when they are near others = time alone away from others. Opposites. Nasty about what's for dinner = they don't get to eat anything. Opposites.

The Difference Between GREEN Boys and GREEN Girls

The difference between a Green boy and a Green girl is more pronounced and more important to understand than gender differences in the other three colors. This section is unique to the Green child.

- Both Green boys and girls will play with toys in unusual, creative ways. They both like experimenting with cause-and-effect. Both Green girls and boys seem to like puzzles and games that include some strategy and they don't like to lose.

- Green girls tend to be a little more bossy about how their friends are supposed to play with them than Green boys are.

- Green boys like to build things from scratch. They like Legos, Lincoln Logs and Erector sets. They may use the directions to build specific models, but after the first original build, they will use their own imagination to create other things with the same building sets.

- Green girls like to build, too, but they will like to build villages out of craft supplies and dollhouses out of shoe boxes. After the building stage, however, they rarely "play house" or "dolls" with it but instead move the pieces around and go on to remodel the whole thing.

- Green girls also build collections. I mean, WHOLE collections of every pocket-sized Polly doll (if you let them) or every little pony, or every outfit for the national look-alike doll of the day. They do this because it's only logical to complete a set—you can't have something missing, that's just stupid! Green girls may catalog their collections but will rarely play with them and may not take very good care of them once they've moved on to a new collection obsession.

- Green girls may also like to "build" their outfit for the day and their choices on what pieces go with what may be very original and creative. You may be very opposed to their style choices, especially if you are a Gold mom with specific, "what's normal" dress code, or a Blue mom who is worried about what the other mothers will think. Either way (and I don't mean to be harsh), you need to let that selfishness on your part go and support your Green daughter's sense of style as long as it's not immodest, needs laundering, or inappropriate for the weather or occasion. If you are critical of her sense of style you will undermine her confidence and she is different enough as it is just being a Green girl. Don't give her more reasons to think that she can't be true to herself!

- Green boys may seem insensitive to others feelings and yet, especially when they are young, have very deep emotions, themselves. As they get into the pre-teen and teen years they will still feel their emotions deeply but will work very hard to cover them up and not share them. A Green 8- to 14-year-old boy will, at times, be very close to tears with frustration or hurt, then become angry for having such feelings. That's when the Wookiee rage appears. They can become physically violent and may throw things, hit, and punch holes in drywall. For more on Wookiee rages see pages 90 to 95.

- Green girls can be very nurturing and may play with very "girlie" toys. They like to play house and prefer to be the mom. They may exhibit what looks like Blue traits, but overall they really are ruled by logic, not feelings. A Green girl Wookiee rage is usually very emotional but not usually violent like a boy's. They may run out of a room, slam a door or drawer, or cry uncontrollably without being comforted.

- When upset with themselves, Green boys will tend to make

excuses, blame others or circumstances, and deny any wrong-doing with some sort of faulty, crazy logic that they will ada-mantly defend to the point of ridiculousness. When they realize that they really are wrong, they can go to the opposite extreme and will beat themselves up without mercy.

- Green girls will cave-in and think they are useless, stupid losers and may even wish they weren't alive. They tend to be unusu-ally self-loathing from the very start of an emotionally overload-ed situation or when they think they've done something stupid. Then some Green girls will do a 180° turn to the opposite and suddenly justify themselves in order to cope. It can surprise you!

- For both Green girls and boys, the behaviors described above are red flags that there is more going on than meets the eye. Don't get frustrated with their behavior. Calmly address any hurtful out of control behaviors with consequences and address any emotions with compassion. Strike a balance between un-derstanding and listening to feelings while absolutely and ada-mantly refusing to allow any inappropriate behaviors.

The Influence of a GREEN'S Second Color and Introvert or Extrovert on Their Behavior and Choices

Greens are future-focused logical thinkers who make decisions based on flexibility or on some sort of structure depending on their second color. A Green's Interaction Style influences how much of their thoughts and feelings they share with you and others.

Extroverted Green-Golds: These children and teens are usually warm, friendly, frank, and decisive. They are natural leaders and usually don't hold back from saying what they think. They are logical thinkers and tend to communicate a lot about logical rules, structure, ways to do things, and what they know better than you. They often try to communicate the "big picture" for themselves and others.

They are usually excellent project managers, even if the given project is how to put together a new set of Legos or their doll house. They are good at puzzles and games that require reasoning and intelligent objectivity. They are often good at giving logical, fact-based, structured speeches or talks but may not be very motivational. They tend to know what is going on and enjoy learning new things.

They often think they know a lot and may sometimes be more confident than their experience in an area warrants. They share their opinions readily and definitely do not have a natural gift for tactfulness. They have a very difficult time with their own emotions and will probably be insensitive to the feelings of others unless you teach them to be. Feelings are not logical and don't fit a natural structure that Green-Golds need and therefore are deemed stupid and not worth their time or effort.

They prefer lots of hands-on activities and will approach sports from a very technical, competent, logical angle. They will get stopped with "analysis paralysis" when they are stressed. To get them out of their "analysis paralysis," get them to tap into their second color Gold by helping them focus on a logical "to do" list, or some other form of structure that seems logical to them. They may prefer to create an outline, mind map, or other structured system before they attack the whole problem. By creating a little needed structure, they will get "moving" before you know it.

Introverted Green-Golds: These are "original thinkers" but they usually keep their ideas to themselves. They may be quiet, less-active dreamers or may be quiet go-getters depending on their level of personal interest in a topic or project. They definitely have an opinion and perspective but rarely will let you in on it, especially if it is about you or you don't directly ask them or seem interested.

They organize their life, their ideas, and their things with their own logic in mind and their logic most likely does not match yours. They are very structured and may exhibit, or Extrovert, this trait more than their logical thinking, although their logical thinking is paramount. They are very focused on their own ideas and needs and really don't care too much about the thoughts, opinions, or feelings of others and may appear to be the most self-centered of all the Greens.

They have a very difficult time with their own emotions and will probably be insensitive to the feelings of others unless you teach them to be. Feelings are not logical and they don't fit a natural structure that Green-Golds need and therefore are deemed stupid and not worth their time or effort.

In areas they are interested, they have a keen ability to organize and complete the job with little or no help from you or others because of their secondary focus on structure. However, if they are not really interested in the task or project their first color Green will become immobilized with "analysis paralysis." They will get stopped with "analysis paralysis" when they are stressed. To get them out of this "analysis paralysis" get them to tap into their second color Gold by helping them focus on a logical "to do" list, or some other form of structure that seems logical to them. They may prefer to create an outline, mind map, or other structured system before they attack the whole problem. By creating a little needed structure, they will get "moving" before you know it. They may often seem generally skeptical, critical, or stubborn but remember they are really just quiet, independent, determined, and don't rely on the thoughts of others.

Extroverted Green-Orange: These Greens are quick, smart, logical, and have a very dry sense of humor. They are always negotiating with you about something because they see everything as being open for debate. They tend to communicate more often than the other three types of Greens and will most often share their ideas, what they've just learned, or how stupid something (or someone) is. They are also resourceful problem solvers and will be constantly thinking about creating, changing, or building something.

They are truly good at many things but will seem afraid to try something new if they don't have the confidence to do it perfectly the first time. They tend to be alert and even outspoken at times. They don't have a natural flair for the social graces and may, at times, embarrass you. They may argue for fun on either side of an issue just to stir up a debate.

While they are resourceful in solving new and challenging problems, they may forget or ignore routine assignments. Because of their second color Orange and their Extroverted focus on things outside their body, they may skip from one interesting activity to another. They are experts at finding or creating a logical reason for getting or taking what they want, when they want it, and in this way they can appear very Orange.

They tend to be interested in very mechanical, techy things, toys, video games, and movies. They like to draw and are usually interested in fantasy books, games, movies, and characters. They prefer lots of hands-on activities and will approach sports from a very technical, competent, logical angle. They have a very difficult time with their own emotions and will probably be insensitive to the feelings of others unless you teach them to be. Feelings are not logical and they certainly do not provide much of the freedom that Green-Oranges need and therefore are deemed stupid and not worth their time or effort. They will get stopped with "analysis paralysis" when they are stressed. To help them out of their "analysis paralysis" get them to tap into their second color Orange by helping them focus on just the first "next action" to be accomplished instead of trying to attack the whole problem. One "next action" at a time will get them "moving" before you know it.

Introverted Green-Orange: These Greens are quiet, reserved, and usually impersonal but are keen observers, so seem to
be a little more tuned in to others around them. They still process
things internally because they are Introverts but part of what they
process will include observations of other things around them a little
more than the other three types of greens.

They have very deep feelings and are constantly thinking but
they will have a very difficult time as they think about their feelings.
When their feelings whoosh over them, they will not know how to
deal with them. They may be brooding and way too serious most of
the time, even as a second color Orange. The combined second
color Orange with the Introvert will appear more quiet, sneaky, and
independent. These are the Greens most likely to look you in the
eye as you tell them not to do something, give very little response
that they've heard you, and then go and do exactly what they think
is logical, smart, or best. They need to suffer logical consequences
right away.

They often enjoy science experiments, technical projects, and
problem solving. They are all about cause-and-effect relationships
and may play the cause-and-effect game with you. Don't get mad.
Be smart and rely on consequences to teach what's right. Don't rely
on logic lectures—they will only backfire. You won't be able to convince these quiet, logical thinking freedom fighters about anything.
When they do talk they will be logical to the point of hair-splitting
and may drive you crazy. Love their smarts and ideas; they will
have tons.

They may also surprise you and may be the most snuggly of
all the Greens. They probably want your approval if you stay smart,
calm, cool, and dish out the consequences when they know they
need them. Being a softy will not win you points; it's not smart and
they know it. They are usually interested in ideas, technical things

like video games (even girls), and fantasy. They will have little patience for birthday parties, small talk, and/or casual get-togethers.

They tend to have specific interests and need to be involved in activities where their interests can be grown and used. They will get stopped with "analysis paralysis" when they are stressed but may not communicate to you how stressed they are. You will need to be on the lookout for their stress behaviors and help them identify and even name their emotions at those times. To help them out of their "analysis paralysis" get them to tap into their second color Orange by helping them focus on just the first "next action" to be accomplished instead of trying to attack the whole problem. Just one "next action" at a time and they will get "moving" before you know it.

How GREEN Children and Teens Behave Badly...

Recognizing <u>GREEN Stress Behaviors</u> helps parents understand that their child is experiencing stress.

When you see these types of misbehaviors, understand that your GREEN is experiencing a lack of INFORMATION, they sense that something is ILLOGICAL, or they need to LEARN by their own EXPERIENCE either through practice or consequence and something is stopping them from this.

- Greens' most common stress behavior is becoming extremely uncompromising and stubborn. This comes in many forms: refuses to help, move, get dressed, stop playing the Wii, run a errand with you and a million other frustrating, "I'm not doing that stupid thing" kind of actions.

- Gets defensive, argumentative, and completely UN-reasonable, even at a young age like 3 or 4. I mean, like REALLY unreasonable! For being so logical, Green kids can be SO illogical! There is NO reasoning with them at this point. Been there, done that, got the t-shirt! (Remember, I'm a Blue in a sea of Green; so yeah, I feel your pain!)

- Says that things, rules, chores, and people are "stupid." Uses the word "stupid" as a substitute for expressing feelings of frustration, anger, and a lack of understanding or knowledge. Things that don't make sense are "stupid" to a Green. In families where the word "stupid" has been outlawed Greens will often stumble around unable to communicate their frustration without saying "stupid," and are thinking it anyway.
- Wants things a very specific way; picky.
- Becomes exacting, splits hairs, wants definitions and details but is not satisfied after you give them, and continues to argue.
- Tries to get what they want through intellectual debate, negotiations, and "one-up-ing" you; always seem to know better than you.
- Gives you that, "you're an idiot" look without saying a word.
- Becomes aloof, withdrawn, indifferent, has "checked-out."
- Experiences "analysis paralysis." May be slow to decide or act.
- Introverts may quietly refuse to act, appear lazy, un-focused.
- All Greens, but mostly Green girls, can be very emotional and even cry. They can shed tears of upset but will also cry with frustration or anger. Green girls tend to melt down and implode but can do the Wookiee rage, too. This is where they may suddenly be physical or violent—throwing, hitting, or destroying objects. However, I've never heard of a Green girl becoming overly violent with another person, all the Green girls I've come in contact with all have a very defined nurturing side and therefore don't have a tendency to lash out physically at people.
- All Greens but mostly boys, can do the Wookiee rage where they may become suddenly physical or violent, throwing, hitting, or destroying objects. However, I've rarely heard of a Green boy becoming overly violent with a person—and then it just about scared them to death and they felt terrible afterward. If a Green boy, after a Wookiee rage, doesn't eventually show,

or feel, true remorse you need to address that right away, either through tough consequences or with counseling if it happens a few times a week.

- A Green toddler or young child may bite, hit, or shove another child occasionally to communicate frustration and needs to have some immediate consequences to learn to handle their frustrations in a better way. A Green 2-year-old is not too young to be taught to not hit or bite.

- If you have a 7- or 8-years-old child or older who is continually acting violently towards people, you have a Green who needs counseling and some serious consequences. Either by being left without severe consequences or by example, they've learned that it is acceptable to be cruel and physically violent. This must be unlearned. Cruelty toward animals by Greens (or any other color) is unacceptable, as well.

- If you have a violent Green please seek professional help. Greens of all ages do have Wookiee rages but they are only occasional (once a month to once a year), they are rarely directed toward people, and followed by periods of true remorse and changed behavior.

Why GREENS Behave Badly...

*Understanding **GREEN Stressors** can help parents figure out WHY their GREEN is experiencing stress and acting out.*

GREENS experience stress when they lack INFORMATION, when people or things are ILLOGICAL to them, or when they are not allowed to LEARN by EXPERIENCE either from being denied the chance to try something new when they are ready, or when they are "saved" from "suffering" the consequences of their negative choices.

- A Green's main stressor is a lack of information one way or another.

- Information, or the lack thereof, comes in hundreds of forms.

Here are several examples:

1. When you go shopping but don't go to the stores in the order you told your Green you would but you don't share with them any information about the change or why the change... they wig.

2. They get mad at themselves for something *they think* is really stupid. You can see, on the other hand, that they just didn't understand how to do it - it's a lack of information.

3. Your Green throws their new trombone on the floor in frustration while practicing because they *don't know* how to play it right. Again, a lack of information.

4. Your Green toddler bites another child at preschool because the other child took your child's toy. They *don't know* why someone would do that and they *don't know* how to get it back, so out of frustration they bite.

- How do you know that it's (most likely) because of a lack of information that Greens do these upsetting things? Very simply. No matter what their age, (if they really are a Green) if you provide the information **they really** need, (not the information you think you want to supply) they don't do the upsetting things anymore. It's really true. I know it sounds too simple but it's true.

- A change in routine (for a Green-Gold) or a change in activity that is enjoyable (Green-Orange) causes great stress.

- Being told what to do without a "why" behind it.

- Being expected to make a quick decision, especially without hearing any details about their choices, situation, who's involved, and why.

- Being told to do things over and over that don't make sense or that don't come with a logical outcome.

- When others are overly emotional and they don't get enough information to understand why.

- Being expected to just trust someone or something without any reasoning or logic behind it.

- Personally doing something really stupid or illogical.

- When other people do or say things that don't make sense, when people are being stupid from your Green's perspective.

- When you don't parent the other children in a logical, "fair," correct way, meaning that the punishment fits the crime in both fact and severity. This is not a power thing like with a Gold child, this is a competency/respect thing for a Green. If they perceive you as being incompetent as a parent (i.e. being too emotional, giving unfair/unequal or illogical punishments, expecting a clean room when your own is a pigsty, changing your mind on what seems to be a whim) your Green will, at least in their mind if not through their words, deem you unfit to be obeyed. They will justify their own misbehavior by your "misbehavior." Don't blame me—I didn't make it up, I'm just sharing what Greens think and will act on whether or not we like it, see it, or agree with it.

- Illogical rules and restrictions of almost any shape or kind.

- Not being able to learn, or try, something new can be very upsetting to a Green, especially if they think they are ready to move on or give it a whirl.

- No time to think and process ANY new information, about ANY thing, change, new situation, people, assignment, chore, project, or emotion (to name just a few!).

- Lack of appreciation for competency or being smart.

- When their ideas, contributions, and competency is ignored.

- Almost anything emotional. Too much "touchy-feely" stuff. Other people being emotional. Worst of all, their own confusing illogical, ever-changing emotions!

- Having "feelings" **without** being able to 1) identify them, 2) categorize them, 3) deal with them in a calm, cool, competent manner, 4) talk about them, and 5) then shut them away. When any part of this very logical process is interrupted, missing, changed, or focused on, it usually brings on a Wookiee rage.

Signs of LOW SELF-ESTEEM in GREENS

- Extreme "Analysis Paralysis" mode about almost everything including what to wear, do, and say.

- Extreme aloofness and separation—or it's opposite extreme, know-it-all-ism.

- Refusal to get along, cooperate, or try something new.

- Sarcasm, especially towards people who have hurt or ignored them, thus contributing to lower self-esteem.

- Giving others and you the silent treatment as a way to inflict hurt when they've been hurt.

- Refusal to communicate, using this as a weapon to hurt back.

- Extreme perfectionism often ending in loads of self-criticism and self-loathing with a very unhealthy dose of complete and utter hopelessness.

- Unusual performance anxiety with extreme symptoms such as recurring stomach aches, crying, or even a highly controlled "teary-eyed" look of frustration from pre-teens and teens, anger that seems very misplaced and out of proportion for the situation.

- Very critical of others without any smidgen of even trying to be understanding.

- A complete shutting out of all information over several

weeks.

- Being very rigid and judgmental about almost everything as a pattern, not just a topic-by-topic annoyance.

- Becomes very withdrawn and immobilized as a pattern of behavior not just an issue-by-issue concern.

- Statements about being weird, odd, or not belonging (even to your family), and thoughts about not being around any-more or suicide are signs of extreme stress. For a Green this is not usually an emotional cry for attention. They don't usu-ally do that. If they are saying it, they are thinking it!. At the same time though, suicide probably seems like an illogical solution to them and they will be torn between their feelings of not belonging but thoughts of valuing life, including their own. That's why they are talking about it. To sort things out. Talking about it is good! Don't freak out. The feelings they are trying to convey are real and serious. Take it seriously but again, don't freak out. They will take that as an emo-tional, and therefore illogical, response from you to a prob-lem that needs solving. They will withdraw from you and the topic. Instead calmly, and right away, institute the changes in YOUR behaviors described in the next section, throughout this book, and in other materials available from "Parenting By Colors". If you do not see a positive change in your Green in a few days or a week, seek professional help right away.

- Generally acting confused, frustrated, angry, and spacey is not just normal Green kid angst but again, it's a pattern of withdrawal and negativism that increases over time. You will see an increase in the frequency, intensity, and duration of Wookiee rages.

- These are all signs of low self-esteem in a Green, but do not confuse them with the normal frustrations that Greens deal with on a daily basis. If you are not sure, just ask your Green when you can catch them in an "up" moment, "Do you like yourself?" A healthy Green child or teen will most likely say something positive, goofy, funny-sarcastic, or highly confident. An unhappy struggling Green will say something negative, self-loathing, or sarcastically arrogant and not nice.

Like it or not, low self-esteem usually stems from controlling and critical behavior from the parent. When kids or teens demonstrate these <u>extreme</u> behaviors, immediately decrease negative criticism and any overly controlling behavior on your part (see page 394 for Command and Control tactics). Increase your time listening and genuinely praising your child or teen for appropriate right choices.

At the same time I am NOT suggesting that you become lax about appropriate discipline but pick your battles and address serious misbehaviors through choices and consequences, never through Command and Control. Don't nit-pick about little annoyances that aren't really hurting anyone or anything. A messy room or mismatched clothes never hurt anyone - let it go and build your child's self-worth when these extreme behaviors are present. If your child or teen continues to demonstrate these behaviors seek additional help from a reputable family counselor or therapist.

Ways to Build SELF-ESTEEM in GREENS

- Increase a **balance** of appropriate praise and rewards for good choices **with** discipline in the form of clear information of what's expected, choices, and immediate consequences for acting out.

- Listen attentively, with your story on hold, when your child is upset. This is crucial!

- Eliminate ALL Command and Control tactics from your parenting efforts. (see page 394).

- Provide lots of information on what they are doing that's smart, useful, creative, and unique.

- Listen to their ideas. Don't criticize or argue how their ideas won't work.

- Play with them, be silly, enjoy their jokes. Hang with your Green teen and play Wii with them. Ask about their studies. Show interest—genuine interest.

- Offer positive and specific feedback when needed but abstain from criticism if at all possible while you work to build their confidence. Issue consequences when necessary in a very businesslike way, but cut out lectures, criticism, put-downs and arguments.

- Go back to understanding their 3 Words and follow the suggestions at the beginning of this chapter.

- Set up rewards for positive choices that mean something to them as a Green. Ask them what is meaningful to them.

- Make sure they get consequences when needed and that those consequences are logical and fit the crimes. For a Green, this builds their self-worth and proves your love and concern for them.

- Encourage them to pursue their dreams and develop their ideas and talents. If they like to draw, get them drawing supplies. Then listen to their explanations of their drawings. Be specific. If they like to build, get them Legos, Lincoln Logs, or even Styrofoam cups, popsicle sticks, and some glue. Then listen as they tell you about their projects.

- Give them age-appropriate problems they can solve, then support their workable ideas.

- Assign them interesting things to do that can help others.

- Invite them to spend time with you one-on-one playing a game or getting ice cream. Do something that gets you talking to each other. Ask what they've been thinking about lately. That usually does the trick with a Green. Then listen, no matter how silly, ridiculous, or outrageous it sounds. Only stop their ramblings if they are inappropriate, hurtful, or highly critical. Quickly redirect their train of thought but don't make a big deal about it. They will usually follow your direction because they just want to be heard and will tailor their talk to be appropriate—just to be listened to.

- Validate their ideas and solutions even if you do not agree with them by saying something like, "I can see that you've really thought about this and I appreciate that. At the same time (don't say "but") let's look at solutions that include your sister in a positive way." Or some such redirection.

- Definitely share your respect and appreciation for their intelligence, creativity, and problem solving abilities. When my son came up with some doozy of an idea, I found myself saying something like, "While I love that you are so creative, we really do need to look at this from a new perspective. One that includes (state the value you are trying to teach here) helping people instead of getting rid of them."

- The trick to building a Green's self-esteem is to appreciate their smarts while redirecting their somewhat darker, negative, or self-deprecating thoughts.

- There is a fine line with a Green's self-esteem that I've not seen in any other color and I've not run into much research on the topic. Here's my observations and my expert evaluation for what it's worth: Green kids and teens go back-and-forth between overconfidence and no confidence. I've come to observe that this is normal. Low self-esteem is an issue if they stay on the negative side of this line and are never over-confident.

    ⇒ <u>When your Green is annoyingly overconfident</u> teach them to be sensitive to others and that they can "brag" to you at home, anytime, but that to others their "bragging" will seem arrogant, unkind, and not the way to make and keep friends. Share this in an informational way and keep it light. You will have to revisit this topic several times as they grow. Be specific about the situation. You won't hurt their feelings. They are analytical about this sort of thing. Put it in terms that this is the smart way to be with people.

    ⇒ When they hit moments of normal Green self-pitying, listen. Don't placate them. They will see right through it. Help them reason through what is logical and positive about themselves and the situation. Follow the suggestions in this section.

- Green self-esteem is all wrapped up in their ability to be competent. Teach them how to be competent in all aspects of their life and you will grow a Green who is healthy, balanced, happy, and a joy to be around.

Best To-Do's For Parents of GREEN Kids

Parenting the GREEN child needs to focus on ALWAYS giving them as much INFORMATION as you possibly can. They value LOGIC. Let them have LEARNING EXERIENCES.

- Greens strive to be competent, even as toddlers. Understand this and always focus your teaching on how the skill or value relates to being competent in different settings, circumstances, or relationships and you've got their ticket!

- Recognize their creative problem solving ability. See their creativity even in their wrongdoing and you will see things from a new perspective. My Green son and second color Green daughter were always outsmarting me. I admire how clever they were about it. I look back now and I wish I'd lightened up a bit. Not compromised on what was right, just lightened up a bit.

- Remember, they have a hard time expressing feelings but they feel things very deeply. You will have to teach them what "feeling" words mean and how to match up a "feeling" word with the emotional sensations they are experiencing.

- They are extremely stressed by rushed decisions, a lack of information, and anything that seems "stupid" to them. Watch for their triggers and help them confront them and learn to handle them competently.

- They usually hold back when they are presented with new information, situations, or trying new things. Remember, they will most often want to hang back and observe, think, process, and then do.

- They may seem lazy, and often suffer from "analysis paralysis." If they will not carryout chores and assignments, see if there is anything stopping them, like a lack of information or resources or even the skill. If not, then issue logical consequences. Don't lecture, nag, cajole, or persuade. This will only teach them how to prolong not working.

- They do better with "flexible" deadlines and assignments rather than "command & control" orders. Give them freedom with HOW they do a task by giving "project constraints," "end results," and "milestones." For cleaning an area of their room, put tasks on index cards and put the index cards on a ring. If your Green is younger, put pictures on the cards; if they are older, have them create their own cards. Then when you ask them to clean their room have them use the cards their way, in their order. Apply this idea to all kinds of things. Greens want the big picture but the independence to do things the way that seems logical to them.

- If you are controlling, illogical, or over-emotional they will lose respect for you and eventually ignore you as much as they can get away with. Be as calm, logical, and as even-tempered as you can be with your Green. They will be the same with you. If they are crazy people at times, think about your own behavior. Model the way you want them to be. It's only logical.

- Greens need to learn by experience either through trying things when they think they are ready, even if they seem too young to you, and by suffering the consequences (and suffer, they will) of their wrong or inappropriate choices. They don't learn from lectures, getting off scott-free, second chances, or your wisdom (until they are much older).

- The Best Formula for Growing a Mature Green: 1) When they are just toddlers and young children provide them with the information of the outcome, good and bad, of their choices as often as you can *before* they make a choice. 2) After a good choice, provide information that connects the good choice to a good consequence or a good "feeling." After a wrong choice, hold your Greens accountable for the wrong choice with a consequence. Don't get upset. It's all about trial and error and Greens are scientists experimenting with trial and error. They *learn* by experimenting. It's actually very simple for a Green: good choices = good outcomes, bad choices = bad outcome, and bad outcome = BIG LEARNING. "Mom and Dad do know what they are talking about and I would be smarter to listen/obey them." So by the time they are pre-teens and teens they will have learned through experience that you really are a wise and worthy authority because you will have provided enough "evidence" to support that fact. Then you end up with Green teens and young adults who are not always challenging you, arguing with you, defying you, and doing their own thing following their own faulty logic. And they are happy! There will still be moments with your Green teen but there won't be near the issues that there could have been.

- A word about consequences, actually a very strong, tough-love sort of word about consequences: If you take away, minimize, undo, or leave out the consequences from a Green's wrong choice, (meaning you rescue them from a learning experience) you might as well strangle them, stunt their growth, hide them in a closet, and throw away the key for all the good you are doing. If you withhold consequences the only one you are making feel better is you. You are being selfish because *you* don't want the conflict, drama, or venom that a Green youngster can create when they have to suffer their consequence. Well, too bad—suck it up! You've got to be tough. Give them those consequences. No rescuing allowed. Hang in there and be the parent. Be tough, but not mean. Calmly, and without emotion, succinctly say, "Since you chose to _____, I'm going to_____. I know that next time you will make a better choice." Then do it and walk away. Later, you can share all the compassion in the world as they process. You can even have them "work" off part of their sentence but no freebies or they will think you don't really mean it in the first place. So listen up Blue moms of Green boys! This is especially true for you. It was for me. I hated giving my son consequences. I could always find a reason to lessen his sentence. But my very Green husband said, "Don't you dare!" I learned by sad experience that if you take away their consequences, you take away their ability to grow and learn. All they learn is how to play you. Greens get choices, sure, but only one chance. Then, it's time to hammer down with a logical or natural consequence. (There will be more about this in my second book.)

- On the other side of the coin, honor their smart choices. Reward them for doing what's right. This, too, serves as "evidence" in the Green mind that good choices = good outcomes, bad choices = bad outcome, and bad outcome = BIG LEARNING. "Mom and Dad do know what they are talking about and I would be smarter to listen/obey them," which leads to few troubles with Green teens. Yeah!

- Ask Greens smart questions. Don't question their smarts, if possible. If you do question their logic (and sometimes, it's questionable) don't argue; you'll only get drama, silence, or defensiveness and where does that get you? Nowhere, fast. Instead, ask them to explain their thinking to you. Don't attack with, "What were you thinking?" Instead say, "I don't understand your perspective, can you share with me what led you to this choice?" Then listen with an open mind. You'll probably be very surprised. I always was! Don't get the wrong idea; I am not implying a soft, warm fuzzy. I'm just saying that there is a good way and a bad way to approach a Green. The good way takes less time, conflict, and drama, and more learning, solutions, and good behavior.

- Don't lead a Green into a lie. Parents floor me with this! They do it all the time. Don't ask a Green if they did or did not do something when the evidence of the truth is all around you. You are just pushing them into a lie. Change two words. That's it. Two little words will take you from heated debate mode to time for a consequence with some teaching. Instead of, "Did you..." (the start of the debate) say, "I can see that..." (the issue of the consequence and the commencement of learning). Here's an example: instead of, "*Did you* carve your name in the hardwood floor here?" with the resulting lie, excuses, blame, and drama, say, "*I can see that* you carved your name in the hardwood floor. Since you chose to do this, I'm going to teach you how to repair it, and you will repair it to my satisfaction on Saturday instead of going to your friend's birthday party. Also, your craft tools will be taken away. I know that next time you will use tools for their intended purpose. Is there anything you want to say to me, respectfully?" Rarely do they have anything to say because Greens know that when you handle things this way you are right and they deserve a consequence—so they go along with it. You will think you have a different kid. They may even be looking forward to learning a new skill and spending time with you and what's wrong with that? Believe me, they will never use their tools, or your tools, in the wrong way again. They will be good as can be for days after a biggie like this. Those Greens are really interesting, counterintuitive kids!

- Understand that "feeling" stupid or "un-knowing"—meaning they are lacking some vital information or knowledge—is very stressful for a Green and will lead to acting out, fighting with you, and becoming rigid and stubborn. When you see these types of bad behavior, instead of dealing with the surface symptom (by trying to reason with them, convincing them of their inappropriate behavior, or bribing them to stop making a scene), try to address the underlying condition. Ask them what's bothering them. Focus on them rather than what you want. Say, "I can see that you are really upset. I would like to listen to what's going on with you if you will calm down and talk. Will you do that?" Depending on their age and ability to calm themselves, you will get one of a few different responses.

  ⇒ **Any age Green who can get themselves calmed down:** They calm down enough to tell you what's bugging them. You get the issue solved quickly without a lot of drama. Yeah! This is where you want to be and happens about 90% of the time but *only after you've trained them to respond this way.* I know, that's quite a catch but the battle is worth it. For ideas on how to get there read on and see which scenario applies to you.

⇒ **Very young Green who is not able to calm down and is still yelling, crying, flailing around:** Say, "I can see that you need some time alone to calm down." As you are taking them to their room at home say, "I will be out in the hall (living room, wherever). When you are ready to talk, come find me, and I will be ready to listen." If you are away from home, as you take them to the car (or the restroom of a store, backyard at a friends house, etc.) say, "I am going to let you sit on this chair (against this wall, on this stair, wherever) and I'm going to turn around and ignore you until you calm down. Then we can talk. Let me know when you are ready."

⇒ 80% of the time the above works and they sit there and calm down. The other 20% of the time they continue to flail around or come out of their room over and over again, or throw things in their room, or try to hit you. There are a number of scenarios and I can't address them all but here's my very successful, workable suggestion: keep your cool. You are untraining a circus lion. Keep putting them in their room, or putting them back on the stair, or sitting against the wall (not nose in, that's just mean and embarrassing) all the while repeating the words, "I will listen when you calm down."

⇒ I would NOT suggest that you try to hold them down with force. You'll have a trapped cat on your hands.

⇒ If they throw things then later they have to pick it up.

⇒ The trick for this last of the young Green 20% is that you've got to outlast them just once or twice and your Green will be "broken" of this pattern for a good period of time. It's worth that first struggle. It's worth the frustration and the time/freedom suck on you. You just have to outlast them once or twice and it will work. The upfront investment of you staying calm-but-determined for even an hour of upset will pay off in that you won't likely visit this type of fit again. I've never heard of it coming back a third or forth time. It's really true.

⇒ I did this with my 3-year-old Green at church. I was so embarrassed when he started to pitch a fit right in the worship service. (In our faith kids attend the worship service at church with the adults so they learn reverence fairly quickly.) I took him out to an empty classroom as far from the chapel as could get. I gently but firmly plopped his little fanny down on top of a table and said "I will listen when you calm down" and turned about 45 degrees so that I could still see him in case he decided to table dive but to him I looked like I turned my back. He kept reaching for me and I'd turn and not say a word and sit him back down about ten times. Twenty minutes later, I was about to lose it but with God's help I didn't. Finally his angry crying turned to a gentle sob and he said, "I weddy now" and he hugged me so fiercely I almost couldn't breath. I started to cry. We got the problem solved. He wanted the blue crayon, not the red one. All that over a crayon! But guess what? That was his last fit—like that—ever. No joke. I outlasted him and he learned by experience that kicking, screaming, and flailing would not work with me. Little did he know—it almost did! (P.S. There were other "fits" later on...Wookiee rages...but the same basic procedure works with those I've already covered.)

⇒ *Young Green child who's pitching a fit, starting to*

revert back to earlier days but has demonstrated an ability to calm down: Say, "I need you to calm down and then I will listen. Are you ready to be calm or do you need to go to your room for a minute to get yourself under control?" They will either calm down on the spot or will go to their room. When they come out be ready to live up to your commitment or set up a time that you can talk—later that same day if possible.

⇒ *Pre-teen or teen who is disrespectful and says that they don't want to calm down:* Say, "I understand you are upset. It's okay to be mad, but in our home, it is not okay to be disrespectful. I will listen if you will be respectful. If you will not be then I'm walking away. What's your decision?" The only time that I've heard of this not working right away with a Green pre-teen or teen is when it was the first time a parent tried this with their Green. At those times you absolutely need to stay calm. If you lose it then, to be honest, why should they respect you? You are not acting worthy of respect. If you can't keep it together and be respectful, then be mature enough to walk away.

⇒ If you can remain calm, you might need to go all the way back to the principles suggested for the "young child who can't calm themselves" and modify it based on the age of your pre-teen or teen. You can't successfully be physical with a pre-teen or teen but remember that while they are being disrespectful they are at least talking to you. That's a good thing. You want your Green to talk to you, but you have every right to have that talk be respectful. What I've counseled parents to do is to keep repeating that you will listen if they will talk respectfully. If they get momentarily mouthy again say, "Hey. Respectfully." as a caution. If they continue to be hurtful, rude, or out of control say, "I really want to hear you out but I refuse to be treated this way. This is not a competent (or smart) way to solve problems with people. Come back later and we will try again." Then walk away. Remember that the bigger picture here is teaching a Green how to fight fair by experiencing it. Don't be hurt or revengeful. Just remember that they are a little scientist groping through life having to learn by trial-and-error. It's a tough way to learn. Have a little compassion with that "tough love" act. It will get you a long way. Don't give up on your Padawan Learner... You're their only hope, Obi Wan Kenobi.

⇒ Ultimately, if your Green is being unreasonable, stubborn, and/or pitching a fit, remember to ASK them what's going on with them. Remember, most of the time they will calm down and tell you. They want to solve their problem, they just don't know how—thus the bad behavior. If ASKING doesn't work, you now have several alternative solutions that will work based on age and ability to calm down.

• Now back to Parenting To-do's... Don't argue with your Green—if you're not a Green you'll never win. I've covered this a lot in the beginning of this chapter. If your Green is arguing with you it's because they think you are missing something and they are desperately trying to inform you of what it is. There's only two ways to go here, 1. stop arguing with an unreasonable child, and 2. listen; hear them out, you might be surprised. If they are rude or disrespectful, you can give them the option to talk respectfully or the conversation is over! Personally, I'd go with listening. I learned a lot when I finally really listened to my Green. You decide what's best for your situation. Just a word of caution: if you always go with the "this conversation is over" thing, they will eventually stop talking to you. Wouldn't you, if you were them?

- When you discipline, teach your Green what's non-negotiable, give them their choice, and ONE chance. If they choose wrong issue a logical, connected consequence and let them suffer. Walk away if you must. Be supportive later.

- After they make a mistake, understand they need quiet time to think, process, and suffer consequences. Remember, they're beating themselves up badly enough; is your lecture really helping?

- Have fun with their "dry" sense of humor.

- Give concrete recognition for logical thinking, intelligent contributions, expertise, and finishing tasks that seem beyond their ability. At the same time, use random positive recognition about non-Green stuff, sparingly. Remember that Green kids and teens really don't care what you think a lot of the time and will tune you out if you go on and on, especially about stuff they don't see as that great. They will think you are patronizing them. Remember, when you praise them sincerely for non-Green things, be short, specific, and link it to being smart or competent.

- Be careful when Green children or teens are upset with themselves. Listen to their ranting and cautiously point out what they've done right but understand they will fight you on it. Try to present a logical case for your perspective. If your words are just fluff to calm them they will see right through it and you will lose their respect. Point out how good their life is and ask if you can do anything to help. Then let them think! Back away and let them simmer on your words for awhile. Check with them thirty minutes later and ask if they have any new thoughts.

- When your Green is upset with others, listen but give them a time limit of one to five minutes to vent their criticisms. Then ask them what they are going to do to fix the situation. Listen to their ideas. Don't comment too much on their ideas because they are mostly brainstorming and processing out loud (unless they are just outright inappropriate or hurtful). As they get older, ask for their permission before you comment on their ideas by saying something like, "Can I share with you an alternative perspective?," or "I'm concerned about one aspect of what you are suggesting, should I share that with you now or later?" I've never heard of a Green teen, or pre-teen, shutting out this kind of grown-up exchange when it's approached this way.

- When a Green is upset about their day, listen first, give a time frame for venting, then redirect their angst by asking them to tell you what went right with their day. Often they don't see the bright side. You must train your Greens to see it and be grateful.

- When their behavior is inappropriate teach them what's right. Give clear expectations and give them their independence in the form of choices. Be prepared for them to do whatever they want, especially Green-Oranges. Then be ready to allow, or create, consequences. Greens often must learn from their own choices, so you have to let them suffer the consequences. Be supportive but a tad aloof during their suffering.

- Green teens will especially test the waters of "free thinking" and may come to think your rules are stupid and that they are smarter. Let them have consequences. But let them help set up some of the rules, boundaries, consequences, and parameters for behavior, communication, curfews, and other such things that concern them. Let them prove to you that you can trust them.

- When your Green pre-teen or teen starts to negotiate with you about anything, turn the tables on them. They will come at you with questions like, "Why can't I go to a girl/boy party? I'm in 6th grade!" Most parents get sucked into their "you have to justify to me, the kid, why your rule is right" vortex. Don't let that happen! See it for what it is, a vortex—a never-ending black hole of Green kid logic. You can't win, so don't try. Instead, turn the tables. Say, "I'm the parent here. I don't need to justify *my* position. *You* need to tell my why you think you should go to that girl/boy, no adults around party as a 6th grader." Their response will either be silence, or ridiculous, or a really, really, REALLY good and wise answer that you can't do anything but see their point-of-view and give them a chance to prove themselves. Mostly though, it's silence and a quick, frustrated turn on their heels never to have the subject come up again. Life with a Green is a kick, if you know the secrets!

- If you will do the above with your Green pre-teens, you will end up with wise Green teens who have learned, by experience, that if they want to negotiate with you they better have a pretty logical, and persuasive argument, and that they better address the topic respectfully and as much like an adult as they can.

- For your Green you might want to take a look at the chapter that explains their second color. For your Greens, that will either be the Gold chapter or the Orange chapter. If they are second color Gold, remember that while they are first-and-foremost logical, strive to be competent, and need information, as a second color Gold they will also desire structure and consistency when it comes to organizing their logic. When your Green gets stuck with "analysis paralysis," teach them to tap into their Gold structure to get moving.

- If your Green is second color Orange remember that while they are first-and-foremost logical, strive to be competent, and need information, as a second color Orange they will also desire freedom when it comes to organizing their logic, life, and world. This secondary need for freedom just accentuates their stubborn independence at times.

- When your Green experiences "analysis paralysis" and gets stuck, teach them to tap into their second color to get moving again. Teach them to use their second color Gold structure to get organized and to list out their ideas, tasks, thoughts, or options. Teach them to use their second color Orange freedom fighter to get moving by just focusing on the "next action" instead of the whole mess of thoughts, tasks, options or details.

- Start as soon as you can, with your Green, to build relationships based on respect through listening and positive recognition for their competence and ideas.

- Most of all, enjoy your Greens. They are clever, funny, and see the world in a wonderful way! Be their advocate in all their different capacities. You may be the only one who really gets them. This will make you seem like the most competent parent in the world to them. You will win them over for life!

Best phrases to use with your GREEN Child

"I have to tell you something and you may not like it."

"I need to give you some information. Ready?"

"Plans have changed. Do you want to know how and why?"

"I don't know right now, but when I do I will tell you."

"In five minutes we are going to…"

A Last Word about GREEN Kids

Most of all, try to provide all the information you possibly can for your Green. Be logical and calm when teaching them and disciplining them. Remember, they don't do emotions graciously, ever (even as an adult), but their feelings are strong and run deep. You will definitely need to teach them how to deal with people appropriately.

Their second color and gender has a huge influence on how they see the world. When they puzzle you, reread this chapter and grow with them. Be their advocate, especially for Green girls who will always feel like an oddity unless you make them feel safe and accepted at home.

Learn to use information before choices and consequences after wrong choices to lead them in the right direction. Don't argue with them and don't let them suck you into the vortex of justifying your stand as a parent. Most of all, listen to their unique ideas, perspectives, dreams, and solutions to problems. Enjoy their sense of humor and be ready at every turn to be surprised by their logic, point-of-view, reactions, and independence. They are old souls in little bodies, so be gentle but firm.

The Quick Answer To BLUE KIDS

Need <u>RELATIONSHIPS</u>
Seeks out and works to create positive relationships. Needs approval and limited conflict. Desires deep connection to others.

Value <u>COMMUNICATION</u>
Responds best to clear, kind, calm communication. Desires lots of "warm fuzzies," hugs. Acts with honesty, openness, trust, and kindness.

Best Discipline Do <u>UNDERSTANDING</u>
Learns best through kind examples and calm requests. Discipline with kind, but firm "redirection" of misbehavior or wrong choices. Continually seeks to please.

The Simple Truth about BLUE KIDS

The Blue child values relationships above all else. Relationships between themselves and other people, between themselves and nature, animals, God and faith, teachers, even their homework. They seek positive connections to almost anything and everything. They see the world and everything in it in terms of relationships—how things interact, how people interact, how they interact with other things or people, how the world interacts with them and itself. Blues need, I mean really CRAVE, those relationships to be nurturing and positive. If any of the Blue child's varied relationships are negative, hurtful, ineffective (mostly for the Blue-Golds), or boring (mostly for the Blue-Oranges) it causes great stress. To understand a Blue, look at what they do and say in terms of "relationships." Look at their world in terms of interactions, influences, feelings, and affiliations. Everything in a Blue's world is either "connected" or "disconnected" in some form or another to something or someone.

First and foremost, parents of Blue children need to know that they are very focused on the future and the potential it carries. This is their overarching approach to the world and makes the Blues appear sort of dreamy or even "spacey." Blue children have a hard time staying focused on things or people in the here-and-now because they are always looking to future connections. They procrastinate doing things right now because they think they will get it done later, in the future, when the task is more connected to the deadline. "Why do it now when it's not due for awhile?" They are connecting the task to the future deadline and connecting their current action to the current moment. That feels more "right" than doing something now that can be done in the future, especially if it's not that fun (for a Blue-Orange) or aligned with their current agenda (for a Blue-Gold). If you want a Blue to do something now, connect it to the now, or how they can feel better about it in the future if it's done now.

Blues like their creature comforts and tend to be nest builders in the here-and-now. That is one way that Blues *seem* very focused on the current moment instead of the future. The truth is actually very future-based. A Blue will work to build their nest of creature comforts to prepare for a loss of comfort in the future and therefore, need everything now. For example, a Blue child who knows you are preparing or packing for vacation may be very adamant about taking everything with them. This can turn into a big battle with tons of tears and no logic in sight. They want every stuffed animal, soft jammies, cute pair of shoes, or every piece of baseball equipment they own. It will definitely seem over-the-top to you but to your Blue, they are just connecting all future possibilities to the things they imagine they need to be happy, comfy, and ready for fun (Blue-Orange), or ready to be comfortably organized and prepared (Blue-Gold) for anything. So you see, what seems to be a very in-the-moment course of action is actually related to future possibilities.

Blues are nest builders or comfort creatures about certain things and not other things based on uncomfortable experiences in their past. It's one way they cope with stress, loss, or a distressing situation. A Blue's action doesn't make sense unless you can connect it to the something or someone that created a "disconnect" for your Blue somewhere in the past. Your 10-year-old Blue boy may be stressed about living up to his perception of his friends' expectations on the ball team. His nervousness leads to several days worth of stomach upset which leads to what I call "stress-a-rhea." A bout of "stress-a-rhea" leads to an accidental mess in his underwear, that he hides because he's embarrassed to be a 10-year-old boy with this problem. So he packs every pair of tighty-whities he owns in a plastic grocery sack so no one can see in his bag. You happen to find them all in his bag and when you ask him about it he either denies it, act like he doesn't have a clue, or gets downright defensive with you asking why you are even looking in his bag. The issue is likely that he had a bout of "stress-a-rhea" earlier, didn't say anything, was totally embarrassed, and either had to stay with the soiled underwear or ditched them in the garbage and went commando without you ever knowing it.

Just in case you are wondering, "stress-a-rhea" can be common for Blue boys or girls who don't feel they can express their feelings openly and honestly. Sure, get them checked out by a doctor, but I bet the problem subsides when someone starts to really listen to the Blue child or teen. Just FYI, "My tummy's upset" is Blue code for "I'm upset and I either don't know why or what it's about, or I don't feel like I can talk to you about it." The simple cure, listen.

To further explain this Blue need for comfort in the future based on scares from their past, I know of one middle school Blue girl who let her friends talk her into wearing a specific kind of dress one day to school saying they all would, too. When she arrived at school that day it was a big joke and none of the other girls wore what they'd promised. She was mortified, made fun of all that day and for several days to come, and felt that life would end. Her Green mother tried to tell her this is what would happen but the Blue girl was adamant that her friends would never do that. So when she called home begging mom to bring her a change of clothes, the Green mom refused, which makes sense for a Green mom, but not what I would recommend for a Blue first offence.

After that, anytime there was a group-established dress code this Blue girl, even through to adulthood, always brought a "back-up" outfit and to this day often over packs out of fear she will be found lacking in the right clothes department.

It's not as crazy as it seems. It's actually a sign of Blue problem-solving and independence. They are trying to cover all the bases alone and by themselves. To alleviate this situation, help your Blues think through their needs but establish a limit for nest-building or creature comforts in terms of time, amount, space, and availability of other options if things become uncomfortable later. You probably guessed that I'm the girl in the story. My sweet husband helped me pack less for trips with his gentle and logical Green attitude of, "If we forget anything or need anything later, we can always go to Wal-Mart and get it." Is he cool or what? Now I can get a week's worth of outfits and stuff in one little overnight carry-on. And I'm certainly not crazy! (or at least not *too* crazy ;-)

Another interesting point about a Blue's future focus is that they are excellent at not only comprehending "big picture" ideals but at creating the "big picture" and communicating "big picture" concepts to others. Blues NEED to dream and dream big! This future focus helps them to see the positive and potential in things and people.

Blues are highly influenced by what is possible. They tend to see the best in other people and will be-friend the outcast or the underdog. They can be naïve and gullible so you need to teach them to be suave without losing their faith in people. A good rule is to teach Blues, even young Blues, that while it's fine to be kind to everyone, only pick close friends that help them do what's right and make them feel happy and good about themselves. Let them politely distance themselves from friends who make them feel fearful, doubtful about themselves, icky, or who make them second guess themselves.

This is very important. Don't force your tenderhearted Blue to stay friends with anyone they are uneasy about. Blues want to be friends with everyone so if your Blues are backing away from someone, don't stop them. Teach them how to do it gracefully. If you get nothing else from this chapter, it needs to be to trust your Blues' intuition and teach them to trust it, too. It will keep them safe and confident. If you undermine their faith in themselves and intuition, forcing them to be logical all the time, you might as well cripple them and their decision-making ability. Don't do it. Watch out for this if you are not a Blue. Green dads can be especially harsh with Blue boys. Gold and Orange moms can be especially tough on Blue girls. Be careful of these combinations.

The second most important thing to understand about Blue children and teens is that they are intuitive "feelers." They gather information about the people and things around them by determining how those people or things make them "feel." Their intuitive feelings are usually right on target and should not be dismissed or belittled by others who approach the world from another frame of reference. Blues in general are deeply concerned about the welfare and feelings of others. They are naturally empathetic and find them-

335

selves acting as the mediator between friends or family members who are in conflict. Blues want to please their parents, teachers, other adults, or friends they've come to care about. This can be a double-edged sword. At the same time, if a Blue child or teen senses the disapproval from those they care about it can be extremely stressful and may let it destroy their self-esteem if they don't have the right coping skills.

As discussed in the Blue adult chapter, think of a Blue's ability to pick up on the emotions of others like a sponge slurps up water and other messes. Let me explain it again, but this time with a Blue child in mind. Think about a sponge that is set in the middle of a puddle of water on the kitchen counter. What does it do? Without prodding or commanding it soaks up all the water as if by magic. Then what do we normally do with that saturated, heavy, bursting sponge? We wring it out. Now there is still some residual water left in it but it can go back to work and soak up more spills. If we let it sit for a time to "recharge" it will dry completely and is doubly efficient the next time it's needed. The dark side of sponges are if they are not wrung out they eventually become saturated and can't soak up anymore and make a mess. On the other hand if they are left to dry completely out in the dark without proper care, it gets musty and sours.

Blues children and teens are definitely like sponges. First of all, they soak up all the emotions, concerns, worries, and stress around them. They keep on soaking up these emotions until, like a sponge, they either get "wrung out" or become so saturated that they can't hold any more. Then they leak (cry or get snippy), burst (have a melt-down or lash out), or stop working altogether (become immobilized or depressed). Add to that soaked sponge an inability to wring themselves out because they don't know how due to their age, pile on a parent that gets upset and angry when the Blue child is saturated and/or emotional, acts powerless, or snippy, and that's too much emotion, too much mess for the Blue sponge to handle, so they breakdown, become immobilized, and eventually sour.

You need to help your Blue sponge learn to wring themselves out. Help them recognize the times when their sponge is saturated. They can easily tell that they are overloaded from emotional input when they are feeling negative feelings like being overwhelmed by a "people problem," feeling overly sad about something a friend did or said, wanting to cry, or when they actually have a meltdown.

Next, you can help wring them out by listening to their concerns, stories about their friends problems, or about what's worrying, upsetting, or frustrating them. Once they start talking about their feelings they will start to feel better. Point out to them that after sharing their feelings with you they feel better. Be very specific that talking to you (or another trusted "right person") about their feelings lead to feeling better... a.k.a. being "wrung out."

I can't stress enough that as a parent of a Blue child you need to approach your Blue from a very different perspective than you've probably read in some tough, hard-liner, parenting book. To change tactics for your Blue, you will find all the tips you need right here. First of all, understand that you can't, and won't, succeed with a Blue if you use a tough, "my way or the highway" punishment-focused parenting style. You will destroy their self-esteem and drive them away—if not physically, then definitely emotionally. They will fall on their face and into the wrong arms as soon as they leave the nest because they will look for love in all the wrong places.

Be firm, for sure. Stand for your values, absolutely. Don't tolerate a smart mouth. But most of all, be tenderhearted in your firmness. Talk, don't yell. Listen, don't lecture. Ere on the side that they were being really dingy and not purposefully disobedient. Validate their emotions while teaching them a better way to handle all those emotions. Teach values when they are young. They will get it earlier than the other three colors. Values will guide their decisions. Don't push them away physically or emotionally. Communicate your need to not be bothered, set limits on snuggle time, don't accommodate the "I can't do it—do it for me" thing (especially if you are an Orange parent and your clingy Blue is a complete freedom suck), but do it with tender communication and address how they can help you meet your needs. Blues love to be helpful and really like to meet the needs of others.

Blues of all ages want approval from you, even when it's not healthy. Being firm but tenderhearted with your Blue will mold them and redirect their behavior while maintaining a healthy, balanced relationship. If you do this you will have minimal problems with your Blue as they grow to maturity.

Blues are instinctually in tune with spiritual matters. They have a natural ability to be faithful. They are very driven by their values, ideals, sense of what feels right, and need for approval. If a Blue grows up with a firm foundation based on everlastingly true principles like honesty, compassion, gratitude, integrity (being willing to do what's right even when no one can see), responsibility, accountability, hard work, mercy, and love, they will be courageous, confident, and calm. If they grow up without such principles and ever changing values they will grow up fearful, doubting themselves, and stressed all the time.

Blues are good at understanding and applying values because they are intuitive and deeply care what others think and feel. At the same time, they can be too worried about what other's think if they are not firmly rooted to a value system they can depend on. Blues are naturally religious and want answers to the big questions. Questions like, "Who am I?," "Why am I here?," "What do I do?," and "Why do you, or do you not, love me?"

Blues are usually easygoing about things if they feel they are loved. While they are easygoing about some things, Blues are very certain and often opinionated about values and ideals, especially principles focused on "people" issues. They are often passionate about human matters, psychology, social issues, and other cultures. Blues are very concerned about societal matters such as racism, poverty, violence, and ethical questions. They want to do something about societal problems at a very young age. Blues want to make a difference and need to have their life mean something. They live to contribute to their family, team, social group, and community.

Part of the Blue's intuitive make-up may cause stress in emotionally-charged situations. Events such as funerals, the death of an animal, the illness of a loved one, finding out a friend is being abused or is going hungry can become overwhelming for a Blue, no matter their age. They truly feel what others feel. Remember, they're a sponge. When the issues are big, heavy-duty, and filled with emotion they may become very quiet and withdrawn or fight and become defensive. These behaviors should be seen as red flags indicating something is hurting them rather than a sign of misbehavior and disobedience. Blues are rarely (if ever) acting out for ornery motives like the Oranges or Greens may. Ere on the side that something's wrong rather than believing they are trying to make your life difficult. That's rarely the case with a Blue, no matter how much of a hardened criminal they seem to act like. They just don't have the heart to be that tough, mean, or ornery.

Blues are authentic and if a Blue lies they are under great stress. They have a very difficult time when others are dishonest and can intuitively feel when someone is dishing out the bologna. It bugs them when others are being untrue—and they tend to not do the same. Because Blues can be sort of dreamy they will often be so honest that they get themselves in trouble without thinking. Blue teens, if they think the solution to whatever dumb thing they've gotten themselves into is to lie, they will often do so, but so badly that you see right through it. They are so authentic that they often give themselves away and don't have a clue how you know. It's actually kind of funny. If you catch a blue in a lie, don't get mad but do call them on it. Explain, gently, that the truth is always better than a lie. Add in a little extra time, or discomfort to their consequence, but when they tell the truth, lessen the consequence to further solidify the lesson.

A final thought about Blues and their intuition: because Blues are intuitive about the world around them, they enjoy nature. The Blue child or teen usually wants to be outside, not for freedom's sake like the Orange child, but because they like being connected to the earth, sky, wind, and rain. They savor a beautiful sunrise and love the roar of the ocean or smell of the earth after a rainstorm. They are very nurturing and may be really drawn to animals. They are caring, naturally kind, and hurt when others are hurt.

Blues handle change very tentatively. It may be different for each blue child or teen, depending on their second color and environment. Blue-Oranges will handle change better than Blue-Golds because they have a bit of freedom fighter in them. Blue-Golds will strive for structure second only to their relationship needs. For more on this check out the section that explains more about their second color. Some change for Blues will be easy to accept, especially when it is a positive, people-focused change. However, change for the sake of change, especially if it hurts people or for the sake of meeting some procedure or rule, will really stress a Blue out!

Blues worry about what others think, even if they don't want to admit it. So when change occurs Blue children will respond in accordance with how safe their parents make them feel. If the change is communicated to be an adventure with lots of opportunity to grow and discover new things or people, and the Blue child/teen is reassured that they will not be deserted (that you, or someone else they feel safe with, will be near) then the Blue child/teen will embrace the change. On the other hand, if little is communicated or only fearful things are associated with the change and the Blue child/teen is afraid they will be left to handle it alone, they will not handle the change very well at all.

The main thing to remember with Blue children is their focus on the future, ability to sense the emotions of others, and that they order the world in terms of relationships. Understand that they are very intuitive and are usually right about what they sense from others.

They are often very hard on themselves and will struggle with self-esteem issues until they learn to not worry about what others think of them. They are naturally and constantly searching for approval from others, so teach them whose opinions are the only ones to worry about (such as their parents') until they reach a certain age or maturity level. As a Christian, I would definitely add God. They can also trust themselves, but not friends, trends, fashion, money, or worldly success. You get the idea. Pick wise ones. If you teach that principle when they are young you will avert a lot of misguided seeking for approval later as a teen. Blues are naturally idealistic. Have that be an advantage.

Bottom line, if your child, boy or girl, young toddler or grumpy teen, is a Blue, no matter how prickly they seem, remember they need tenderness and understanding and the skills to wring themselves out. They don't need yelling, harshness, command and control tactics, or over the top groundings, severe time-outs, the silent treatment, or tough boot camp consequences.

Blues need you to listen to them. They need a once-in-while start over (not to be confused with a series of second chances that don't help at all). They need forgiveness and cheerleading. They need approval and to be included. They definitely need boundaries if they are Blue-Orange or a plan and some structure if they are Blue-Gold. More than anything, they need you to have faith in them.

Teach them to balance kindness for others with preserving their own energy. This way you will teach your Blues that they can and should say "no" at times. Teaching your Blue worthy values will definitely help them know when to say "yes" and when to say "no."

Be aware that Blue boys and Blue young men have it really tough in our society. They are not "allowed" to be emotional or sensitive. Let home be a safe haven for them to show their real selves and teach them skills for balancing the "macho" guy stuff with being an "intuitive feeler."

Remind all Blue kids that their "intuitive feelings" about something is as valid as another's logic or rules. Show your Blue lots of love and they will open your world to the finer things that relationships can bring. Enjoy your warm, sensitive, often light-hearted, positive Blue!

A BLUE'S Greatest Need:
Positive RELATIONSHIPS

RELATIONSHIPS, for a Blue child or teen, is often their only focus, though they don't realize it. They are intuitive feelers, highly in tune to the emotions of others. Conflict in RELATIONSHIPS is their biggest stressor.

- Blues see everything in terms of how different things, people, events, feelings, and actions are connected or disconnected. It's all about relationships. Their relationship with you, their friends, brothers, sisters, the Earth, ocean, nature, animals, values, personal "mission," a higher purpose, and God.

- They are very focused on whether or not people are happy or not happy. If they sense that someone around them is not happy they tend to think it's because of something they've done or didn't do. They go into "fix-it" mode and try to do something to either make the other person happy or alleviate their own stress that comes from another's upset with no solution in sight.

- That's why (I think) Blue toddlers and small children get clingy and want you to do stuff for them. They sense your upset and mistakenly think if you do stuff for them it will soothe them and get your mind off what's bugging you. It probably worked a few times when they first started using that tactic when they were a 3-year-old, but at age six it backfires and makes you more irritated—creating a vicious cycle. They're acting like a baby, you get upset (or upset-er!), they cave-in or melt down and you get more frustrated and... ICK! What a mess!

- To break the "I want to be the baby" cycle, in a nutshell, when you have time (not on your way out the door) and NOT when they are begging for attention, explain that from now on you are not going to be babying them by brushing their teeth, putting away their clothes, carrying them—whatever the babying is— and that you will ignore them when they beg until they choose to act their age. Be gentle but firm in your tone with lots of encouragement that they can do it. During this preventative chat you could even set up some sort of gentle signal, say a look, or a phrase, that will let them know they are crossing into "BabyLand" and you are not going to stand for it. When they start begging for babying, give the look or the phrase and say, "I'm going to ignore your actions right now until you can be the grown up girl I know you are." Then walk away. As soon as they switch to "big girl/boy" mode, be very excited and complimentary. In other words, make a big deal of their choice and voila—you have the start of a better pattern. You may have to do this a few times to really solidify the pattern of acceptable behavior in their mind, but it will work!

- The above suggestion will work with Blues and not with the other colors for a few very uniquely Blue reasons. First of all, Blues really want to please you. The other colors don't really care about pleasing you past a certain age—sometimes never. When you gently let them know the best way to get your positive attention and the ways that will alienate you, they will comply—especially when they also get a double dose of encouragement for doing what's right. Second, Blues just want to be loved, happy, and have others feel the same positive stuff. If you keep things positive, you will train your Blue how to be even-tempered, independent, and self-reliant. If you are harsh, negative, yell, or demand, you will create a scared, co-dependent, wimp of a thing with no gumption. It's really up to you. It's all about the relationship.

- Set aside time to build your relationship with your Blue. Go on Daddy-Daughter Dates and Mom/Son Outings. Talk, joke, dream, and dream BIG. Do this when they are young and you will build a strong foundation for when things get tougher during the teen years.

- Blue teens *will* have a tough time. They probably need a book that's all about them. I'll work on that as soon as I can. Even the most loved and approved-of teen, with the best parent-child relationship, will have a rocky time learning to *appropriately* separate from their parents (without losing themselves or their values), without making a big mistake or two, and learning to lose a wrong friend or two or ten along the way. They will hit emotional times as well as spacey, dingy times. But here's a positive word, your Blue teen will have rocky times but they will scale those moments with grace and courage because you will continue to apply what you are learning here and in my next book. Love them unconditionally and communicate with them at every turn. You will come out of the teen years just fine and so will your Blue.

- All Blues are very sensitive to negative feelings. Remember the sponge concept. Somehow Blue sponges tend to hang on to negative emotions easier than to positive emotions. Even a very young Blue toddler will react adversely to the negative feelings they pick up on from a parent or sibling. They will experience stress and react to it themselves with crying, tension, irritability, or stomachaches. They want to be cuddled and will appear very clingy. Their clingy reaction is a cry for safety from the negative feelings that they are too young to understand and unable to fix. At those moments, they need security from you.

- To preserve your relationship during these filled-up-sponge times use communication skills to help your Blue "wring out." Ask them to talk about their feelings, be brave, and ask for what they need. When you listen to your Blue, don't interrupt or second guess them and don't jump to conclusions. Hear them all the way out. Listen with an open mind and heart. If you do this, especially as they get older, they will deal bravely and appropriately with their filled-up sponge and you will keep your relationship healthy and intact even during the toughest of times.

- Blue children and teens are very focused on how others feel and react to their actions, words, and choices. This can plague the mind of a Blue; especially if they live in a home where a parent or sibling is constantly on an emotional roller coaster with little or no communication about the emotionally charged situation. Blue children need to be loved and know that the people they live with love each other.

- Blue children and teens can handle conflict in relationships if it is talked about, resolved, and with good times in between the conflict.

- Blues are usually easygoing as long as their "relationship" needs are met. Remember, if you ask a Blue child at which fast -food restaurant they want to eat, they will often answer, "I don't care." They probably don't care as long as they are not stressed about something. What they DO care about is going WITH YOU or with specific friends. It's ALL about the relationships.

- If you focus on seeing all the "relationship" ties that influence a Blue, from a Blue's perspective, you will be amazed and maybe even a bit tired when you realize how plugged in they are to every person and feeling going on around them and throughout their little world.

- Blues will do amazingly wonderful, and amazingly dumb, things just to keep others happy and keep their relationships from falling into conflict. Go to the section on "Best To-Do's for Parenting Blues" for ideas on how to help your Blue learn to balance their own needs and feelings with the needs and feelings of others. You will find ideas for teaching them to be helpful and understanding but appropriately independent when it comes to relationships, feelings, and friends.

A BLUE'S Strongest Value: Authentic COMMUNICATION

A BLUE'S need for positive RELATIONSHIPS is always intertwined with their need for authentic COMMUNICATION. If you COMMUNICATE calmly and balance understanding with firmness, you can guide your BLUE and teach them to be balanced, independent, and courageous for years to come!

- Blues build relationships through communication. The two are interconnected. To a Blue, a lack of communication means no relationship.

- Blues are usually natural communicators whether they are Introverted or Extroverted. They want to tell you everything and anything that is going on with them, because relationships are built and strengthened through communication for a Blue.

- They will enjoy telling you about their dreams and fantasies. Don't get too upset if they share make-believe stories with you and think they are real. Parents really worry that their Blue is lying or living in a fantasy world. As your Blue grows from child to pre-teen, they will grow to differentiate between their fantasy stories that seem real to them and what is pretend. Many innocent 8- to 12-year-old Blues, mostly girls, still play teacher, house, or fashion show but realize they are pretending. Blue boys will tell tales of fighting off dragons and bad guys. When they are young they may tell you amazingly vivid stories and adamantly defend they ARE real. It's really not a problem; they are just having fun and being very creative. If you actually wrote down some of their stories you might have the next Harry Potter on your hands. Enjoy their stories. As they mature, gently help them learn to differentiate fantasy from reality.

- If you are an Introvert and not very talkative, your Blue will take that quiet and interpret it to mean distance, separation, dislike, and disapproval from you. Little and big Blues will think you are mad at them. If they seem particularly whiny, stressed, or clingy, talk to them and find out if they think you are mad at them. If they do, it's probably more that they misinterpreted your quietness as mad. Tell them you are just quiet and not mad at all and that you will tell them if something is wrong. Then you need to do just that. If you are upset, be gentle but specific and authentic and let them know what you need from them. They are people pleasers and will most likely try to do what you ask.

- At the same time, tell your Blue child or teen daily that you love them. Let them know that you approve of them without making them dependent on you for their self-esteem. In my next book you will learn how "Cheer Talk" is different from praise, and builds self-esteem. For now, give sincere compliments that don't depend on your positive judgments like, "You're so pretty!," or "That's a good boy." Use this format instead: "I'm so happy when you help me do the dishes because now I can have time to read you a book." Use the underlined words as the format. Doing this creates a self-esteem building compliment without making a Blue, who is constantly seeking approval from you, dependent on your good opinion. I explain this in great detail in my next book. Make it a point to give them one real heartfelt compliment at least every few days.

- Non-verbal communication is very important to a Blue. They naturally pick up on the nuances of a look, hand gesture, sign, and tone of voice. First of all, do your best to be authentic. In other words, make your tone of voice and your words match. For example, don't say, "NO! I'm NOT MAD!" Yelling the words "I'm NOT MAD!" is not authentic. Yelling is a negative expression and even if you really aren't mad, the Blue is still going to absorb that negativity—and still feel as though you are mad. Ultimately, the words don't match the tone. When words and tones don't match it causes a Blue to be confused and act out.

- One very important nonverbal for a Blue is a smile. Especially if you are more of an Introvert, smile often at your Blue. This will communicate approval and closeness without a lot of talking.

- If your younger Blue is being a baby, constantly following you around, talking at you, or just generally being annoying and underfoot they are seeking approval and attention. If you can, stop what you are doing and don't discipline the annoying behavior. Ignore it if possible and give them some appropriate attention. Read a book or take a five minute snuggle break. The dishes can wait, the bills can be taken care of in five minutes. Pay a little attention to your Blue youngster. A little bit every day will keep the Blue "Attention Monster" away!

- If your Blue Attention Monster soaks up your attention and they don't want it to end when you try the above suggestion, you have some repairing to do. What their annoying attention grabbing behavior is telling you is they feel insecure in their relationship with you. They need your approval. They are starving. When you first start this, you do need to end the attention session (book reading time) so you can balance your life and get other things done while understanding you have some serious changes to make. You need to build into your schedule or into your day some time for your Blue and you. As you do this you will see that the baby-like annoying attention grabbing behaviors will lesson and be replaced with independence and confidence. You can, and must, make the difference or you will end up with a Blue teen, girl or boy, who is looking for attention in all of the wrong places.

- Give your Blue the safety and freedom to communicate openly and freely with you when they need to. If their timing is bad, communicate that and set a better time to talk. This is especially important for Blue boys and all Blue teens. Younger Blue girls are more likely to just talk at you, even if the timing is wrong but Blue boys, Blue teens with a "they don't care about me anyway" attitude, and Blue Introverts won't force their talk on you, especially if they have felt pushed away before or for a long time.

- Blues will most often be tactful in their communication but not always forthcoming if they are afraid of the reaction they might get from you and others.

- They may also be annoyingly timid and beat around the bush when you just wish they would spit it out. Don't get frustrated. Keep your cool. If you push or blow up they will back even further away or completely lash out. Instead of saying, "Will you just SPIT IT OUT!" gently and quietly say, "Honey, I really want to hear what you have to say, but I need you to get to the point." Or you could say, "You seem to be worrying about what you want to say. You are safe with me, I won't get mad. I'm listening." Either firm but gentle response will promote communication.

- If your young Blue wants to communicate through timid whispering (which can be so annoying), remember they are embarrassed or scared or something. At the same time, *you* need them to just spit it out. Be patient but firm. Gently say, "I want to hear what you want to say but I will not tolerate whispering. If it's private, tell me so, but say it in a regular voice." This way you teach them to be assertive *and* polite.

- If you are upset with your Blue you need to communicate that to them. But you need to be calm in your communication. Yelling does not help a Blue change their behavior. It only makes them sacred and... dumber? They will do dumber things trying to not make you madder. It's like throwing gasoline on a fire. If you yell at them for spilling some milk, they will suddenly get dumber and clumsier and turn around and accidentally knock over something bigger and messier causing more upset. It's a vicious cycle.

- Blues can be ditzy and clumsy so when they do things like spill the milk just smile and hand them the paper towel. It's that simple. Don't get mad. You'll just make the problem worse. They will clean it up without a problem as long as you can handle it with perspective and calm. This gentle way of teaching your Blue communicates loads! It lets them fix the problem and builds their confidence. It communicates your approval even when making a mistake. That's important for later when your Blues are teens and do dumb things. If they know you will love them anyway they will turn to you in a crisis. If they learn you cannot be trusted to communicate approval, they will run to someone else when they suspect you will be upset or disapproving of them.

- Don't be afraid to communication your frustration. Just do it calmly and without blame, lecture, or negative judgments. Be matter of fact. Tell them what you need and they will try to please you. Unlike a Green, they will try right way and may need several tries to get it right. Don't settle for less than what you know to be their best; but don't criticize failures. Be encouraging while holding true to your expectations.

- Be very careful how you word criticism. Blues want to improve, and please, but need encouragement or they will easily give up. Let's say you are teaching your Blue boy or girl to catch a baseball and they keep missing it. Sometimes it's because they are just not concentrating and sometimes it's because Blues are not always natural athletes but they want to be. Instead of yelling, "Hey! You're not concentrating. Pay attention!," be gentle but firm and say, "I know you want to do this **so** (not "but") you need to keep your eyes on the ball. That will help you concentrate on where it's going so you can catch it better." Can you see how the second response firmly teaches what needs to be done but takes into account their willingness and is more positive? Don't sugarcoat things for your Blue—just soften the blow.

- The most important thing to remember about Blues and communication is that if you cut off communication, are stingy with it, inauthentic (like saying, "NO! I AM NOT UPSET!), and/or trying to not tell them everything, they can sense that something is up anyway. They will assume the worst and make up the rest and imagine stuff way worse than it probably is. So just spit it out. Your Blue is tougher than you think. They may be emotional, but they can handle stuff with positive-ness if you teach them how!

The BIG Discipline Strategy for BLUES:
Be Firm but UNDERSTANDING

*BLUE children and teens need to feel UNDERSTANDING
from you. They need to know that you love them
Unconditionally, even when they are acting badly.
They need you to set boundaries or expectations for them
depending on their second color, but need you to be
gentle in your discipline with them so they have the courage
to change without the fear of losing your approval.*

- Blue kids are generally pretty good kids. What they do wrong is not usually "naughty" but more annoying and overly emotional. Teens will not usually be disrespectful or disobedient, but instead be forgetful, undependable, change their mind a lot, be wishy-washy, and procrastinate.

- If you do have a mouthy Blue teen, then they've learned they can get away with it—probably because you've not called them on it. If you do have a Blue teen that is habitually acting out, there is a deeper meaning to their misbehavior. Look for approval clues. They are likely seeking approval from their friends and doing dumb things. A heartfelt, gentle talk with you doing a lot of listening can do more to turn them around than all the yelling or groundings in the world. Blue teens, especially Blue teen girls, just want to be loved, understood, and accepted and will do really dumb things to win approval.

- Blues are not really disobedient because they really do want to please you and that means they will do what's right for you. But they will mess up if they are unclear about what they think you think is the right thing to do. Remember, they are Blues, not Golds, so they are not concerned about doing what's right for the sake of doing what's right—they are concerned about doing what they think YOU think is right to please you. There's a big difference there. They will be very stressed and highly conflicted if they don't know what YOU want them to do. In other words, they will do what they think you think is the right thing so that you won't be mad. Be plain with your Blue about what you want and what you think is right.

- Blues don't see absolutes, don't *feel* in terms of right and wrong, black and white. They *feel* in terms of what they feel you want from them. If you tell them to speak up one day, but the next day you say, be quiet, they will be completely over-whelmed and immobilized not knowing when they should speak up or shut up. Out of fear of disappointing you they will get all befuddled and do the wrong one at the wrong time until they get older and figure out the nuances and details of what you really mean. I know, if you are not a Blue, it's really tough to get your head around how complicated a Blue child or teen is. But the solution is simple. Keep their 3 Words in mind as you parent them: Relationships, communication and understanding.

- The biggest way to show you understand your Blue is to be sensitive to their emotions, worries, and concerns for others. Remember, they feel deeply what others are experiencing even if *you* don't sense any underlying emotional tension or conflict. If they come to you with worries or concerns, listen intently to their perspective and don't dismiss their feelings just because you don't see it. Help them "wring out" their sponge. Help them appropriately decide to let it go or help out with the problem. Even at a young age you must help your Blue learn they are not responsible for fixing everyone's feelings.

- Listen to their dreams, ideas, and opinions. They just want you to understand who they really are. It's about being authentic and loved. As they feel more understood and close to you, they will be more and more devoted to doing whatever you need from them. They are gentle spir-its.

- Pay attention to them when they are being good and you

will get more good. It's so easy to ignore a good Blue until they are annoying. Then you get after them for being clingy, but you've given them attention, and even if it's negative attention *it is* attention, so what do you think they will do to get you to notice them later? The good things you ignore or the annoying, whiney, clingy behaviors that you get after them about? Blues are funny about attention, they will repeat whatever gets them noticed. You decide what gets noticed.

- Teach Blues to seek attention appropriately. Even when they are very young kindly discuss any obnoxious attention-seeking behavior and give gentle but firm consequences for it. Heap on the positive recognition for mature behaviors. You will train your Blue very quickly to not be attention-grabbing.

- Understand that meanness and fighting are very stressful to Blues of any age, whether they are boys or girls. If there is tension between parents they will think it is them that caused it. Blues will literally run and hide from conflict, meanness, yelling, or what they perceive as conflict. A loud relative (who is not really yelling, but seems like it) will upset a young Blue.

- Blue teens on the other hand will first run from conflict one moment, then completely surprise you by being right in the middle of the mean-teen crap. Blue teen girls especially will fight nasty if they feel boxed-in or face rejection if they don't go along with the meanness.   Here's the kicker: the whole time they are in the thick of being the mean teen they will be triple stressed out because 1) they hate themselves for doing it, 2) they know they are being hurtful, and 3) they are afraid that at any moment the tables can turn and they could become the victim. Your job in all of this is to first listen, then help them come up with a solution—a gracious and a not too obvious way out of the mess. Bravery comes later. First just help them learn to find a gracious escape route. Discipline your Blue with firm understanding and a chance to fix it.

- When you are frustrated with your Blue's illogical logic don't argue your point with facts and logic. Share your feelings, even if you are deeply disappointed in them, and ask about theirs. Be understanding. Don't take me the wrong way here, I'm not saying that you have to agree or go along with bad choices or behavior. All I'm saying is that if you want a Blue to change, at any age, you must approach them with understanding first, gently listening, and then you will gain insight into how to address the problem. Be firm in what you expect and teach your family's values.

- You want to know what your greatest advantage is with a Blue? If I share this with you, you must use it sparingly and in the right way or it will backfire and become a complete de-motivator and be downright emotionally abusive. It's when you are disappointed in them, or they lose your trust. When your Blue, whether they are young, a pre-teen, or teenager, and they've done a BIG dumb, and a usually loving parents says either, "I'm very disappointed in your choice." or they say, "I don't know if I can trust you right now because of this choice." Holy cow, you've got their full attention! Your Blue is completely humbled and will do anything to win back your approval and trust. But you must reference their choice! NOT them as a person. That's the first, and only, rule to doing this right. If you talk about being disappointed in their CHOICE they feel encouraged to change because they know deep down inside they can make a better choice. On the other hand (and this is SO important), if you refer to being disappointed in THEM, you've demoralized them and immobilized them to the point of giving up because they won't know how to change who they are. That's why you have to refer to being disappointed in (or not trusting) their CHOICE. Blues can be encouraged to change a choice, but will be discouraged and immobilized to change WHO they ARE. Use this only sparingly, too. If you communicate that you are constantly disappointed in them you will send a message that they can never do anything right and you are stripping them of their self-esteem. If you really ARE continually disappointed in them, then you own the problem, not your Blue, and you need to change.

- Work on problems together. Blues are all about the relationship but they can get overwhelmed by big problems. Working with you can teach them several important things. They can see by watching you that problems are fixable, that together it's not so overwhelming, and they will learn the process of problem-solving. They can learn how to work through steps such as brainstorming, deciding on a course of action, and then working to accomplish the plan through your example.

- If there are conflicts or relationship problems at home, don't keep secrets about what's going on. Provide honest, age-appropriate information to your Blue. Your Blue can already feel that something is going on. Talking about it will help them understand their role in it (or not) and what, if anything, they can, or should do, to fix the situation.

- Be careful not to burden your Blue with people problems beyond their capacity to understand or solve. They will try to take them on but protect them while balancing honesty.

- Don't make your Blue guess what you are thinking or feeling, about anything. Tell them. Their imagination can run wild and surprise you by where it ends up.

- Be their parent first, but also their friend when appropriate. If they feel safe with you they will rarely disobey and meltdowns will be kept to a minimum.

- Ask for their help, but teach them not to give too much of themselves to their friends and those they want to please.

- Remember, they don't care WHAT they do with you as long as it's WITH you.

- To sum things up, when your Blue is upset, or acting up, if you listen first, then discipline, and teach or correct them with gentle firmness you will see great changes in their behavior. When they are timid, unsure, or fearful, reassure them with, "It will be okay!" It works every time. Finally, trust THEM to solve their problem. Don't do it for them. Expect them to be courageous and they will.

- Being understanding of your Blue will get you further than lectures, commands, yelling, or control ever will.

- Just love them. Be mushy with them. Hug them. Smile at them. They need to be loved and to feel love from you, everyday! If you do this, they will be putty in your hands and a joy in your life.

A Few Words about BLUE Boys

The difference between a Blue boy and a Blue girl is more pronounced as they mature. This section is unique to the Blue boy.

Blue Boys are rare but awesome! They are a wonderful mix of careful sensitivity and all BOY. Blue boys care deeply about their families and want to be close to their parents at any age. Blue boys, like Blue girls, will seek the approval of their parents and peers. Young Blue boys will, at times, be much more obnoxious than Blue girls when seeking for attention. They can act all tough as if they don't care one minute, then the next be a bundle of emotions and even tears. Blue boys, from 2-years to 10-ish can be loving and snuggly but also tough, rambunctious, and playful.

As Blue boys mature into their pre-teen and teenage years they may become tougher and more competitive if that's what you expect from them. When it comes to sports, understand that if your Blue boy seems to be all hyped about crushing the other team you would be wise to see that his bravado is more about pleasing you, winning your approval, and not seeming weak rather than ever really being about annihilating the competition. It's not a bad thing to have your Blue child, boy or girl, involved in sports. Actually, it's great. Just let them approach it from a Blue point-of-view. Understand that they will focus on what the team needs. They will be self-sacrificing if they are not the best player on the team and that conflict and "crushing the enemy" will never be their objective. It's more likely that they are in it to please you, hang with friends, or to have an activity that you two have in common. It's all about relationships!

The most important thing to understand about raising a Blue boy is balancing their Blueness with teaching them how to be a man in a dog-eat-dog world.

The easiest way to do this is to make home a safe place for them, whatever happens to them in the big bad world. Give them permission to share and show their emotions with you, no matter their age. At the same time, help them understand that when they are out in the world (meaning away from home) they probably have to suck it up and be tough without being a bully and overcompensating, or obnoxious and attention-seeking. Let them know that "real men" are kind and stand up for the underdog, but they don't have to be walked-on or bullied. Help them understand that being gentle and quiet is not weakness but takes great courage and strength. Define for your Blue boy (and girl) what it means in your family to fight fair. Define (and even role play) situations when it's best to walk away.

Blue boys can be obnoxious when they are young. If it's not dealt with by a courageous parent who balances fairness with understanding and who holds them accountable for their inappropriate attention seeking behavior, they can turn into a bully as a pre-teen or teen. Blue boys will do this to overcompensate for their past hurts and deep feelings of rejection. This hurt is often because a parent, most likely a dad, was a bully to them by not understanding their Blueness and demanding that they "man-up" and stop being such a "cry-baby." Demanding such toughness in such abrupt ways when the Blue boy is too young to understand will cause him to suppress his feelings and act out opposite to his true nature.

This is one of the most hurtful things a parent can do "accidentally" to their child without realizing it. When a Blue boy is expected to hide his emotions in these less-than-healthy ways there are consequences that affect the Blue boy for the rest of his life. I understand that parents who do this are well-meaning but if they are not careful to teach their Blue boy to balance sensitivity with becoming a man then the Blue boy is forced to suppress his very nature, the very traits that make him who he is. This causes great stress and confusion, leading to a serious identity crisis as an older teen and they may adopt very self-destructive life paths.

Teach your Blue boy to embrace his intuitive ability to read other's emotions. Teach him to use his natural ability to authentically share his own feelings with a courageous understanding of when, where, and with whom to share their talents and feelings. Often a Blue boy learns instinctually to develop and show more of his second color Gold or Orange in an effort to balance his intuitive, sensitive nature to seem tough enough to his peers. This can be a healthy process if it's accompanied by a conscious choice by you and them to continue to value their Blueness. On the other hand, this can be an unhealthy development if they unconsciously choose to *be* more of their second color in an effort to suppress who they really are because they are afraid of someone's disapproval.

Blue boys tend to often show, or Extrovert, their second color—especially if they get the "feeling" that being sensitive is not accepted, misjudged, or misunderstood by their fathers or other boys. Remember, they are very intuitive to the feelings of others and have very deep feelings of their own. This will NEVER change, even if they suppress it or ignore it. They will, however, learn very quickly, very intuitively, whether they are safe in sharing their feelings or insights with you, their friends, or in various environments. In the end, help your Blue boy balance his intuitive, sensitive nature with becoming a tough, go-to guy.

A Few Words about BLUE Girls

The difference between a Blue boy and Blue girl is more pronounced as they mature. This section is unique to the Blue girl.

The only thing I can think to share specifically about Blue girls is focused on two concerns that will affect your Blue girl when she is a pre-teen and teen. The first is about dealing with the "mean girl" games of middle school and high school, and the second is focused on Blue teen girl vulnerability of seeking approval.

When it comes to "mean girl" games, Blue girls are especially affected because the conflict is so hurtful. All of the "mean girl" stuff is hard on a Blue because she will be stressed on one level or another by the conflict and meanness and will hurt for the victim (target) of the "mean girl" stuff, even if she's the one causing it.

There are three possible roles that a Blue teenage girl may play in the "mean girl" game and each will bring it's own unique set of stressors. First, your Blue girl will be stressed and very uncomfortable as she watches the meanness unfold. She may feel hurt for the victim and ashamed she didn't intervene and stop it. By her very nature a Blue girl will not naturally intervene. She will have to learn that behavior and grow her courage over time.

When this hits your daughter it's time to listen to her feelings but don't scold her for not stepping in. Remember, it's not a natural thing for a Blue to create conflict. By jumping in, she's creating new conflict, a possible new victim, and a new target: herself. Be gentle and encouraging. Ask her how she wants to handle the situation before you go telling her how she should. Then role play with her for possible things to say and/or do, including walking away if that is the most courageous thing she can muster at age 11 or 12. Believe me, she'll grow into her ability to stand up for the underdog by the time she's a 16- or 17-year-old if you start out slow, encouraging, and letting her be brave at her own pace.

In the second "mean girl" scenario, a Blue girl may be devastated if she becomes the victim. She may act like a scolded puppy and go back for more. When this happens, DON'T overreact and head off to the principles office or the phone to call the mean girl's parents. If you do, you will sever all communication with your daughter, the current victim. She won't trust you. She wants and needs you to listen and sympathize, not attack, possibly making things worse for her. So, listen first and ask her how she wants to solve this. If you do, you will give her the courage to handle it her way and she won't likely go back for more since you are on her side at home.

Continue to build her self-esteem. Protect her by giving her appropriate "outs" that she suggests like picking her up from practice instead of having her ride with the other girls, even if they are not the mean ones. Discuss without ridicule her ideas for "rescuing." They may not make sense to you but they do for her and if she is asking for what she thinks will be best, trust her. Believe me, she HAS thought it through. It's tough for a Blue to ask for help so if she's asking for it, give it if you can. At the same time, help, her to stretch and grow by teaching her to do things that may be uncomfortable or cause her to learn to let it go or see another point-of-view. It's okay to expect her to get out of her comfort zone, but don't feed her to the sharks just to make her tough. A shark feeding will destroy a Blue girl, it won't toughen her up.

The third possible "mean girl" scenario is in an attempt to not be the victim, your Blue girl may be very un-true to herself and actually participate in, or even instigate, the "mean girl" stuff. If you find out this is the case don't be shocked. It is totally possible and can be more debilitating to her self-esteem than being the victim or standing by and letting it happen. It's a cry for self-esteem building. If your Blue girl is the one stirring the pot then there is a lot of negative stuff going on in her head and heart. Something is amiss. I don't have the psychology degree or room to explain it all here.

Here's my parenting advice, don't be shocked or in denial that it's your sweet daughter being the mean one. Deal with it. Deal with it the same way as anything else with a Blue, understanding. Something's going on. Something not good. First, listen to her. Don't lecture about how wrong it is to be mean. She knows. Listen to what's hurting her, even as she's defensive. Fight the impulse to lecture, give tough consequences, and overreact because you are embarrassed. All of that is "your story" and your story is irrelevant right now if you really want to help your Blue girl who is crying out for help. You'll have your say in a while. Listen, now, and get her WHOLE story.

When she gets it all out (the hurt, anger, blame, fear) she will seem calmer and may be crying. When that happens you've hit a wonderful turning point. It's time for "your story." Say this firmly but calmly and quietly, "I am extremely disappointed that you chose to be so hurtful to someone that … (used to be your friend; is less fortunate than you; needs your help; whatever the case may be). I expect it to stop and stop now. Do you understand me?" (Answer will be a quiet "yes"). Continue with, "Will you stop?" (Answer will again be a quiet, "yes"). Then pause, and with all the kindness you can muster say, "Okay, I'm very proud of your decision. How do you want to fix this? Do you need my help?"

This is an example of "Coach Talk." It is so effective with a Blue. I promise, if you will handle your discipline this way you will have the Blue girl (or boy for that matter) of your dreams AND you will have taught them how to be mature and balanced. Your Blue girl will find a way to NEVER, EVER be the "mean girl" ring leader, again. You may even find out she's said the above words to other "mean girls" to get them to change their ways. Interesting, huh?

The second issue that seems to affect Blue girls in their pre-teen and teen years and looking for love in all the wrong places. This is directly linked to a Blue girl's need to seek approval. Bottom line, if a Blue girl (or boy) feels brushed aside, misunderstood, constantly criticized, ignored, or unloved as they are growing up, they will seek for that love and approval from any source that becomes available.

I know of a Blue girl, a real sweetie actually, from a completely dysfunctional home, who at 15 was hanging with the wrong crowd and met an older man who said he loved her. He eventually led her away from home, got her hooked on drugs and turned her into a prostitute. About the same time, the police *just happened* to be watching this terrible man, arrested him, and "released" all the girls in his "care," including the girl I am speaking of. A few days later, as the girl was de-toxing, she was literally fighting to get back to the man "who loved her." My heart broke when I heard this. This Blue girl just wanted to be loved and accepted for who she was. I tell you this not to scare you but to have you understand that having a teen-age Blue girl go looking for love in all the wrong places is real. Teenage Blue girls who strive to get this need met as they are growing can range from just annoyingly boy crazy (with loving parents who keep close tabs on her relationships without being smothering) to as scary as the above story illustrates.

How do you guard against this? It's simple. First of all, build her self-worth at home. Let her know that she is worth being treated with respect and dignity. Help her develop her intuitive sense of who is a good person with values and who is not. Don't worry about her being judgmental. That's not usually a problem for Blues, young or old. They are often *too* forgiving, *too* naive. Blue's learn to be judgmental from others or having it happen to them, for the most part. Trust her instincts from a young age. If she shy's away from an older boy, an older male friend or relative, or other women, don't try to force her to "be nice." She's getting creeped out for a reason. Listen to her concerns. If you negate that feeling when she's 4, you short circuit it for when she's 14 and 24. Not a good thing. Beware.

Second, set very specific boundaries for your Blue, especially your Blue-Orange about what's allowed when it comes to relationships with boys. Set an age for dating (many say 16) and talk about it just being a fact from the time they are three years old. Decide, and talk early, about phone rules, texting, email access, and Facebook. (I know of another very desperate and lonely 17-year-old Blue girl who found her 43-year-old boyfriend - yes, that's 43, not a typo - on Facebook, left on a bus to go marry him, and I've not heard how that turned out. No joke.)

Set boundaries on other social events and what to do on a date. Be very careful about sleepovers, even other girls can be predators now. Sleepovers are not always a wise thing. Don't feel bad about protecting your child, or about saying "no." It's your job. Later, be very specific about kissing and other activities and physical expressions of affection according to your family's values. We had a rule, according to our family's values with our Orange daughter as she was an older teen that really helped her know a "kissing" boundary. It would work well for a Blue girl, too, if this is aligned with your family's value. The rule was you never lay down to kiss until you are married (yes, we eventually covered that you can get in trouble standing up, too, but she was older and knew what we

364

meant!) As a side note, our kids had great success in the dating years. They made awesome choices and came through happy and healthy. If you are interested in specifics and the boundaries that we personally implemented, contact me through our website.

The last thing is, from a very young age, help your Blue girl define who is worthy of providing their approval of her. In other words, help her define whose opinion of her counts, and whose doesn't. Certainly you would be on that list until she is much older. Then, at some point, you need to teach her to separate even from needing your approval. Her own approval is worthy, especially as she learns to compare her choices and motives to a set of worthy personal values such as honesty, integrity, dependability, and so on. For me, personally, as a Blue and a very devout Christian, I was taught to look to God for love and approval. For me, when all else fails, I know that I have God's approval as I strive to do what's right. God is truly a worthy source for approval. When your Blue is young you will need to provide her with worthy sources of approval. As she matures you need to teach her how to decide who is a worthy source of approval and who is not.

When it comes to seeking approval there are two things to understand, especially if you are not Blue. First of all, Blues will always seek approval. You cannot erase their need for approval. You can only teach your Blue to focus on worthy sources. Second, Blues who don't have worthy sources of approval will not simply go without. They will fill the void with unworthy sources of approval. Decide now how best to help your Blue girl determine healthy sources of approval so that she can live a happy and healthy life.

When it comes to the very serious emotional trials that hit all Blue pre-teen and teenage girls, ere on the side of listening first, understanding second, teaching what's right, and giving the tools to handle their problems with maturity, grace, and poise. Be firm but gentle and expect the best. Your Blue girl wants to live up to your ideal.

Influence of a BLUE'S Second Color on Their Behavior and Choices

Blues are always focused on relationships and constantly seeking understanding in one form or another. How they do this will be influenced by their second color.

Introverted Blue / Extroverted Blue: Introvert and Extrovert for a Blue doesn't have a lot of extra influence on their behavior, except that Introvert Blues will be more introspective and a little less talkative than Extrovert Blues. Both Introvert and Extrovert Blues will communicate rather effectively and more often than any of the other colors because they are focused on relationships and understanding. Those things grow *through* communication for Blues. Introvert Blues tend to hold back their real feelings more than Extrovert Blues. However, this can be overcome by asking your Introvert Blue about their feelings. They will talk quickly and easily because their need for understanding overrides their preference for being an Introvert. According to years of observation, this trait appears to be unique to Blues.

A bit about a Blue's Second Color: For the Blues, their second color shows up more pronounced than with some of the other colors. The strong influence of a Blue's second color often makes Blue-Oranges seem inconsistent, emotional, and sort of all over the place. This can make them somewhat difficult to understand and very different from Blue-Golds as a group. Blue-Golds can be a bit confusing because Blues are supposed to be "people-people," but can actually be controlling and sometimes not very nice, even demanding and bossy. Once you understand the influence of their second color, a Blue child's or teen's behavior seems to follow a pattern.

Extroverted Blue-Golds tend to be more traditional and try desperately to be organized. They will become overwhelmed by the need to clean a messy room or to complete a big project. They are a little more focused and responsible than a Blue-Orange but can still be preoccupied by people watching. They are definitely a combination of people-focused and structured, which can lead them to be a bit controlling of people, or at least they try. They have very specific ideas of how people should be, act, and even feel. They are very responsive to people's needs and hurts. They are usually very responsible and care deeply about doing a good job.

They tend to talk a lot about what they need and how they feel and what others need to be doing and feeling. They generally feel real concern for what others want or think. They usually try to handle emotional situations with kindness and concern for the other person's feelings but can become bossy, demanding, and even abrupt under extreme stress. They tend to communicate emotions easily, sometimes dramatically.

They are usually a good leader and often will "direct" the play of their friends. They talk easily with others and are usually tactful. They tend to be very social and enjoy organizing parties but end up having high expectations that can be frustrated if others don't go along with the plan. They can be a little self-absorbed. As they grow they can become very popular with their peers and with adults who see them as polite and organized. They want to be good students but may struggle with technical subjects. They are usually sympathetic and service-oriented. They truly take praise and criticism to heart and work hard to please others.

Introverted Blue-Golds: Blue-Golds tend to be more traditional about their values and behaviors. They can be more organized but are still first color Blues and will get overwhelmed and immobilized, especially by cleaning a messy room. They are definitely the most focused and responsible of all the Blues and the most serious because they are more introspective as Introverts.

They, too, are a combination of people-focused and structured. They tend to have very high expectations for everything but especially for themselves. Introverted Blue-Golds are quietly concerned for others but may not communicate their emotions easily. They may talk quite often but you will notice it's not very personal. They keep that more to themselves, yet desperately want to feel connected and will share if asked.

They will show great compassion and kindness to others through their service for those around them. They usually stick to an assignment and want to do whatever is needed. They will put their best effort into their work because they are secretly striving for your approval, even if you don't realize it. If you fail to notice they will be secretly hurt and tend to withdraw. When this happens, you may not notice it for weeks and when you do, you won't know what's wrong. Invite these children to talk with you often. They will be easy to ignore but they are not oblivious to your inattention and it's hurting them. When they are upset they may quietly pout or stand stubbornly resisting what you want them to do. They will quietly refuse to do something they think is wrong but will be torn by worrying what others are thinking of them. They are very conscientious about pleasing you, their teachers, and friends that they find worthy of admiration. These children and teens are often respected for quietly doing what's right but may be secretly battling inwardly about balancing doing what's right and pleasing others. Often others look up to them and they may feel even greater stress to not let anyone down. They are very kind, caring, and service-oriented.

Extroverted Blue-Oranges: Blue-Oranges are creative, energetic, imaginative, fun, and freedom-seeking. They strive to be very individualistic and hope to change the world. They desperately want to make a difference. They are a combination of people-focused and freedom-loving, which means they can be swayed into doing dumb things with friends. Extroverted Blue-Oranges are the ones most likely to jump into new situations, especially when those new situations are people-oriented or a friend is joining in, too.

These children and teens are warmly enthusiastic, high-spirited, ingenious, and imaginative. As young children they can come up with some wild tales. They are able to do almost anything that interests them. They are very quick with a solution for any problem, especially people problems. They don't like to see people hurting and tend to jump in and rescue the wounded, the strays, and the underdog. They are ready and willing to help anyone in need and will give away whatever they have to make a difference for even one person.

They are deeply affected by hurtful images, starving children, or scary movies and may have bad dreams from such things. They often rely on their ability to improvise in-the-moment instead of really preparing in advance. They tend to be on their own time schedule. They are persuasive negotiators and can usually find compelling reasons for whatever they want. They are very flexible, usually fun, kind, and good communicators.

They have never met a stranger. They can jump in and be too trusting or give the wrong people chance after chance to be their friend. They can also get easily overwhelmed and immobilized by a messy room, messy people problems, or big projects. Because they have no natural structure they will be especially susceptible to disorganization, collecting stuff, and running on the spur of the moment whim of all Blue-Oranges. These Blues need concrete boundaries almost as much as the Oranges do.

Introverted Blue-Oranges are also creative, imaginative, and freedom seeking but will be more quiet about how they go about doing it than the Extroverted Blue-Oranges. They, too, are a combination of people-focused and freedom-loving but are much more introspective. Introverted Blue-Oranges are less likely ones to jump into new situations, even when those new situations are people-oriented or a friend is joining in, too. They want to see how it will all work, first, but will be all in if it seems doable. They are full of enthusiasm and loyalties, but will seldom talk of these things unless they trust you. You can see their excitement more in their twinkly eyes rather than in their excited talk. They care deeply about learning new things, great ideas, language, and projects of their own but may not be very talkative about any of this unless you ask.

As with all Blues they tend to take on too many things at one time. They will feel great stress from that but will somehow quietly get it all done; then crash. These children and teens are friendly but may focus more intently on their projects or playing by themselves, first. Extroverting with others will come secondary to them. As teens, because they are a combination of Introvert and people-focused-but-flexible, they really have little concern for being in charge of a group, the "social status" of their peers in high school, or in collecting expensive things. They will be more concerned with activities like humanitarian efforts and art projects. These Introvert Blue-Oranges need your understanding and love.

How BLUE Children and Teens Behave Badly...

Recognizing <u>BLUE Stress Behaviors</u> helps parents understand that their child is experiencing stress.

When you see these types of misbehaviors, understand that your BLUE is experiencing a threat to one of their RELATIONSHIPS, or they feel that they are going to upset a RELATIONSHIP. They may be feeling that there is a breakdown in COMMUNICATION, and therefore, a lack of UNDERSTANDING or they feel MIS-UNDERSTOOD by you.

- A Blue's most common stress behavior, is becoming overwhelmed and immobilized; they don't know what to do next. This happens all the time for Blues. If you see your Blue stopped in their tracks and unable to make the next move in their messy room, homework, with a friend, in any form—they are under stress.

- Becomes overly compliant, says "yes" to too many things, over-extends themselves with no thought to how they can accomplish all their commitments.

- Blues become reactive and depressed, feels "blue," may create dependencies in order to "manufacture" relationships that are not real. This happens when your young Blue acts helpless and whines that you need to tie their shoes or brush their teeth. Build your relationship by first praising their independent actions and gently-but-firmly refusing to do what they can do for themselves. Try not to get upset with them. This will only lead to some real immobilization on their part. Be encouraging without rescuing.

- Not firm with self or others, acts like a "push-over," seems wishy-washy about what they want to do or where they want to be. They may be slow to make decisions because they don't want to let anyone down.

- Weak at goal setting, undisciplined with time, and may be disorganized to an extreme.

- May become overly emotional, dramatic, cries about everything, and can't seem to calm themselves down.

- Can be too helpful and rescuing, seems to be in the middle of all the drama, may even stir things up.

- Shows/picks favorites – a Blue show of power, can play one friend against another, becomes "passive-aggressive" or plays the "martyr."

- These last few bullet points happen less often and are more often a sign of stress caused by, and compounded by, low self-esteem and negative thinking.

Why BLUES Behave Badly...

Understanding <u>BLUE Stressors</u> can help parents figure out WHY their BLUE is experiencing stress and acting out.

BLUES experience stress when they feel a threat or loss of a positive RELATIONSHIP, especially if they fear they are causing the problem. They will also experience stress when COMMUNICATION breaks down or when there is a MIS-UNDERSTANDING. They also will be extremely stressed when they are personally MIS-UNDERSTOOD.

- Lack of positive relationships, especially when parents fight or don't get along. When they feel that they have no friends or anyone who loves them. This can destroy a Blue. Relationships are their lifeline. Without them, they die emotionally.

- People fighting, mean people, personal rejection, being physically pushed away. For a little Blue this is especially hurtful and they don't understand why.

- Insincerity, people who lie, lack of authenticity, dishonesty. This is very stressful for a Blue, especially a young Blue because they can feel that something is not right but they can't figure out what is wrong.

- Being ignored or unappreciated. Feeling as though they have no special value.

- Feeling criticism from parents, teachers, or coaches.

- Loud, negative remarks, actual yelling and sarcasm are very hard for a Blue to handle because they would never communicate that way and it speaks volumes about the lack of a positive relationship. Any harsh communication will be described by a Blue as yelling, even if you actually never raise your voice.

- Trying to please too many people is overwhelming to a Blue. They can't decide who to please and then feel like they are disappointing everyone.

- Repetitive work is especially stressful for the Blue-Oranges because there is a lack of freedom in it.

- Bossy, controlling people are mean, hurtful, and unkind to a Blue. They instinctually feel that it's contrary to building positive relationships.

- Feelings of confusion are very disconcerting to a Blue because they feel there is a loss of connection to something safe and real. They are especially immobilized by confusion when it comes to people problems.

- Disharmony between family members and friends will be very upsetting to a Blue, young or old, because they will feel compelled to somehow fix it and will not know how.

- Insensitivity and insincerity is just mean to a Blue. Because they are so naturally sensitive they can't comprehend someone who can't pick up on the feelings of others or worse, someone who doesn't care about the feelings of others.

- Time limits and pressure to decide quickly will stress a Blue to no end because they don't have time to consider everyone's feelings and needs. They are fearful that they will either make a wrong choice or may hurt someone's feelings.

- Impersonal treatment, social exclusion, isolation conveys a lack of understanding of people and will upset a Blue if they see it or are a victim of it.

- Personal criticism or disapproval, non-supportive behavior, and discouraging remarks hurt relationships and are upsetting forms of communication that the Blue can feel upsets others.

- When rules matter more than people, the Blue always sides with the underdog. Rules tend to exclude the individual.

- Unresolved conflict - Blues have a very difficult time dealing with the "elephant" in the middle of the room that everyone is ignoring. What I mean by that is Blues, young and old, have a very stressful time when they can sense that there are underlying issues not discussed in a family or group but that those underlying issues influence everyone's feelings, attitudes, and conversations. The Blue wants to talk it out but generally no one else wants to bring it out in the open.

- Blues really hate competition because someone always must lose. Many Blue boys and some Blue girls will play sports but will have a hard time tearing up the other team. They are too soft-hearted and once they know how it feels to lose they don't want to inflict that on others.

- Abuse and aggression toward others is about the most stressful thing that a Blue might have to deal with. It just destroys everything a Blue holds dear... relationships, communication, and understanding.

Signs of LOW SELF-ESTEEM in BLUES

- Extreme attention getting behavior.

- Exhibits a pattern of complete immobilization to make any decision for fear of upsetting someone or that they won't be able to make a good enough choice to please you, their parents.

- Unable to set and work toward goals because they have become completely undisciplined and disorganized to an extreme.

- Very emotional, never seems happy, and can't seem to calm themselves down, depressed.

- Lying to save face.

- Withdrawal, extreme day-dreaming, always crying (girls), getting lost in inactivity like video games (boys), or books (girls).

- Passive aggressive behaviors, uncharacteristic emotional outbursts.

- Extreme inertia, little self-confidence, and complete inability to get moving, even with little things.

- Demanding you do things for them that they can, or have done, for themselves in the past.

- As a pre-teen or teen: A lack of interest in their own appearance, believing and acting on negative self-judgments. (Believing that negative "voice" in their head that says they are no good. Talking about a voice in their head does not mean they are crazy. Blues have a negative self-talk "voice" in their head that can berate them constantly if not keep in check. Ask any adult Blue. Blues really are about communication and often it's self-communication. Interesting, huh? I suggest a remedy in the next section.)

- Extremely focused on what others think of them to the point of acting in ways that are contrary to what they know is right or best.

- Seeking approval, acceptance from inappropriate people.

- For teen Blues... looking for "love" in the wrong places in ways that are immature, overly emotional, not smart, and embarrassing to themselves and to others by "chasing" after those of the opposite sex or by getting involved in same-sex relationships for approval and a way to be accepted as sensitive.

- They may appear lazy and unmotivated but really they are overwhelmed and immobilized without goals, priorities, or self-direction.

- Playing the victim in that they are SO abused, SO left-out, SO misunderstood, that NO-ONE understands now, or ever will, that they fall pray to defeatism: "I can't do anything right." "Nobody loves me."

  Like it or not, low self-esteem usually stems from controlling and critical behavior from the parent. When kids or teens demonstrate these <u>extreme</u> behaviors, immediately decrease negative criticism and any overly controlling behavior on your part (see page 394 for Command and Control tactics). Increase your time listening and genuinely praising your child or teen for appropriate right choices.

At the same time I am NOT suggesting that you become lax about appropriate discipline but pick your battles and address serious misbehaviors through choices and consequences, never through Command and Control (page 394). Don't nit-pick about little annoyances that aren't really hurting anyone or anything. A messy room or mismatched clothes never hurt anyone - let it go and build your child's self-worth when these extreme behaviors, are present. If your child or teen continues to demonstrate these behaviors seek additional help from a reputable family counselor or therapist.

Ways to Build SELF-ESTEEM in BLUES

- Increase a **balance** of appropriate praise and rewards for good choices **with** discipline in the form of clear boundaries, choices, and consequences for acting out.

- Listen attentively, with your story on hold, when your child is upset. This is crucial!

- Eliminate ALL Command and Control tactics from your parenting efforts. (see page 394).

- Lots of unconditional acceptance without using positive judgments that make them even more dependent on your good opinion. Instead of saying, "You are such a sweet girl." say, "I'm so excited to have you sit next to me."

- Teach how to recognize the negative self-talk "voice" in their head. Help them know they are not crazy. Teach them to replace negative thoughts with positive, comforting ways they can control, and can have their power to choose. Put positive phrases on a mirror for them to see every morning. This will build self-esteem while giving a tool to use the rest of their life when that negative self-talk invades.

- Provide opportunities for your Blue to be recognized in some sort of public forum without embarrassing them like a small recognition party at your house with family or a few friends. With a teen, send them flowers at school. Bring the treats to soccer practice and have your Blue hand them out.

- Call them by name and comment on how much you appreciate their individual-ness.

- Give very personal compliments describing how their positive actions affect you and others for good.

- Let them be a teacher to you about something they love or something they've learned.

- Teach them to be independent and do things for themselves. Don't coddle them at a young age. If you do, they will become dependent on you for things they can do and should do. This will lower their self-confidence.

- Listen to them. I mean, really focus and listen to them. Look them in the eye. Stop doing whatever you are doing and turn your whole body to pay attention to them as they talk. Ask questions.

- If you don't have time to listen, sincerely explain that and set a follow-up time to talk. Then do it and follow the listening suggestions in the previous bullet point.

- Have them be your helper and errand running partner. Sincerely praise them on how they really helped you.

- Ask them to tell you how they feel about a specific situation. Ask for their "advice" for handling something age-appropriate that you are struggling with.

- Be supportive when they try something new. Let them know you think they can do it. Let them know what they did right, even if the "try-out" was not successful. Describe how you were proud of their willingness to try and for their courage.

- Provide them with opportunities to be of service and build the self-esteem of others. Help them do things that make them feel they are making a difference.

- Teach them how to positively handle conflict, self-doubt, and "the blues."

- Even at a young age help them learn to balance pleasing others with appropriately meeting their own needs.

- Use "Cheer Talk" as described in the next book or a "Parenting By Colors" class (see website for more information).

- Give them jobs they can succeed at. Praise them for the smallest of successes.

Best To-Do's For Parents of BLUE Kids

Parenting the BLUE child needs to be focused on preserving your parent-child RELATIONSHIP through firm but gentle COMMUNICATION where UNDERSTANDING is the overarching discipline approach.

- They desperately need YOUR approval or they will seek it from others. Be sure to communicate appreciation of their individual contributions and help them know they are valued and loved by you. Say, "I love you" at least once a day. Give physical and verbal hugs.

- They are tenderhearted, but don't underestimate their toughness. Be firm about what is okay and not okay, but be careful to use a non-yelling level or tone. Be authentic by having your words match your tone. Don't say confusing things like, "NO! I'm NOT MAD!"

- You can say what needs to be said. Just realize their feelings are close to the surface, so you might see tears. Don't assume they are being weak and don't demand they stop crying. It's not an act unless you turn it into a weapon by drawing too much attention to it when they are young. Praise them for getting themselves under control. Blues just cry. Don't make a big deal about it and it won't be a big deal.

- If they are overly emotional, give them a few minutes "to get it out" by listening to their concerns but don't let them wallow. If they are out of control, send or take them to be alone and get themselves under control. Most Blues don't want to be alone when they are upset. If you don't give audience to their emotional outburst and praise them when they are more contained, you will help them learn to communicate with words rather than emotions.

- Teach age-appropriate coping skills such as snuggling with a favorite toy, singing to themselves, listening to soft music, praying, writing in a journal, talking it out with you.

- Validate their feelings but promote independence by supporting them while they try to solve their own problems as mentioned several times in this chapter.

- If they "tattle" or blame others, ignore what you can and refocus them on their own choices and behaviors.

- They can be strong if you help them have faith in their own ability to cope and solve problems. Help them learn how to do things for themselves but don't be critical as they work on the skills. If they feel they can't do anything right, they will give up very easily. It's hard to get them to get moving again.

- They actively sense the feelings of others, including you. If something is upsetting you (even if it has very little or nothing to do with them) you need to address it because they can sense that something is wrong, anyway. Don't tip-toe around elephants. Make your talk age-appropriate and, depending on the problem, have them be part of the solution. Whatever you do, help them understand they are not the cause of the problem when they aren't.

- When conflicts arise, they need your listening ear first.

- Be very careful with criticism.

- Give them gentle consequences ONLY AFTER you've taught them what is right, given them a choice, and they STILL overtly do something naughty, inappropriate, or wrong. Don't be overly harsh. Give them a chance to "fix it" if possible. Then let it go. Blues rarely overtly disobey. They often act in emotional stressed-out ways, but rarely engage in calculated misbehavior the way an Orange or a Green might.

- Give concrete recognition for almost anything. Blues seem needy in this area. Concentrate on building their self-esteem through "positive reinforcement" of anything good while they are young. As they grow, give them more and more chances to succeed. When the rewards are more of the good feeling of accomplishment and quiet recognition, you will have a very happy, very cooperative Blue teen who gets their own self-esteem from doing what's right.

- They just want to please you. Use this appropriately to your advantage by asking them to do what's right. Be positive with them. Tell them you have faith in them to do the right thing and they will most likely live up to it.

- One word of caution: balance self-esteem building without making your Blue dependent on you for approval by providing positive recognition for good choices that is not founded on positive *judgments.* For example, don't say, "That's such a pretty picture." Say instead, "I love to look at this picture, it makes me feel happy." Don't say, "Your room looks good." Say instead, "I love it when your room is all picked up. Doesn't it make you feel happy and organized?" Don't say, "You are such a good friend!" Say instead, "I am very grateful to see you helping your friend, even though I know you don't really have time right now. Doing the right thing feels good." <u>Positive reinforcement without positive judgments</u> is focused on how YOU FEEL about their actions or choices, not on your assessment of their value. "Pretty picture," "room looks good," and "such a good friend" are all accessing value. "I love to look" and "I am grateful" are expressing your feelings about how their actions make you feel good. Praising without judgment not only builds a Blue's self-esteem but fosters independence and encourages them to form their own good opinion of themselves. This is your best tool for helping a Blue learn balance!

- When your Blue is upset communicate acceptance, understanding, and sensitivity first, then work on correcting bad behavior. They will change faster when they feel accepted and understood for who they are but have a clear understanding of what's acceptable and what's not.

- When they are upset listen to them attentively and don't dismiss their feelings, instead validate their feelings and teach them coping skills. Then let them have a chance to come up with their own solution. If they can't think of what to do next then give them ideas. Be cooperative not commanding. If you are commanding they will knuckle under and do what you want for years, out of fear, but there will come a day when they will openly or secretly defy you.

- Give them the freedom to communicate openly and freely, they will usually be tactful but not always forthcoming if they are afraid of the reaction they might get from you and others.

- Discipline <u>firmly</u> but with kindness. Remember, "understanding" is the key to teaching a Blue their whole life. That doesn't mean that you give in, give repeated chances, rescue, or ignore bad behavior. It just means that you will get far better results with understanding than with meanness. Blues are such gentle souls, you don't want to break them, you want to guide them to greatness.

- Provide lots of opportunity for Blues to learn time management skills. Connect their success to feelings of peace and calm they get from not procrastinating. Help them see that their lack of real organization can frustrate others and can create conflict — this is your best bet for helping them choose to change.

- Prepare Extroverted Blue kids for time alone, teach them coping skills, and how to entertain themselves. Reward quiet time with family time.

- Teach communication skills for times of stress so that Blue kids and teens can release pressure appropriately without lashing out suddenly or imploding destructively. Teach them to recognize the early signs of their stress triggers. Teach them to balance meeting the needs of others with meeting their own needs appropriately. Most of all, help them minimize the "drama" through recognition, communication, time management, exercise, positive thinking, and letting go.

- When they are young use time-outs carefully. Keep the times short, especially for Blue-Oranges, and always show more love and tenderness after the time-out or drama. If left too long in time-out Blues feel abandoned. If they feel abandoned, their subsequent misbehaviors will be far worse than whatever they did to be in time-out in the first place. Reinforce your expectations, kindly and without loudness, then immediately give them the chance to "fix it." Remember, to a Blue, it's all about the relationship. "Fixing" the thing they did wrong = "fixing it" with you!

- Be as consistent as you can with a Blue child or teen. If you are not, they won't understand how to please you and they are all about trying to please you. Not knowing what someone else wants from them is very stressful for a Blue. Change doesn't freak out a Blue as much as mixed messages do.

- If your Blue is second color Gold remember that while they are first and foremost seeking to build happy relationships, as a second color Gold they will also desire structure and consistency when it comes to their relationship with you. This secondary need for structure just accentuates their drive for approval and safety from you.

- If your Blue is second color Orange remember that while they are first and foremost seeking to build happy relationships, as a second color Orange they will also desire freedom when it comes to everything in their life and their world. This secondary need for freedom just accentuates their need to be themselves and to be loved unconditionally for who they are.

- When your Blue experiences feelings of being overwhelmed and immobilized they will be stuck. Teach them to tap into their second color to get moving again. If they are second color Gold teach them to use their Gold structure to get organized and to list out their ideas, tasks, thoughts, or options. If they are second color Orange teach them to use their Orange freedom fighter to get moving by just focusing on the "next action," instead of the whole mess of thoughts, tasks, options, or details. Do just that first next thing. Then when that's done, do just the next thing. When that's done, do just the next thing after that. Before you and they know it, they're moving.

- Always listen to a Blue's perspective when they do something wrong. Chances are they didn't realize what you meant or wanted, especially young Blues. They are very tenderhearted.

- When a teen is acting out and gets overly upset when you confront them they might be manipulating you, but most will tell you why they did what they did it if you ask. A Blue teen wants so badly to have a loving relationships with you that if you even give them a chance to really talk they will fall right into it, even against their tough bravado. A troubled Blue teen will most likely be acting out because they are looking for love and acceptance from you anyway. I'd still ere on the side of listening, I mean real listening.

- In the end, when you discipline a Blue, young or teen, have a listening ear, understanding mind, and an open heart. Be willing to change your opinion of them and their action as you hear their side. Even be willing to lighten the consequences or to bend the rules with new information from your Blue. (Now you can only do this on a first offence with a Blue and never with the other colors.)

- Remember to never waver on values or principles, but change the rules when it's the right thing to do for your Blue and ALWAYS explain the difference!

Best phrases to use with your BLUE Child

"It's going to be okay, I know you can handle this!"

With a kind tone, "You have two (five, ten, whatever) minutes to be sad and I will listen, then we need to find a way to fix this."

"I'm sorry, I can't listen to Wendy/Walter Whiner. When my sweet daughter/son comes back, I will listen to her."

Also with a kind but firm tone, "I'm very disappointed in your choice. I need you to … instead. Will you do that for me?"

"I'm very worried that you seem so upset about this. I need you to calm down and see this from a more logical point of view. Will you do that for me?"

"I need to tell you something but I don't want to hurt your feelings. Tell me when you are ready to be strong and hear me out."

Gently, "I know that it hurt your feelings. Let's stop and look at what's really important here. What did you do that was ... (kind, right, best, brave, strong, or wrong, mean, hurtful, a little wimpy)? What will you (can you) do next time?"

"I think that you are feeling overwhelmed with ... (this chore, your friend's actions, your Spanish project, etc.). Let's use your second color (Gold, Orange) to get you moving."
To a Blue-Orange, "What's the 'next action' that you need to do to get you closer to being done?" (child answers or you give an idea) "Okay, that's great! Do just that one thing, then we'll think of the 'next action' and that will help."
To a Blue-Gold, "Let's come up with a list of things that you need to do to get you closer to being done." (child works with you to create a "To-Do list") "Okay, that's great! Now start at the top and do each one. If you get stuck come get me. That should help."

A Last Word about BLUE Kids

Most of all LOVE your tender Blues. Give them a safe haven from the cruel world. By protecting their marshmallow inside at home you give them the courage and gumption to go out into the world and be tough. Communicate love and acceptance through words, hugs, and small surprises. Appeal to their mushy insides. Draw them to you with love rather than push them away with harshness. Nurture their nature and see them blossom and grow.

Parenting by PERSONALITY

What's Left?

The Ugly Boxes,
3 Word Chart & Discipline Do's,
Contact us!
Reference Pages

Check out our

COLORWORKS Circle

member site with parenting answers just
for you and your child 24/7
Check out www.colorworkscircle.com

Also join our mailing list at
ColorWorksGroup.com

Command & Control Tactics... or Ugly Gray Boxes

I shouldn't use these but I probably do. We all do.

To learn a better way than using Command & Control, read the "Lower Your Stress" section of your color and the "Best To-Do's For Parents" section of your child's color.

THE MOVER & SHAKER
Interested in getting things done in a hurry

Uses action commands, strict how-to's, needs people to move, NOW! Usually is yelling.

"Just get in the van now, we have to go!" "I said get that room cleaned, NOW!" "Just do it, don't argue!" "I said, 'MOVE'!"

THE GENERAL
Interested in keeping things well under control, on time, on schedule

Uses orders, threats, commands

"Stop crying right now or I'll give you something to cry about!"

THE JUDGE SUPREME
Interested in proving themselves right and the child wrong

Uses judgments, comparisons, unrealistic expectations

"You're going about this all the wrong way." "You know your brother would never have done this." "This must be why you're not getting straight A's."

THE THERAPIST
Interested in analyzing the child, or the child's problem, makes excuses for child's bad behavior, rescues from consequences

Uses diagnosis, judgments from parent's perspective, questions motives, uses conditions (disorders, tired)

"Maybe your teacher just doesn't understand you."

THE PREACHER
Interested in moralizing, likes to be heard

Uses lecturing, self as good example, scripture*, guilt

"Now, I wouldn't do that if I were you." "When I was your age..."
"In the bible it says that we need to honor our parents, are you honoring me by not getting your work done?"

THE MOVIE CRITIC
Interested in the same things as the Preacher and the Judge Supreme but uses different tools

Uses ridicule, name-calling, sarcasm, jokes

"Oh come on, how hard can your math be?" "What...oh, oh, you gonna cry now, too?" "You are so lazy, sit up and do it now!"

THE PROFESSOR
Interested in sharing all they know about how the child should change, be better, or improve

Uses questioning, advice-giving, logical appeals, superiority

"You know what? You need to turn around and focus. You can't watch TV and do your math at the same time." "That makes no sense. There is no way you can think like that?"

When you are upset with your child's actions what

COMMAND & CONTROL

tactics do you use?

THE BEST FRIEND
Interested in getting the problem over with quickly, treats the situation lightly

Uses simplistic reassurances, manipulative praise, surface listening

"Come on, math isn't that hard, you can do it. Just hurry up and get it done so you can go outside."

The 3 Words

Are a simpler way to remember why
our kid's do what they do.

These words can help you remember your
child's COLOR needs, values, and Discipline Do's.
Remembering your child's 3 Words can help you
understand WHY they do what they do when
things are upsetting or stressful to them.

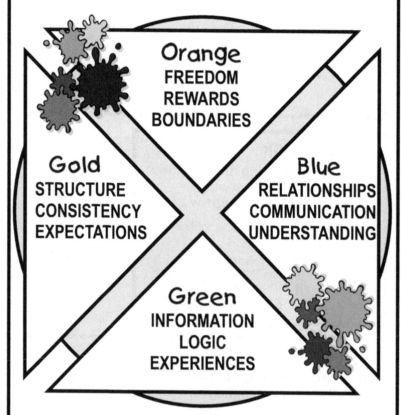

Orange
FREEDOM
REWARDS
BOUNDARIES

Gold
STRUCTURE
CONSISTENCY
EXPECTATIONS

Blue
RELATIONSHIPS
COMMUNICATION
UNDERSTANDING

Green
INFORMATION
LOGIC
EXPERIENCES

Remember these "3 WORDS" summarize each color's basic need,
value, and "Discipline Do". When these needs are violated,
you, or your child, will experience "stress" and will act in
ways to get those needs meet. These ideas are explained in
detail in the color sections of this book.

DISCIPLINE DO'S... Each **COLOR** learns to change their behavior in different ways. Some change once they learn what's right, others only after suffering consequences, other's need extra doses of understanding. You get better results when you discipline WITH your child's **COLOR** in mind.

THE ORANGE CHILD

Needs *FREEDOM*:
Freedom to act and to be themselves. Grateful for the ability to "move on."

Values *REWARDS*:
Likes actions over words and quick results. Enjoys new freedoms and fun.

Discipline Do: *BOUNDARIES*
Learns best by doing, needs clear boundaries (rules you can see) explained BEFORE they make the choice, if possible. Focus on rewards for good behavior, not Punishment for bad choices.

THE GOLD CHILD

Needs *STRUCTURE*:
Structure, order, and plans that make sense. dependability from others.

Values *CONSISTENCY*:
Respects things that stay the same, rules, order, conformity and tradition. Change is very stressful, needs time to adjust.

Discipline Do: *EXPECTATIONS*
Learns best by understanding specifically what is expected from them before they have to commit to, or complete, a task.

THE BLUE CHILD

Needs *RELATIONSHIPS*:
Positive relationships. Limited conflict. Peace and calm. Connection to others.

Values *COMMUNICATION*:
Clear, kind, calm communication. Lots of "warm fuzzies", hugs. Honesty, openness, trust, and kindness.

Discipline Do: *UNDERSTANDING*
Learns best through kind examples and calm requests. Discipline with kind, but firm 'redirection" of misbehavior or wrong choices .

THE GREEN CHILD

Needs *INFORMATION*:
Lots of info, data, facts, and to know why. Needs "big picture".

Values *LOGIC*:
Information that make sense, independence and autonomy. Respects logical communication, and problem solving.

Discipline Do: *EXPERIENCES*
Learns best by experience and thru consequences. Must be allowed to suffer consequences for choices. Lecturing at, or using adult reasons rarely works.

```
┌─────────────────────────────────────────────────────────┐
│          The complete Parenting by PERSONALITY          │
│                     Reference List                      │
│            (In case you want to learn more ;-)          │
└─────────────────────────────────────────────────────────┘
```

Reference List

Arliss, L. P. (1993). *Contemporary Family Communication: Messages and Meanings.* New York, NY: St. Martin's Press.

Bowman-Kruhm, M., & Wirths, C. G. (1992). *Are You My Type or Why Aren't You More Like Me?* Palo Alto, CA: Consulting Psychologists Press.

Buckingham, M., & Clifton, D. O. (2001). *Now, Discover Your Strengths.* New York, NY: The Free Press.

Buckingham, M., & Coffman, C. (1999). *First, Break All the Rules: What the World's Greatest Leaders Do Differently.* New York, NY: Simon & Schuster.

Cline, F. W., & Fay, J. (1990). *Parenting with Love and Logic.* Colorado Springs, CO: Pinion Press.

Cogen, V. (1990). *Boosting the Underachiever: How Busy Parents Can Unlock Their Child's Potential.* New York, NY: Berkley Books.

Covey, S. R. (2004). *The 8th Habit: From Effectiveness to Greatness.* New York, NY: Golden Books.

Covey, S. R. (1997). *The Seven Habits of Highly Effective Families.* Salt Lake City, UT: Deseret Books.

Covey, S. R. (1970). *Spiritual Roots of Human Relationships.* New York, NY: Golden Books.

DiRienzo, C., Das, J., Wonhi, S., Kitts, J., & McGrath, K. (2010). The Relationship Between MBTI and Academic Performance: A Study Across Academic Disciplines. *Journal of Psychological Type, 70*(5), 53-67.

Dobson, J. (2003). *Parents' Answer Book.* Wheaton, IL: Tyndale House Publishers, Inc.

Embree, M. C. (2011). Psychological Type and Student Views of the Origins Debate: Understanding the Culture Wars. *Journal of Psychological Type, 71*(1), 1-11.

Engstrom, M. C., Boozer, R. W., Maddox, E. N., & Forte, M. (2010). Psychological Type, Emotional Intelligence, and the Work Outcomes of Job Satisfaction and Organization Commitment. *Journal of Psychological Type, 70*(11), 123-133.

Eyre, L., & Eyre, R. (1984). *Teaching Your Children Responsibility.* New York, NY: Simon & Schuster.

Eyre, L., & Eyre, R. (1993). *Teaching Your Children Values.* New York, NY: Simon & Schuster.

Fay, J., & Cline, F. W. (2000). *Pearls of Love and Logic for Parents and Teachers*. Golden, CO: Love and Logic Press, Inc.

Fenell, D. L., Weinhold, B. K. (1997). *Counseling Families: An Introduction to Marriage and Family Therapy*. Denver, CO: Love Publishing Company.

Galvin, D. (1994). *Emotional Intelligence: Why It Can Matter More Than IQ*. New York, NY: Bantam Books.

Galvin, K. M. (1982). *Family Communication: Cohesion and Change*. Glenview, IL: Scott, Foresman and Company.

Goleman, T. (1975). *P.E.T.: Parent Effectiveness Training*. New York, NY: Plume Books.

Gordon, J., & Lott, L. (2000). *Positive Discipline for Teenagers*. New York, NY: Three Rivers Press.

Hayword, K. (2005). *True Parenting*. Santa Ana, CA: True Colors, Inc. Publishing.

Hirsh, S., & Kummerow, J. (1989). *Lifetypes*. New York, NY: Warner Books.

Jung, C. (1979). *Psychological Type*. Princeton, New Jersey? Princeton University Press.

Kise, J. A. G. (2005). Coaching teachers for change: using the concepts of psychological type to reframe teacher resistance. *Journal of Psychological Type*, 65(6), 47-58.

Keirsey, D. (1998). *Please Understand Me II*. Del Mar, CA: Prometheus Nemesis.

Keirsey, D., & Bates, M. (1978). *Please Understand Me*. Del Mar, CA: Prometheus Nemesis.

Kench, B. T., Beekman, R. L., Wynn, G. A., & Niman, N. B. (2010). The Influence of Psychological Type and Interpersonal Needs in Social Dilemmas: A Public Goods Experiment With Punishment. *Journal of Psychological Type*, 70 (1), 1-17.

Lawrence, G. (2010). Refining the Language of Type Descriptions. *Journal of Psychological Type*, 70(12), 135-140.

Loffredo, D. A., & Opt, S. K. (2006). Argumentativeness and Myers-Briggs Type Indicator preference. *Journal of Psychological Type*. 66(7), 59-68.

Maslow, A. H. (1970). *Motivation and Personality*. New York, NY: Harper & Row, Publishers.

McMahon, T. (1996). *Teen Tips: A Practical Survival Guide for Parents with Kids 11 to 19*. New York, NY: Pocket Books.

Mitchell, W. D. (2006). Validation of the Full Dynamic Model of Type. *Journal of Psychological Type*, 66(5), 35-48.

Murphy, E. (1992). *The Developing Child: Using Jungian Type to Understand Children*. Palo Alto, CA: Consulting Psychologists Press.

Myers, I. B., & Myers, P. (1980). *Gifts Differing*. Palo Alto, CA: Consulting Psychologists Press.

Nelsen, J. (1996). *Positive Discipline*. New York, NY: Ballantine Books.

Nelsen, J., & Lott, L. (2000). *Positive Discipline for Teenagers*. New York, NY: Three Rivers Press.

Niven, D. (2001). *The 100 Simple Secrets of Happy People: What Scientists Have Learned and How You Can Use It*. San Francisco, CA: Harper.

Noller, P., Fitzpatrick, M. A. (1993). *Communication In Family Relationships*. Englewood Cliffs, NJ: Prentice Hall.

Papazova, E., & Pencheva, E. (2008). Adolescent Self-Esteem and Psychological Type. *Journal of Psychological Type, 68*(8), 68-76.

Pearson, J. C. (1989). *Communication in the Family: Seeking Satisfaction in Changing Times*. New York, NY: Harper & Row Publishers.

Reynierse, J. H., (2009). The Case Against Type Dynamics. *Journal of Psychological Type, 69*(1), 1-21.

Rimm, S. B. (1994). *Keys to Parenting the Gifted Child*. Hauppauge, NY: Barron's Educational Series, Inc.

Schullery, N. M., Schullery, S. E., Knudstrup, P., & Pfaff, L. A., (2009). The Relationship Between Personality Type and 360-degree Evaluation of Management Skills. *Journal of Psychological Type, 69*(11), 141-155.

Sullivan, E., Sullivan, J., & Leafgren, F. (1998). *Communicating and Relating*. Dallas, TX: RAI Communications, Inc.

Sullivan, J., & Whitaker, J. (1996). *Learning and Personality Styles*. Dallas, TX: RAI Communications, Inc.

Tieger, P. D., & Barron-Teiger, B. (1997). *Nurture By Nature*. Boston, MA: Little, Brown and Company.

Thompson, C. L., & Rudolph, L. B. (1996). *Counseling Children*. Pacific Grove, CA: Brookays/Cole Publishing Company.

Tobias, C. U. (2000). *How Your Child Learns and Succeeds*. New York, NY: Galahad Books.

Trachtenberg, J. (2007). *Good Kids Bad Habits. New York, NY*: HarperCollins Publishers, Inc.

Wadsworth, B. J. (1989). *Piaget's Theory of Cognitive and Affective Development*. New York, NY: Longman.

Yerby, J., Buerkel-Rothfuss, N. & Bochner, A. P. (1995). *Understanding Family Communication*. Scottsdale, Arizona: Gorsuch Scarisbrick, Publishers, 1995.

Questions? Kudos? Concerns? Contact us!

Shannon Ward, M.A.

Family Life Coach, Creator of Family COLOR WORKS Courses
Owner of Family COLOR WORKS, LLC
Shannon: 402-510-2800
shannon@colorworksgroup.com

Rebecca Bockart

Certified Family COLOR WORKS Trainer
Family Life Coach for Family COLOR WORKS, LLC
Rebecca: 402-278-1448
rebecca@colorworksgroup.com

www.colorworksgroup.com
2211 Crestridge Drive, Blair, NE 68008

Made in the USA
Middletown, DE
24 January 2023

22999151R00225